WORLD CLASS SPEAKING *in* ACTION

WORLD CLASS SPEAKING
in ACTION

50 Certified World Class
Speaking Coaches Show You
How to Present, Persuade, and Profit

CRAIG VALENTINE
and MITCH MEYERSON

NEW YORK

WORLD CLASS SPEAKING *in* ACTION
50 Certified World Class Speaking Coaches Show You How to Present, Persuade, and Profit

© 2015 Craig Valentine & Mitch Meyerson.

Published in New York, New York, by Morgan James Publishing. Morgan James and The Entrepreneurial Publisher are trademarks of Morgan James, LLC. www.MorganJamesPublishing.com

The Morgan James Speakers Group can bring authors to your live event. For more information or to book an event visit The Morgan James Speakers Group at www.TheMorganJamesSpeakersGroup.com.

A FREE eBook edition is available
with the purchase of this print book

CLEARLY PRINT YOUR NAME IN THE BOX ABOVE

Instructions to claim your free eBook edition:
1. Download the BitLit app for Android or iOS
2. Write your name in UPPER CASE in the box
3. Use the BitLit app to submit a photo
4. Download your eBook to any device

ISBN 978-1-63047-073-9 paperback
ISBN 978-1-63047-074-6 eBook
ISBN 978-1-63047-075-3 hardcover
Library of Congress Control Number:
2014937575

Cover Design by:
Rachel Lopez
www.r2cdesign.com

Interior Design by:
Bonnie Bushman
bonnie@caboodlegraphics.com

In an effort to support local communities, raise awareness and funds, Morgan James Publishing donates a percentage of all book sales for the life of each book to Habitat for Humanity Peninsula and Greater Williamsburg.

Get involved today, visit
www.MorganJamesBuilds.com

Contents

Acknowledgments

Thanks to the World Class Speaking Coaches for their great energy, insights, and talent.

To Amanda Rooker and her team at SplitSeed for their excellent work in editing this book.

And to the talented team at Morgan James Publishing for getting this book into the hands of future World Class Speakers around the world.

Introduction

It was late summer 2007. Mitch was finishing up the last stage of his *Entrepreneur* magazine Mastering Online Marketing tour in Washington, DC, and Craig had just returned home from one of his many national speaking engagements.

We sat down at a small outdoor cafe in Maryland to enjoy the crisp, invigorating air of early fall, and to create something new, something exciting—something that would change lives.

We had met two years prior, co-leading the Guerrilla Marketing Coach Certification Program, and shared a creative vision for teaching, coaching, and inspiring entrepreneurs. Craig had a loyal following in the speakers world, just as Mitch did in the online marketing and coaching world.

At that outdoor café, in a moment of inspiration and synergy, World Class Speaking was born.

The first World Class Speaking book was published in early 2009, followed by the World Class Speaking Coach Certification Program. In this 12-week intensive program, entrepreneurs, coaches, and speakers learn powerful speaking and coaching skills as they build their own business as a Certified World Class Speaking Coach.

At the time of this writing, we have certified over 150 World Class Speaking Coaches in over 15 countries. And this is only the beginning. This active community of Certified World Class Speaking Coaches are helping speakers worldwide to become more dynamic and powerful using the 12 World Class Speaking competences that you will learn in this book.

Get ready to experience real case studies and hands-on teachings that will help you:

- build stellar presentations that will keep your audience on the edge of their seats
- turn presentations into dozens of profitable income streams
- master leading-edge technologies and speak to thousands without ever leaving home
- and much more

However, World Class Speaking is more than a system; it is a mindset. In the pages that follow, you will hear the words, experiences, and teachings of 50 of the best speaking coaches in the world.

Let their long road inspire you, and become your shortcut to success.

Craig Valentine and Mitch Meyerson
www.CertifiedSpeakingCoach.com

Part 1

THE WORLD CLASS WAY

1

The 12 World Class Speaking Competencies

Craig Valentine and Mitch Meyerson

Craig's Story

At ten years old, something disturbing happened to me. Walking through the Mall in Columbia (Maryland) by myself, I ran into my friend's father. He asked about my family. I don't remember what I said, but I never forgot his response. He fixed me in his gaze and said, "Do you know you have a serious lisp? Craig, if I were you, I wouldn't talk anymore, because every time you open your mouth, you remind me of Daffy Duck!"

My heart dropped. My confidence and esteem plummeted, and for the next five years you couldn't get a word out of me. But by age fifteen I was sick of voluntarily muting myself, so I started striving to become empowered rather than embarrassed as a communicator.

Eighteen years later, on August 21, 1999, I stood on stage in Chicago being crowned as Toastmasters International's 1999 World Champion of Public Speaking. That's a long way from Daffy Duck! Out of 25,000 contestants in 14 countries, I came home with the first prize trophy.

Since 1999, I have used the art of public speaking to become:

- the three-time Salesperson of the Year for the Mid-Atlantic Division of Glencoe/McGraw-Hill
- an award-winning management trainer for one of the largest seminar training firms in the United States
- a full-time professional speaker delivering hundreds of speeches per year all around the globe

You Want Me To Do What?!

My biggest surprise after winning the World Championship was getting a phone call from Wade Randolph. I hadn't heard of Wade, but he had heard of me! He said, "Craig, I'm from down in Richmond, Virginia, and I was wondering if you'd be willing to coach me in speaking?" I said, "Wade, I don't coach speakers." He said, "I'll pay you good money." I said, "Let me get my whistle!" Little did I know Wade would be one of thousands of speakers, from Toronto to Taipei, I would eventually coach or teach.

My success has very little to do with any innate special speaking talent. In fact, I believe speaking is 10 percent talent and 90 percent tools. Here's the tricky part: you have to have the *right* tools.

Mitch's Story

It was January 1998, and it was yet another cold, gray, bitter day in Chicago. My low-grade depression had become a little too familiar.

By some people's standards, I had it all—a successful psychotherapy practice, three psychology books published, good friends, and a wonderful wife.

But like a fish out of water, I craved the sunlight and warmth that seemed to be all too elusive for eight months of the year in this northern city.

Time and time again I pondered a move to a warmer climate, but my wife had a solid business in Chicago, and to be honest, I just didn't want to start a brick-and-mortar counseling business over in a new location. I felt helpless and started to wonder, *Is this as good as it gets?*

Fast forward to today, where I live in the warm, sunny climate of Scottsdale, Arizona, where and I enjoy a six-figure home-based business writing books and teaching online courses to excited students across the globe.

My lifestyle has lots of time for tennis, recording, performing music, and spending time with friends. I am very happy.

As a self-employed entrepreneur, I have been able to:

- co-author 11 books, including *Mastering Online Marketing, Six Keys to Creating the Life You Desire, When Is Enough Enough?, When Parents Love Too Much, Success Secrets of the Online Marketing Superstars, Success Secrets of the Social Media Marketing Superstars, Guerrilla Marketing on the Front Lines, Guerrilla Marketing on the Internet,* and *World Class Speaking.*
- co-create 5 online programs, including the Guerrilla Marketing Coach Certification Program, the 90 Day Product Factory, the World Class Product Creation Program, the Online Traffic School, and the World Class Speaking Coach Certification Program.
- be the featured expert for a six-city national tour with *Entrepreneur* magazine called Boost Your Sales by Mastering Online Marketing

How was I able to make this transition to living the life of my dreams? Five things come to mind: I developed a world-class mindset, I used the power and leverage of the Internet, I developing powerful partnerships, I took consistent, strategic action and used the 12 World Class Speaking Competencies. If you follow the system outlined, you can do the same.

Avoid This Painful Lesson

Some people think success in speaking is something you're born with or that you can simply get better at with practice. But what if you're practicing the wrong things?

> *"Practice doesn't make perfect; practice makes permanent."*
> —**Larry Gelwix**, former coach of the Highland Rugby Team

Craig's Daughter's Story

When my daughter Tori was eight months old, she started crawling. However, to our surprise, she could only crawl backwards. To get Tori crawling forward, my wife and I put the TV remote control on the floor in front of her because we knew that was the one item she wanted most in life. Guess what she did? She crawled backwards faster! She had the ability, but not the skill, to grasp what was right in front of her. The more she tried, the farther away she got from her goal.

This is exactly what happens to those who think they can practice blindly and become better speakers. If they use the wrong tools, they only get better at getting worse. They go backwards faster. Even though the prizes of potential income, recognition, and rewards are directly in front of them, they are not able to reach them. Plus, when they reinforce these backward habits, it becomes harder to turn around and head in the right direction. It's not enough to speak. You must speak using the right tools if you want to make the right impact. It's not about talent; it's about tools.

The Right Direction

The right tools are in this book waiting for you to uncover them. Like the forty-nine Certified Speaking Coaches featured in this book, you too can use these tools to become a World Class Speaker. To make sure you're going in the right direction, we've established 12 World Class Speaking Competencies that you can master to become the kind of speaker others sign up and line up to see. Think of these competencies as muscles. The stronger you get with each of them, the more impact you will have on your audiences and the more income you will have in your bank account.

The 12 World Class Speaking Competencies:
Your Speaking Muscles

We strongly suggest that you keep these 12 World Class Speaking Competencies in a visible place so you can chart your progress and build your speaking muscles each and every time you take the stage. Because World Class Speaking is about action, take a moment to do the following activity, which will be invaluable to you moving forward.

For each competency, rate yourself from 1 to 10. Give yourself a 1 if you are very poor at the competency, and give yourself a 10 if you are great at it. Chances are you will fall somewhere in between. Also, this is not a wish list. In other words, don't rate how you wish you were. Rate how you currently are. It just might open your eyes to an area you need to improve. Ready? Let's go.

1. **Storytelling.** Bill Gove, the first president of the National Speakers Association, said that the essence of public speaking is being able to "Tell

a story and make a point." To be a World Class Speaker, you must become a world-class storyteller. On a scale from 1 to 10, how well do you feel you use *stories* to keep your audience on the edge of their seats and to illustrate your points?

2. **Selling**. Every presentation is selling something, whether it is an idea, product, or service, or it's simply getting your audience to understand the benefit of listening to your message. World Class Speakers embrace this and integrate proven selling tools into every message. Their audiences know what's in it for them to follow the speaker's advice. How well do you feel you sell your idea, product, service, or message?

3. **Process driven**. We always tell speakers, "When you lift yourself up, you let your audience down." Instead of selling your audience on how great you are (which is what lots of speakers do), you can sell them on how great your *process,* or formula, or recipe is.

4. **Next steps**. World Class Speakers have one exact, defined next step they get their audiences to take immediately following their presentation. They build their entire speech around getting their audiences to take that specific next step. This next step should involve you in some way.

5. **Anchor driven**. We have a saying that "What's loose is lost." This means that what's not tied to an anchor gets forgotten by your audience. Anchors are whatever helps your audience remember your message. How well do you use anchors (stories, analogies, activities, acronyms, visuals, etc.) to illustrate each point you make and make it memorable?

6. **Begin with a bang**. Did you know your audience members will decide whether or not they like you within the first 7 seconds of your speech? Within the first 30 seconds, they'll decide whether or not they want to hear more. Most speakers open with a whimper. World Class Speakers open with a *bang*. How well do you use the first 30 seconds of your speech to make the audience thirst for more?

7. **Succinct**. One of the biggest problems we see with presenters is that too many speakers try to get across too much information in too little time. The old speaker proverb states, "When you squeeze your information in, you squeeze your audience out." We tell speakers, "You can't rush and resonate." How well do you get your information across in a tightly focused and succinct way?

8. **You focused**. World Class Speakers know that it is never about what they give, but what the audience gets. Therefore, instead of saying, "I would like to share with you three ideas…" they say, "You're about to receive three ideas…" The focus is always on "you" (the audience). How "you focused" is your message?

9. **Dynamic.** Renowned speaker Patricia Fripp says, "The enemy of a speaker is sameness." Many speakers mistakenly believe that if you're always at the highest level of energy, and you're using vocal variety throughout the entire speech, that's being dynamic. Guess what? Even that gets tiring. That's sameness! On a scale from 1 to 10, how truly dynamic are you in your delivery?

10. **Involvement**. World Class Speakers constantly get and keep their audiences involved from the beginning to the end of their presentations. They realize that people buy into what they help create and making their audience part of the process helps to sell their message. How well do you keep your audiences involved all the way through your speeches?

11. **Staging.** Audience members remember what they see when you speak. Many speakers are so concerned with what they plan to say that they neglect to pay attention to what the audience will see. There are many ways to use the stage to clarify your message. How well do you move with a purpose and physically use the stage to increase the impact and clarity of your presentation?

12. **Research/assessment**. World Class Speakers meet their audiences where they are by doing pre-speech research and by assessing the energy of the audience throughout the speech. They find the pain and turn that pain into their promise. How diligently do you research your audience before you present to them?

Build Your Muscle and Better Your Impact

Here comes the magical part. As you measure and strengthen each of these competencies, you will automatically find yourself speaking at a much higher level, making a much deeper impact, and attracting much more lucrative opportunities. There's magic in these speaking muscles, as long as you build them.

How do you strengthen them? That's what *World Class Speaking in Action* is all about! From 49 of our Certified World Class Speaking Coaches, you'll pick up tools, processes, formulas, recipes, and steps for mastering each of these competencies, and you will see how they work in the real world.

When we say "world," we do mean "world," because these coaches are from the United States, Canada, the United Kingdom, Bahrain, Japan, Australia, Saudi Arabia, Indonesia, and more, and they all share something in common. They use the World Class Speaking tools. This goes to show you that, in a global economy, these tools work wherever you go. Whenever we speak, we use these tools every time. Don't go into your next speech without them.

Let Our Long Road Lead to Your Shortcut

So whatever happened to Wade Randolph, the man who asked Craig to coach him back in 1999? Well, fifteen years later, he's a well-known professional speaker and Certified World Class Speaking Coach, and he has written a powerful chapter for this book! These tools worked for us, they worked for Wade, and they've worked for countless other speakers who are standing in front of audiences right now changing lives.

Like us, these Certified Coaches are in the trenches, practicing what they preach. And, just like Craig's daughter, who has gone way beyond crawling to become one of the top track stars in the country, picking up these tools will help you hit your stride and separate yourself from the pack. As a speaker, they will truly help you become World Class.

Craig Valentine is the 1999 World Champion of Public Speaking for Toastmasters International. He has spoken in 19 countries and is a world-renowned expert on presenting with impact and persuading with ease. He lives in Ellicott City, Maryland. For more information, visit www.craigvalentine.com.

Mitch Meyerson is the co-author of 11 books and 5 online programs. He a recognized leader in online education and Internet marketing. He is also a musician and lives in Scottsdale, Arizona. For more information, visit www.MasteringOnlineMarketing.com.

2

Four Words That Make
a World Class Speaker

Sarah Hilton

It's true: you can have all the speaking tools in the world and still be a terrible speaker.

Imagine speaking to audiences of all sizes across the world and getting paid your desired amount—but never being called to speak again. That becomes a marketing nightmare. Marketing to a new audience or a new customer every time can be exhausting, overwhelming, time consuming, and a financial drain on your bottom line.

Now picture yourself speaking, and when you finish you discover a line has formed of interested individuals. Each of them wants you to speak at their event or coach them on that exact message you just shared, or buy your product to ensure they keep a small part of you with them. Presto! Repeat business. How do the best speakers, the successful speakers, do it? It's a process I like to call "Go BALD."

B = Believe
A = Authentic
L = Learn
D = Dream

Are you a BALD speaker? Follow the checklist below and ask yourself honestly.

Believe

1. Do you believe in your message? Is your message something you are excited about?
2. Do you believe in yourself to overcome challenges, obstacles, and hard times in your speaking business?
3. Does your belief system meet your message?

Authentic

1. Are you speaking as you and not as an actor?
2. Do you feel comfortable practicing vulnerability onstage by sharing your stories?
3. Are you comfortable saying "I don't know" or "I'm not sure" even when you are supposed to be the expert?

Learn

1. Do you practice the saying "learn something new every day"? Or "I am always a student"?
2. Do you include reading as a regular activity in your week?
3. Do you walk away from your presentations asking yourself, *What did I learn from my audience today?*

Dream

1. Have you decided on your professional dreams?
2. Do you have a design to help you reach those dreams?
3. Do you take time to celebrate those dreams?

> *Are you speaking as you and not as an actor?*

If you answered yes, great! You may not have known it, but you are a BALD speaker in my book. You might have answered no to one or more of the questions.

That's okay. Most speakers are in the same position. As speakers we often focus on the skills it takes rather than the foundation we need.

The foundation is going BALD!

Going BALD is a lifestyle; it's a commitment and an important awakening. It took me two years to realize this need and to understand speaking from a place of depth instead of wondering what an opening looks like or how I should end my speech. It took many challenges, heartache, and pain for me to realize how important going BALD is in the speaking business. It took time to dig deep into the lives of speakers I considered mentors to see what made them successful. I realized it all came down to the person, their personality, and their presence as a speaker. I summed this up and created the process called BALD, and now I apply going BALD to all aspects of my life.

Getting Real, Getting BALD

Two years ago I was ready to take the stage for a talk on mental health in the workplace when a pain struck me in my face. It felt like a knife jabbing into my jaw, or at times an electric shock jolting me to the point that I fell to my knees in agony. I learned later I had an illness called trigeminal neuralgia, otherwise known as "suicide disease."

This malady affected me every time I spoke; it also affected me when I ate, when a breeze brushed past me, when I brushed my teeth, or when someone touched me at the point of pain. Not great for the love life, and to make matters worse the neuralgia would come out of nowhere. I couldn't even be sure I would get through a shopping outing. I was trapped, never knowing when it would hit.

My dream was about to die. One grumpy old doctor even said, "Sarah, dreams are destined to destroy you. Give it up."

I knew the importance of going BALD as a speaker. So I practiced the process. If it didn't work, I knew my business was doomed. First I asked myself, *Do I believe I am meant to do this work?* Absolutely; I had never been happier. I practiced vulnerability and authenticity. I told everyone I knew about my pain, my illness. It became my story.

I called my coach, Craig Valentine, the co-author of this book and the 1999 World Champion of Public Speaking. "Craig, I think my business is doomed," I said.

His reply changed everything. "Sarah, your message is not in your voice, it is in your heart and your head. Find a new way to share your message."

And I did just that. I learned everything I could from my coaches, the books I read, the mentors I spoke to, and my family who knew me. I shared my message in a new way.

1. I coached individuals online; they would send in their video and I would critique it and send back suggestions for growth.
2. I started writing books, blogs, newsletters, and articles.
3. I used social media to share my message.
4. When I was having a good moment, I would call clients to check in and help them (again being authentic, explaining I might have to go if I was struck with pain)
5. I made videos, which allowed me to stop when I needed to.

Keep Your Dream Alive

And finally I kept the dream alive. I lived the dream. Two years ago I had surgery, and now I am pain free.

By going BALD I developed a new way of doing business. I was able to once again speak and conduct face-to-face coaching, doubling my business that year.

How do you go BALD? Here is your five-step process:

Believe. A belief from Rosita Hall: "I will guard my tongue and only allow it to speak in a way that builds up and does not tear down."

1. Get Coached

- If your past is holding you back from believing in yourself, talk to a counselor, close friend, coach, or clergy. I often coach others to create their life cocktail. This does not mean adding every experience you've ever had, or adding every person that has been a part of your life. If your mother constantly belittled you or told you you're not good enough, leave her out of your cocktail of life. Your life cocktail represents the great moments, the moments that taught you something, the moments you want to carry on with you. Leave the other experiences and people out of your life cocktail.
- If you struggle to believe in your message, be honest with yourself. Is this really your message to share? If not, sit down with your coach and see what you bring to the world and how that fits with speaking. This is often the case when you are asked to make a presentation for work. What happens if

you do not believe in the idea or the content? Well, I am here to say *your audience will know*. Your audience will pick up your doubt through your voice, your body language, and your facial expressions. To believe, you must be passionate about your topic and live your message.

Authentic. Author and speaker Brené Brown has said "vulnerability is the birthplace of innovation, creativity, and change."

To be authentic, you must be vulnerable.

2. Build a Team

- Sometimes your fiends will be the right audience to tell you "hey, you are so different on stage." Take this as a clue that you need to look deep inside and find "you" in your speaking. Are you an actor? Speaking is a conversation, only with more than one person. If you find yourself acting differently on stage, ask yourself why. The answer may not be what you want to hear, but are you really a speaker or do you belong onstage to portray different characters?

- When you run into challenges, share them. There is a network of answers and resources for the taking. Every challenge has a choice. Be authentic and share your story of challenge. Speakers who stay silent on their struggles and challenges are the ones who fail. As a speaker it is usually your challenges in life that give flesh and blood to your message.

Learn. Dale Carnegie said, "Take heart from the experience of others."

3. Set Yourself a Goal

- Learn something new every day, whether through a book, your audience, or a coach/mentor. For example, I encourage my children to read a book, mark a book, recite a book, and reread that book. The books I love all have markings in them, in different colors. I find ways to use what I have learned instead of reading books and then leaving them sitting on a shelf. "Read, write, and recite" is the way to learn through books.

- Meet someone new every day because when you do you will learn through his or her stories. Some of my greatest stories and learning have come from the people I meet every day. One day I spoke to a business owner about the work I do in mental health. She shared her story about her mother, who has depression. That story is now one that touches audiences every time.

Dream. As Dr. Seuss writes in *Oh, the Places You'll Go!*—

> So be sure when you step.
> Step with care and great tact
> And remember that Life's
> A Great Balancing Act.
> And will you succeed?
> Yes! You will, indeed!
> (98 and ¾ percent guaranteed.)

4. Create a Dream Board

- Remember doing collages in school? Visuals are powerful. This dream board could be a collage of all your business dreams. Imagine a picture of you in front of a thousand people, sharing your story. And a picture of a $1,000,000 bill. The more you have on your dream board, the more likely you will live your dream.

- Your dream board could be a card in your wallet with a written list of all the pieces of your dream you want to accomplish. Looking at your dream every day when you go for coffee will help your dream become your destiny. What's visible is viable. The biggest challenge with dreams is that we lose sight of them when life gets busy. Unfortunately this is the exact time you could benefit from living your dream. Have you ever had a day when you just knew you wouldn't get everything done and you started to panic? Now imagine looking at your dream board and recognizing that some of the "to do" list did not fit with the journey to your dreams. You will find that your list of "shoulds" will not be as important anymore.

5. Check in with Yourself Weekly

- Ask yourself the questions of going BALD. These questions will keep you on track and help you stay fresh and inspired to move forward. Every day I ask myself, *Do I believe this is the right thing to do to move me forward in my business? Am I being true to myself? What have I learned today that will move me toward my goals as a speaker? Have I taken action on my dream today?* What is your list of questions to keep you on track?

- When times get tough, know you are not alone. Think *I believe*, be authentic, and share your challenges. Learn new ways of doing things and keep the dream alive. Remember that dream. This is the time to call on someone. My coaches are the reason I am living my dream today, every day, and when someone says "Your dreams are destined to destroy you," I say "My dreams are my destiny. So sad for you."

> *Vulnerability is the birthplace of*
> *innovation, creativity, and change.*
> **—Brené Brown**

Going BALD kept my business alive. Going BALD drives repeat business my way, connects me to my audience, makes it easy to answer those difficult questions, keeps me focused on the dream, and reminds me every day why I am meant to be a speaker and coach.

Go BALD…

Because when you *believe* in you and your material,

You will be *authentic* and true to yourself on and offstage,

You will *learn* from your audience, your mentors, and others,

And through challenges and your journey you will keep focused on your *dream* so that you can live it every day.

Dreams are your destiny; your destiny becomes your legacy. Make your legacy linger through your children, your children's children, and onward. As speakers you have this gift every time you share your message—if it's a message that starts by going BALD.

Sarah Hilton has studied human behavior and communication styles through her twenty years of working in the mental health industry. The result is an uncanny knack for communication and creating messages that are memorable whether speaking to one or one thousand. Sarah has spent the last five years coaching and teaching presentation techniques that lead audiences to change, grow, and discover new ideas.

3

Phenomenal Action
the World Class Way

Teri Kingston

I n the introduction to *World Class Speaking* (WCS), co-author Craig Valentine proclaims that the best part of using the WCS tools is that we will "touch many lives along the way." When I first read those words in 2009, I knew immediately that that is what I wanted to do as a speaker and coach. Finding words to move people into action, creating compelling stories and speeches, making a difference—this is the work that would be my "third career," my post-retirement passion, my opportunity to earn a living doing what I love.

Have you ever thought you were taking on something for one reason only to find out years later that the real reasons were totally different? Leadership guru Zig Ziglar tells us that "Every single thing that has ever happened in your life is preparing you for your greatest moment that is yet to come." Life has a funny trick of twisting in unexpected directions, causing plans to change in ways that we cannot even begin to imagine. In 2009 I thought I needed the WCS coaching certification to build a business, a new career, while in actuality I was being perfectly prepared to put my passions and skills into play three years down the line with the hardest story I have ever been asked to tell.

I was fifty years old when I married the man of my dreams. We had no illusions at that age of reaching our fiftieth anniversary but often joked that we wanted at least thirty good years together. We were only seven years into our dream marriage when, in November 2012, we received medical news that plunged us into a whole new world and threatened to put a full stop to our thirty-year plan. As we sat in the doctor's office at the Ottawa Heart Institute, listening to the news, I felt like a character in a crazy cartoon with "balloon bubbles of words" floating around the room. Nothing was making sense.

The doctor sat down across from both of us and, in a serious but warm voice, said, "Harry, you don't have cancer, but you do have a serious disease called pulmonary hypertension."

While hugely relieved that he did not have cancer, we were puzzled by this new condition with the strange name. What was she talking about?

The doctor continued. "Pulmonary hypertension is a general term used to describe high blood pressure in the lungs from any cause. Pulmonary arterial hypertension is a chronic and currently incurable disease."

"Incurable? What do you mean by incurable?" we both asked at the same time.

With great compassion, she said, "There is no cure at this time, but treatment can extend and improve quality of life."

She went on to explain that pulmonary hypertension can strike anyone regardless of age, sex, or social or ethnic background. In pulmonary hypertension, the arteries of the lungs become narrowed and scarred. This can result in almost complete closing of the arteries and may lead to heart failure. She listed the symptoms that would plague Harry—many of which already did: shortness of breath; bluish hands, feet, and lips; swelling of hands and feet; lightheadedness and dizziness; chest pain; exhaustion and fainting.

This was to be our new life? This is what our "golden years" would have in store for us?

Putting the WCS Skills into Action—Personally

As speakers and speaking coaches we are trained to zoom in on life's defining moments as the best sources for stories and lessons that will create the most powerful connections possible with our audiences. Believe me when I say there is no more powerful defining moment in life than the frozen segment of time surrounding a doctor's diagnosis of a loved one's incurable disease.

> *As speakers and coaches we are trained to zoom in on life's defining moments as the best sources for stories that will create the most powerful connections with our audiences.*

Almost a full year later, Harry and I attended a conference for people affected by or involved with pulmonary hypertension (PH). This conference is hosted every two years by the national association for PH in Canada, and for the first time it was being held in our hometown of Ottawa. The theme for the 2013 conference was "Keeping the PHlame of Hope Alive." As the weekend unfolded a picture started forming in my heart. There I was, a certified WCS coach and trained public speaker, bowled over by the many stories of courage in the face of huge adversity told with varying degrees of effectiveness and impact.

I also heard loud and clear a cry from those attending for more exposure, more awareness, and more opportunities for patients, family, caregivers, and medical staff to speak out about PH. Was this what I was being prepared for over all the years of speaking training? Not a moment of personal greatness but the opportunity to change lives through speaking and storytelling skills to create change for an entire community?

The Pulmonary Hypertension Association of Canada website (www.phacanada.ca) puts it this way:

As patients, caregivers, family members and friends, we all have a right to fight back and raise our voices to assist all those living with pulmonary hypertension to get the care that they need. Raising awareness starts at home and in your community. There are many ways that you can assist in this project. You can choose to raise awareness by telling your story, talking to the media, presenting at a local event or reaching out to others living with the disease. Nothing is more powerful and educates better than sharing the story of how PH has affected your life whether you are a patient, a caregiver or a family member. By getting active and educating others, the advocates within the PH community are transforming attitudes and helping to build awareness.

By educating others about PH, you can help to save lives. Education leads to earlier diagnosis and more effective treatment. By raising your voice, you can help us to shine a spotlight on this disease and make everyone from health care practitioners to politicians take notice and pay attention.

Phenomenal Courage Calls for Phenomenal Action

The PH community uses the word "phenomenal" to describe the many daily acts of courage and persistence that patients and their families exhibit day after day, and I have witnessed many such moments myself since Harry joined in on this unplanned journey. His way of dealing with this disease was to get voted in as a member of the board of directors for PHA Canada at the same conference where I had my "aha" moment. I now work hand-in-hand with a core group of patients and caregivers as we prepare to launch a new support group in Ottawa.

This is my opportunity to live out Craig's words—the opportunity to touch many lives is here and now. Not only could I put the WCS system (competence plus confidence plus credibility) to work, but I am ideally placed to help my fellow PH community members develop their skills as well.

One of the most powerful lessons Craig and Mitch teach their WCS coaches is not just to "get ready" to speak but to "stay ready." I plan to use all the tools in the World Class Speaking toolkit to help the PH community members develop powerful storytelling techniques, create compelling messages, and strengthen their speaking skills through coaching and workshops so that together, as a community, we can become even more powerful advocates. Using all these tools helps me to stay ready to help, stay ready to advocate, stay ready to fight for patients and families who need a strong community around them simply to survive.

> *One of the most powerful lessons Craig and Mitch teach their WCS coaches is not just to "get ready" to speak but to "stay ready."*

What Is Your Cause?

I have chosen a very personal story to illustrate how I intend to put my WCS skills into action to create real opportunities to change lives and make a difference. My cause may have nothing to do with anything you are experiencing in your own life. But is there something in your life, your neighborhood, your community that needs you to raise your voice? Is there a cause you identify with that calls for above-ordinary speaking and communicating skills—World Class speaking skills? Do you have a defining moment that you can amplify through excellent advocacy?

Steve Jobs puts it this way: "Remembering that I'll be dead soon is the most important tool I've ever encountered to help me make the big choices in life. Because almost everything—all external expectations, all pride, all fear of embarrassment or failure—these things just fall away in the face of death, leaving only what is truly important."

What is truly important in your life? I know what is important in mine, and I have every intention of putting all my skills into play to create phenomenal action—the World Class Way.

Teri Kingston, DTM, BMus, is a certified World Class Speaking coach. For more information about her coaching business, visit www.terikingston.ca.

Part 2

WORLD CLASS SPEAKING STRUCTURE

4

Structure: Your
ROADMAP to Success

Teresa Dukes

tructure is the SatNav of speaking! A World Class Speaker will take you on a content-rich journey that is approached through a visual ROADMAP. Many people I have coached are shocked at the difference this one key process makes when developing their speeches and presentations.

This chapter will open your eyes to the power of a visual ROADMAP structure that engages your audience from beginning to end. Adding this step into your speech-building process will enable you to produce an end product that you and your audience can follow, understand, and remember easily. If you want an added edge that will keep you in the minds of your listeners long after you have left the stage, follow me on *your* ROADMAP to success.

In this chapter you will learn to develop a structure that:

- generates interest and creates curiosity among your audience
- keeps your audience on the right track
- produces an end product that you and your audience can follow, understand, and remember easily

Let's get started on your ROADMAP journey!

R—Remember

Wouldn't it be nice to entice the audience into your speech before you even start speaking? I would go so far as to say it isn't just nice but essential for an effective speech or presentation. If you don't hook them at the beginning they won't follow you to the end. So how can you generate interest and create curiosity from the very first step? When coaching clients I ask them: "Think about how you can entice the listener even before you start—can you give them something to *remember?*"

You can do this within the title, at the very beginning of the speech (creating the BANG discussed in the next chapter by Jeremy Tracey, "The ABCs for Your BANG Beginning"), or by taking them on a visual journey they can follow each step of the way. You are helping them reach your message in the most efficient and imaginative way!

Every time I'm asked to stand up and speak I always go straight to the place in my head where the journey begins. When I was a little girl I used to love to go on vacation. It was a very special treat because we didn't always get a vacation, so the times we actually did go made it that much more special.

Can you remember the buildup that always came before that wonderful day when you jumped in the car and started your vacation journey? I think I enjoyed counting down the days as much as I loved going on the trip. It was like a pre-journey experience. The same thing happens for me in speeches and presentations. *R—Remember* is the first step in giving the audience something to think about, which helps you as a speaker know they are following you each step of the way.

O—Opinion

When my mama would tell my sisters and me where we were going on holiday you can bet your bottom dollar we all had different expectations and opinions about the destination. Even at a young age my older sister, Selena, wanted culture and history; my younger sister, Anetta, required quiet and secluded surroundings; and I needed excitement! Can you imagine what my mama went through to plan our holidays?

Forming an opinion is something you do every time you listen to a speaker, and you do this without even thinking. That's why this step is so important. You want to create curiosity through the use of opinion forming and the expectations your audience may have. *O—Opinion* is the second step. You can do this by teasing a little—leave them wondering what your opinion is and thinking about the one they have just formed. One way I have found to help clients create curiosity and form opinions is through the use of acronyms, and, you guessed it, that's the next step.

> *Leave them wondering what your opinion is and*
> *thinking about the one they have just formed.*

A—Acronyms

Acronyms are one of the most powerful tools we have and can be used to entice your listeners to follow you without any question. I recently delivered a workshop to a group of wedding business professionals. This group was looking for concrete ideas to improve their individual presence within their core market. The idea they wanted me to focus on was helping them make their sixty-second pitch more effective.

Now these professionals have all expertly developed their businesses and know exactly what they are good at, but they are still a bit shy or conservative in blowing their own trumpet (they are all English, which may help to explain this!). They asked me to help them promote themselves without coming across as arrogant or pompous. So I came up with a workshop they would *remember* that would cause them to form an *opinion*, and to which I could apply an *acronym*. And boy did I get it right, because they absolutely weren't expecting "Perfecting Your Pitch through OCD."

They got it and were able to follow me from the beginning of the workshop to the very end. *O for Opening* with a personal flare; *C for Clients* you've worked with, the problem solved, and their story; *D for Differentiate* yourself from others. I still have people asking me about that OCD workshop! Acronyms help you with the next step: *D—Demonstrate* the power of your message and keep your audience on the right track.

D—Demonstrate

Demonstrating your ROADMAP really does bring your audience along with you. It reinforces the point that your message has to be easy to follow, so make the structure an overt part of the presentation rather than something hidden away in your notes.

I was invited to a monthly breakfast meeting to share a fifteen-minute talk on public speaking. What better way for me to demonstrate the ROADMAP than to deliver my talk "The MOT of Public Speaking"? Because the talk was so short it was important to identify something that could be demonstrated quickly and that they would talk about in the future. I love acronyms because they make your talk even more interesting and keep the audience on track. The MOT stood for:

- **M—Minutes (one to ten rule).** For every ten minutes you speak, deliver one point effectively.
- **O—One next step.** End your speech succinctly with only one action you want the audience to take.
- **T—Tell a story.** The stories are what help your audience connect and retain your message.

When coaching my clients on the World Class Speaking techniques I always demonstrate the ROADMAP. This helps them realize that I practice what I preach—if you get my meaning!

How many opportunities do you have on a weekly or monthly basis to blow your own trumpet? There are many places for you to demonstrate your journey, whether at a weekly breakfast meeting, a monthly team meeting, or as a guest speaker. These opportunities give you the chance to stand out from the crowd, from your peers, and from your colleagues—helping you to be *remembered*, have *opinions* formed, *acronyms* used, and your message *demonstrated* easily in a different way.

Another way to help your audience connect with you is through storytelling. The next step offers a chance for you to turn your speech into a story that is both exciting and thought provoking by capturing it with a metaphor. Yes, *M—Metaphors* can be real "light bulb moments" for your audience.

M—Metaphors

Through the use of *metaphors* you can ensure you will be followed, understood, and remembered. Metaphors give the audience a chance to reflect on what you are saying and make a connection at the same time.

"The World Is Your OYSTER—Start Cultivating Your PEARLS" was a workshop I delivered at a conference in England. The idea behind the workshop was to give the audience a way of identifying their dreams (their OYSTER) and then acting upon them (cultivating their PEARLS). I started the workshop by giving the audience a chance to identify with what I had gone through. Here is a small clip of the opening after setting the scene:

When I tasted oysters for the very first time they left a bitter, salty taste in my mouth. Why is it that the world is called our oyster when they are such disgusting things?

The interesting thing about oysters is the beautiful gem they could make if they get irritated! Because do you know how oysters make pearls? Well, what happens is the oyster gets an irritation; something like sand gets underneath its skin, between the shell and the mollusk, and the oyster can't get rid of it. The irritation just keeps digging at it and digging at it. This is exactly what happened to me when I went for promotion and nobody could see me as anything but the secretary I had been for four years. They kept rejecting me again and again.

But the oyster doesn't let a little irritation stop it. No, it starts to attack it with layers and layers of nacre to protect itself and eventually turns what is perceived as a real irritation into something as beautiful as a pearl. The rejection and the role of secretary was the sand of my oyster, but with the help of my mentor we added layer after layer of nacre, or new skills, to turn it into promotion after promotion until we were able to produce the best pearl yet: Dukes Consultancy.

This is a simple example that helped lay out the ROADMAP for the audience to follow, understand, and remember: OYSTER to PEARLS. By the way, I still don't like the taste of oysters, but I love their ability to overcome any obstacle and take action! Guess what? *A—Action* is our next step.

A—Action

The most important thing your audience is looking for is a good return on their investment. They need to leave with a new opinion, a new skill, or a new desire to change something in their life. In other words, you want to inspire them to take action. But before they can be inspired, they have to sign up for your workshop or presentation in the first place!

> *Your audience needs to leave with a new opinion, a new skill, or a new desire to change something in their life.*

You may have regular followers who already know you and enjoy hearing you speak. They have already taken their first action by showing up to listen to you again. To reach others who may not know you yet, you can build in a step calling them to *action* within your ROADMAP. The action has to connect with them, so your speech will need to help them overcome the pain or problem they are facing. Your ROADMAP can become part of your title to help you reach this new audience.

Whenever I attend a seminar I analyze all the workshops on the agenda before choosing the ones I want to attend. They have to resonate with me on something I want to improve, something I need to fix, or maybe even just something to make me laugh. I usually make my choices by the title. Titles that grab my interest are the workshops I will choose to attend. Some have included:

1. Six Steps to Corporate Club Success
2. From OYSTER to PEARLS
3. How to Demystify Successful Communication

As a speaker you hold the power in your hands to attract even more people by using your ROADMAP, not only to form the structure of your speech but within the title itself. Your title is crucial so don't rush it. You may want to leave that step for last because until you know exactly where you want to take your audience, how can you choose the right title?

So the next time you start developing a new speech, forget about the title until you have truly developed the message, the key points you want to make, and the action you want to inspire them to take. No process would be complete without spending a bit of time honing the techniques you've learned and making them your own. And that takes us to the final ROADMAP step: *P—Practice.*

P—Practice

Within the World Class Speaking program there are three parts to the opening of a speech: the BANG which grabs and keeps their attention; the Big Promise that ensures they know what they are going to get from you; and the ROADMAP that guides them along the journey visually. Practice makes perfect, as you know, so the more you get used to including a ROADMAP in your speech, presentation, or workshop, the easier it will become. Putting all seven steps together will help you link your message to a structure that your audience will follow, understand, and remember.

Once again, here are the seven ROADMAP steps summarized:

R—Remember. Give them something to remember.

O—Opinion. Help them reflect and form an opinion.

A—Acronyms. Use acronyms to create curiosity and intrigue.

D—Demonstrate. Think of how you can easily demonstrate your structure.

M—Metaphors. Bring it alive with a metaphor, allowing your audience to relate.

A—Action. Inspire your audience to take action.

P—Practice. Perfect this process with practice and reach your destination—success!

Teresa Dukes is the founding director of Dukes Consultancy, located in the United Kingdom. Her specialty is "Sowing the Seeds of Confidence" that help bring out her clients' natural qualities to communicate more effectively. She has over sixteen years of corporate and public speaking experience and provides coaching, speaking, and training services to her clients. As a certified World Class Speaking coach, Teresa works with individuals at all levels from apprentice to CEO, helping them to be heard, understood, and most importantly remembered. Find out more about Teresa and Dukes Consultancy at www.dukesconsultancy.co.uk.

5

The ABCs for Your
Bang Beginning

Jeremy Tracey

If you read two or three paragraphs into this chapter and still had not found anything of value, how would you feel? Would you keep reading? Would you put the book down and never pick it up again? Would you feel annoyed?

These are some of the emotions your audience may feel if you are one, two, or ten minutes into your keynote and you haven't really said anything or shared some sort of value.

Many speakers begin a presentation with what I like to call "unpleasant pleasantries." Have you ever heard a speaker start with

- "Hi, my name is_____" (followed by a list of credentials).
- "What beautiful weather…"
- "It is such an honor to be here…"
- "I would like to say thank you to _____ for asking me to speak."
- "A priest, a nun, and a rabbi walk into a bar…" (or another joke from *Reader's Digest*).

If you begin your presentations with any of the above, please stop immediately.

You are about to learn the three most powerful ways to begin any speech with a bang and get your audience engaged and excited to hear what you have to share. When you apply any one of the techniques below, your audience will know right away that your presentation will be different and that you are worth listening to. You will literally see them sit up and engage within seconds.

Here are the ABCs for opening your presentation with a bang. I do not mean after you have shared unpleasant pleasantries of any kind. I mean the very first words out of your mouth.

A: Ask a Question

B: Big Bang Statement

C: Create a Compelling Story

Option A: Ask a Question

There are three considerations when formulating your opening questions. First, are you casting a wide enough net? Second, is it really a question? Third, how long should you give your audience to answer your question?

First Consideration: Are You Casting a Wide Enough Net?

The purpose of the opening is to engage your entire audience. A question like "Did you watch the hockey games last night?" may not be your best question. You want to ask a question that will elicit an emotional response from almost everyone in the room. Always consider your audience and decide what question will be best for that particular group.

Example

The opening question I initially used for my keynote "Learning to Soar" was "Do you remember when you first discovered personal development?" A fellow speaking coach told me this was not a good question. His theory was that such a small percentage of people are familiar with personal development that it would fall flat. Being a bit stubborn, I moved forward with my question only to discover that he was absolutely right. When I posed my question I would get a few nods, maybe 10 to 15 percent engagement, but mostly blank stares.

By the way, that is the best way to know for sure if you have an effective question—go test it on a real live audience. With the goal of casting a wider net I tried a new opening question: "Do you remember a time when you felt motivated to create a positive change?" Even if my audience had never heard the term *personal development* everyone has likely felt motivated at some point. This created a much better response. More nods, more agreement, more engagement from the audience.

Advanced Tip for Casting a Wider Net

There are three little words that will make almost any question more effective and automatically engage more of your audience: "Have you ever…?" Consider these two examples.

1. "Do you feel frustrated?"

Audience response: some nods of agreement, but many may be thinking *no, I'm pretty content,* equaling low or no engagement with you or your speech.

2. "Have you ever felt frustrated?"

Audience response: everybody in the audience will begin to think about the most recent frustrations in their life. *Yeah, with my boss* or *My new client is a real pain* or *You try getting three kids out the door* or *The traffic around here is awful.* This equals a room full of engaged people waiting to hear what you will say next.

Second Consideration: Is It Really a Question?

You should be aware that it is completely possible to tell someone who you think they are or what they should or shouldn't want/do in the form of a question. Make sure your question does not define the listener. For example, I worked as a trainer with an international fitness consulting company and the owner, Paul Brown, shared a story of what not to ask. Paul told me of a personal trainer who made the mistake of asking a very solidly built female gym member "How much weight do you want to lose?" What he didn't realize was that she was an Olympic discus athlete. She leaned forward and said, "Listen punk, if you take one pound off this body I will ring your scrawny little neck."

> *Most likely your audience won't threaten your life if you ask a poorly worded question, but they will tune out, sit back, and cross their arms.*

Most likely your audience won't threaten your life if you ask a poorly worded question, but they will tune out, sit back, and cross their arms. Make sure your questions are actually questions and not assumptions that could be considered offensive.

Third Consideration: How Long Should You Give Your Audience to Answer Your Question?

The quick answer is as long as it takes.

Let me take you into one of the speaking boot camp sessions I ran with fellow World Class Speaking Coach Sarah Hilton. One particular participant, a phenomenal speaker, was asking brilliant questions but not giving her audience time to respond or even think about their answer. She was sharing a portion of her speech when I interrupted to demonstrate this point.

"Okay," I said, "I want you to repeat that question, *but* you are not allowed to continue until I tap you on the back." Sheepishly, she asked her question again.

...

...

...

Finally, I tapped her on the back. "Seriously," she said, "I have to wait that long?" I had only counted to three, which felt like an eternity for her. I said, "Don't take my word for it, ask your audience." That is one of the great benefits of the workshop setting, the immediate feedback from fellow participants who are your audience. "Yeah, that was about right for me" was the general response. This simple technique helped make a great speaker even stronger.

Option B: The Big Bang Statement

Imagine a speaker who started her speech by walking onstage with a big smile, looking around, and then saying "I am *awesome*!" What would you think? Would this grab your attention? Why is she awesome? This opening is unexpected, and that is what a Big Bang statement is all about. What is a statement that would catch your audience a bit off guard?

One of my favorite speeches was from back when I was still a personal trainer. The opening line was "Personal trainers are *perfect*!" When you use an opening like this, you do need to choose your next words carefully; let them know you are not the most conceited person on the face of the earth. The next lines of my speech are "that is not true, but it is what so many people think, believing that I work out and eat salad every day—and that I am happy about it."

I worked with a client named Susan who sells Norwex products. As we talked, I learned that one of her products called the body cloth eliminated the need to use soap. The opening line of her speech became "I have not used soap [pause] for thirty-seven days. [pause] My name is Susan McQuay, and I bet you think that's gross. I did too until I discovered Norwex and this amazing body cloth...." This opening line has a great bang. Who would expect a woman to stand up and confess that she does not use soap? Who would ever see (or smell) that one coming?

Imagine you are sitting in her audience; during her pauses, what are you thinking? Are you thinking *That's kinda gross*? If you are, then her next line of "I bet you think that's gross" will create an even stronger connection and her speech will be off to an amazing start.

Another one of my clients is a tax accountant, and her opening is a bit different: "Raise your hand if you would like to add stress to your business."

With your next presentation, is there a bang opening that will grab your audience's attention in a fun and exciting way? The goal is to be unexpected—surprising but hopefully not offensive.

Option C: Create a Compelling Story

When I listen to speakers it's interesting to watch for when they relax—when they go from talking *to* their audience and settle into talking *with* their audience. Most speakers become more comfortable when they share a story. Even the most nervous speaker can appear to be having fun when they simply tell a story. Why not start with a great story that sets up the rest of your presentation.

> *When I listen to speakers it's interesting to watch for when they relax—when they go from talking to their audience and settle into talking with their audience.*

When I share a keynote on speaking skills, I often open with the story of my very first speaking experience. The first words out of my mouth, with an imaginary phone held to my head, are, "Hey, Jeremy, will you go to Rotary and tell them about our fitness center?"

When you jump into your story with a line of dialogue, your audience may be curious as to what you're talking about. That's a good thing. It is easy to take a step back and explain the situation. With my example above I continue with "It was my boss calling, and even though I was not a speaker at the time, it made sense that he called me. I was the lead trainer in his club, I am very passionate about fitness, and most importantly, [pause] I like to talk." This answers the question *what is going on?* But it leaves the curiosity of what happens next.

Stories are an incredible tool for any speaker. If you have a story that your audiences love to hear, consider using it as your opening to set the tone. Please know that having an opening story is not enough; to accomplish your goal of beginning with a bang you must jump right in. If you open with "I'm going to start by telling you a story…" you will have lost much of the impact.

An alternative to beginning your story with a line of dialogue is to start by inviting your listeners into the situation. One of my stories is about how my youngest son becomes an unexpected guru, and it begins like this: "If you had been standing on the side of the road in Elmira, you would have seen me and our nine-year-old son, Nolan, driving toward you [pause] on our unicycles." Yes, I have the added benefit of surprise because most people are not expecting us to be on unicycles. Even without that advantage, can you see how I invited you to be there to witness this story unfold?

Recap of the ABCs for Your Bang Beginning

You only need to apply one of the techniques, not all three, in the opening of your speech. Either…

A: Ask a question that casts a wide net, or
B: Begin with a bang statement that catches your audience off guard, or
C: Create a compelling story and jump right in.

The openings we have talked about are to set you, the speaker, at ease and get you in the groove. The added benefit is that your audience can be set at ease as well, which is a real win-win.

Consider testing out your opening question, bang statement, or story on friends and family. How many of them answer yes or engage? A word of caution: you might have people say things like "don't you have to tell them your name?" or "you have to thank whoever asked you to speak" or "that's not how a speaker is supposed to start."

If you want to be boring and ordinary then yes, you should state your name and credentials, tell a bad joke or two, and remember to talk about the weather. But if you want to be World Class, go out there and put the ABCs of opening your speech to work. Enjoy the benefits of being able to connect faster and engage your audience more fully.

Jeremy Tracey is a keynote speaker and certified World Class Speaking coach who offers one-to-one coaching, teleclasses, and speaking boot camps. As a holistic lifestyle and neuro-linguistic programming (NLP) coach, he helps his clients not only master the techniques for effective speaking and sales but also develop the confidence and mindset to reach their goals.

6

Transitions: The Most Neglected Part of a Speech

Kathryn MacKenzie

Imagine this: You're on a roller coaster ride in an amusement park. Seeing the upcoming twists and turns ahead is what keeps you filled with anticipation and excitement throughout the entire journey!

Many speakers, though they work hard on the structure, content, and delivery of their speeches, pay little to no attention to their turns, or their transitions, from one point to the next. In fact, transitions may be the most neglected part of a speech or presentation.

To take your audience on exciting rides with your own speeches, filled with anticipation and curiosity from beginning to end, you need to understand the importance of transitions and how to use them. This chapter will cover:

- what transitions are
- why they are important
- the three factors transitions must incorporate
- two World Class approaches to weaving these three factors into your transitions
- examples of how to use these two approaches

What Are Transitions?

Transitions are simply the spaces between one point and the next. Unfortunately, many speakers ignore the opportunity these spaces provide and move abruptly from one point to the next, assuming not only that the audience wants to move on, but also that the audience actually is still with them!

Taking all this for granted, they may say these same mundane phrases:

"My next point is…"

or

"Point #3 is…"

or

"Let's move on to the next step of…"

Why Transitions Are Important

If we want to have our audiences at the edge of their seats, intrigued, enthused, and excited to hear more of our presentation, our transitions need to be both sharp and exciting, as well as the segue that allows a seamless flow from one point to the next.

World Class speakers know that it is their job to bridge their points in a fluid motion—first, to ensure that the audience is still with them, and second, to ensure that the audience wants to continue on with them.

> *World Class speakers know that it is their job to bridge their points in a fluid motion—first, to ensure that the audience is still with them, and second, to ensure that the audience wants to continue on with them.*

Three Factors Transitions Must Incorporate

So how do we clearly and effectively alert the audience that they are transitioning to a slightly different but related theme, while maintaining their interest and curiosity? World Class speakers create speeches that flow, ensuring that the transitions are smooth and tie all points together to a central theme.

This is achieved by carefully and conscientiously weaving in three factors:

- call back to where they've been
- tease them to where they're going
- show why it's important to go there with the speaker

More specifically, great transitions wrap up the previous point by reminding the audience where they've been by calling up a past event, character, or message, teasing them towards the next point, and then emphasizing its importance and how it will benefit their lives.

Two World Class Approaches to Weaving the Three Factors into Your Transitions

Two World Class approaches to creating great transitions are the *Verbal Knife* and the *Silver Spoon*. Both tease the audience into wanting to hear more and take heed.

When using the Verbal Knife approach, the speaker discusses the common pain(s) of the audience they want to avoid, such as frustration, profit loss, stress, poor health, social isolation, or not achieving goals.

In contrast, the Silver Spoon approach teases the audience into listening to the upcoming message by promising what we know that particular audience wishes to attain. This approach entices them using the Build on Benefits (BOB) formula. Combining both the Verbal Knife and the Silver Spoon approaches emphatically and effectively reminds the audience of both the consequences they want to avoid and the beneficial, life-changing results they want to attain.

Please note: In order for people to take action, they need to hear the pain before the gain.

- Hearing the painful consequences of not heeding the message *motivates them to move.*
- Hearing the benefits of heeding the message gives them *a direction towards which to move.*

People are motivated more by the fear of loss than hope of gain. Using the Silver Spoon approach alone, without mentioning the possible loss(es) if they do not heed your advice, is not as effective.

People are motivated more by the fear of loss than hope of gain.

How to Use the *Verbal Knife* and the *Silver Spoon* in Your Transitions

Here is an example taken from one of my keynotes titled "The ABC Guide to Greatness" (A = Attitude, B = work/life Balance, and C = Courage to change).

My first two major points were about committing to a mental action of having a positive Attitude, and then committing to the physical actions of planning, setting priorities, and time management—in other words, work/life Balance. The two points could be connected with a transition that purposely weaves in the three aforementioned factors.

To be more specific, my transition between my first point ("A") and second point ("B") went as follows:

1. *Remind* the audience where they have been. I returned to my first point of having a positive Attitude.

We've established the fact that winning at anything starts as an inner game of the mind, and that life is not a physical journey but a mental construct, so we can rightly assume that attitude towards anything is everything. After examining the devastating effects of holding onto a negative attitude and the winning effects of a positive attitude, it is obvious why winners have positive attitudes...

Now I ask you, what good is having a positive mental attitude...?

2. *Show* them where they are going. I stated the next point by connecting it to the previous sentence.

...if it's not followed by this next point, which necessitates the physical action of doing. Without it, you may very well reach your goals or destinations, in isolation of others, but not fully enjoy your ride along the way, since your motive was success, not happiness with those around you.

3. *Tell* them *why* it's important for them to come along with you. Build on benefits for them: explain what they will get by coming with you—in this case, by listening to my personal story.

> *We all have the potential to be winners, and winners believe that there is no road to happiness—happiness is the road! Does that make sense? Can I assume that you want both success and happiness? Well, you can when you exercise this next step.*
>
> *Let me ask you this. Have you ever reflected on possibly missing out on important matters simply by mentally turning your clock ahead as you rushed towards the finish line? I invite you to step back with me about fifteen years ago, when my grown daughter, Carolyn, taught me a huge life lesson…*

The transition from my second point ("B") to my third point ("C") followed the same process.

1. *Remind* the audience where they have been. I returned to the first two points of positive Attitude and work/life Balance.

> *Earlier we noted that our attitude affects our expectations, which affect our behaviors, which affect our outcomes. So because your Attitude affects your expectations and the behaviors you choose to perform as you pursue work/life Balance, you also know that your future outcomes will also be affected by these choices… So how do you think you can exercise the third action with ease?*

2. *Show* them where they are going.

> *Again, we return to a possibly new mindset for you in order for you to take action in doing new things. Let me ask you a question: What often stops us in our tracks from doing something?*
>
> *[Audience: "Fear!"]*
>
> *When was the last time you experienced being fearful of doing something for the first time, but you did it, and you not only survived, but thrived?*

3. *Tell* them *why* it's important for them to come along with you.

The next section will lead into a discussion of the third point, which is the Courage to change what is not working for us.

> *...Let me take you back twelve years, when a friend helped me discover the wonderful benefits of great joy and self-fulfillment by exercising the courage to explore new things, in spite of the fear I was experiencing. Had I not taken her advice, I know I would now be living in regret, as so many people do, stopped by a fear of change and trying new things, saying: I wish I had...!*
>   *In July of 2001, I had just...*

Here are a few bonus reminders to help you further ease the audience's journey from one point to the next:

- Memorize your transitions (I highlight the entire transition paragraph in my speeches)
- Use You-Focused questions and/or tell a story/vignette stating the benefits for the audience
- Change stage locations to visually represent the verbal transition with a physical transition
- Consider transitions as potentially good opportunities for using humor

The next time you work on a speech or presentation, I invite you to breathe new life into your speech by paying close attention to your transitions. Your audience will not only stick with you, but be excited to make the next turn on the roller coaster. As you use these World Class approaches to ease their journey to the next point, you will be remembered as a speaker who can skillfully captivate your audiences throughout your entire speech or presentation and bring them safely back home to a more enlightened state.

Discovering these three steps in creating transitions—

1. *Remind* the audience where they have been
2. *Show* them where they are going
3. *Tell* them *why* it's important for them to come along with you

—and utilizing these two approaches—

1. The Verbal Knife
2. The Silver Spoon

—were great "aha" moments for me and transformed my keynote speeches into those that held my audiences' attention by easing them and teasing them into the next point.

Remember: It's all about where you took them, where you're taking them next, and why they should go there with you!

Kathryn MacKenzie, MEd, is an award-winning international speaker, member of CAPS, and author of Speeches That Will Leave Them Speechless. A former educator and stage actress, she has the ability to "edu-tain" her audiences as she helps them find their personal or speaking magnificence. For more information visit her website at www.KathrynMacKenzie.com.

7

Use Callbacks
to Connect

Wade Randolph

Several years ago, I attended a program for an accounting group. I was sitting in the conference room with about sixty other people, waiting eagerly for the next portion of the program. The topic—how to save money when filing taxes—couldn't have been more relevant, and the speaker was well qualified.

Finally, the speaker took the stage. We leaned forward in anticipation, completely silent and attentive. He began by telling a canned joke—and it bombed. Based on the speaker's body language, you could tell he knew it bombed, too. We began to fidget, feeling uncomfortable. He tried again, this time with another canned joke about the weather, which of course also bombed. It was all uphill from there.

This speaker began with a fresh and attentive audience. He had a topic that was interesting and relevant. He was well qualified to speak on the topic. He was likely even well prepared to deliver this particular speech. But when he couldn't make a connection with his audience, he was put at a disadvantage that was nearly impossible to recover from.

When taking the stage, one of the first things speakers ask themselves is, "How do I quickly create rapport with this audience?" Some speakers resort to telling jokes to create rapport, yet as we saw above, telling jokes often fails and creates an even greater disconnection than what you started with.

A far more effective rapport building strategy is to use *callbacks*. A callback is a reference to a positive or humorous experience that will connect with your audience emotionally as well as intellectually.

In this chapter, you will learn how to use callbacks to:

- create instant rapport with your audience from the moment you take the stage
- create memorable moments to deepen your connection with your audience throughout your presentation
- make the major points of your speech unforgettable long after you leave the stage

> *A callback is a reference to a positive or humorous experience that will connect with your audience emotionally as well as intellectually.*

Create Instant Rapport with Your Audience

From the moment you take the stage, your audience is already asking three major questions:

1. Who are you?
2. Why should I listen?
3. Does this person connect with me?

Questions 1 and 2 should be answered by the person who introduces you, or at least by the program handout. Answering question 3 is up to you, and you need to answer it with the very first words of your speech. Using callbacks is a great way to create an instant connection with your audience and set yourself up for success.

I was once hired by a real estate firm to speak to their sales associates. During the pre-planning meeting, Thomas, one of the senior executives, joked that I had been around for years. To be exact, he said, "Wade has been around since dinosaurs roamed the earth."

On the day of the presentation, I began my talk by calling back to Thomas's earlier comment. The audience erupted in laughter. This created my initial connection with the audience that led to a great presentation.

You can also reference shared history between you and your audience. I once saw speaker Charlie "Tremendous" Jones use this technique by referencing the words of the person who introduced him. When he came on stage after the introduction, he said, "What the introducer failed to tell you is that I only had a shoestring budget, but I still got here. What the introducer failed to tell you is that I'm just a country boy, but through hard work and perseverance, look at where I am now. What the introducer failed to tell you is that if it's possible for me to make it, then it's possible for you." We were hooked!

In truth, to create instant rapport, you can use a callback to refer to any kind of shared experience—besides the weather! Just make it simple so your audience can easily connect. I've found that a humorous shared experience works best, especially if it's self-deprecating.

Create Memorable Moments to Deepen Your Connection with Your Audience

As important as rapport is, it is a surface connection. If you lose that connection, you will lose your audience. To keep your audience connected, you need to take rapport to another level by *creating memorable moments*. Here are five ways you can use callbacks to deepen your connection with your audience throughout your presentation:

1. Empower your audience. As you're crafting your speech, take a moment and reflect on the experience you will have had at this point with your audience. What does the audience need to hear that will make them feel empowered about themselves and their situation? If you help people feel better about themselves, they will continue to want to listen.

Tawana Williams is a motivational speaker who was born without arms. In one of her presentations, she uses her audience's personal experiences to create an empowering moment of gratitude. She asks her audience something like the following: "I want you to put your arms behind your back and think about, If you were thirsty, how would you drink, if you had no arms? How would you swat a fly? How would you get a teaspoon of sugar?"

This callback to the audience's inward experience allows the audience to reflect on what they have, and come up with their own private insights that result in a new, empowering perspective. As the audience also notices how much Tawana is enjoying life without arms, and realizes they tend to complain about little things that truly don't matter, they become even more grateful and empowered—without the speaker saying a word.

> *To keep your audience connected, you need to take rapport to another level by creating memorable moments.*

2. Evoke an emotion. Many people come into a presentation on automatic pilot. They're thinking about everything else except the presentation. To shake them out of automatic pilot, evoke a positive emotion with a short and unexpected callback. For example, you can call back to a story or illustration you've used and have them repeat back to you a key word or phrase from a story or illustration you've used to heighten their level of energy, such as, "I'm strong." Several rounds of this can't help but change their emotional state. Anything short and unexpected, referring back to a shared experience or shared information, will shake people out of automatic pilot.

3. Inspire reflection. This approach is the exact opposite of our typical greeting, "How was your day?" It's a surface question that doesn't really invite reflection or deeper thought and almost always results in an automatic, unconsidered response. For an impactful presentation, ask deeper, meaningful questions that make your audience stop and think.

For example, what lesson did you learn from overcoming a certain situation or challenge? What will you do with your day—in the next few hours or even the next few minutes—to make it enjoyable and empowering? The deeper questions you ask, the greater the connection.

Motivational speaker Les Brown is great at this technique, often asking questions such as, "If you had your life to live over, what would you do differently?" These kinds of questions create what we call the "silent hum," an internal pause where your audience begins to reflect on their life.

4. Call to action. Once you've explained a concept, ask yourself, what action steps do you want your audience to take to move them to a positive outcome? Here's an example from one of my own presentations:

Sometimes you have to ask yourself what kind of people you want in your life. Who do you want to count in, and who do you want to count out? If people can't be with you in the hard times, why would you want them with you in the good times?

Ask yourself the hard question: Are there people in my life who aren't good for me? You have to make the tough decision to separate yourself from those people and simply choose not to be in their company. You must take the responsibility to use your time wisely to empower yourself.

5. Deepen relationships among your audience. Certain people stand out in any organization, whether through position or personality. The more you can call back to that shared relationship in your presentation and make that person a part of your presentation, the more meaningful your presentation can becomes.

I used this technique when I was retained by a health-care company to speak to their employees about how to make the upcoming year outstanding. On a few occasions I had already had the pleasure of meeting with Valerie, a well-respected director of the health-care facility. During one of my meetings with Valerie to gather information to prepare for the upcoming presentation, she became teary-eyed when we talked about her love for her employees and passion for the company.

On the day of the presentation, I planned to emphasize the importance of caring and supporting each team member. To make the point, I told the audience about my conversation with Valerie. When I finished this relational "callback," the audience erupted in applause. I asked Valerie to join me on stage. The audience applauded more loudly and started to cheer her name. This created a special moment for everyone.

Make Your Speech Memorable Long After You Leave the Stage

I have heard that most people tend to forget 50 percent of the information they hear. Using a callback can also increase your audience's long-term retention of your information.

One way to increase retention is to use a callback for the main points in your presentation. For example, many say it's difficult to teach young people anything. So if you're giving a presentation to teenagers, you never want to have them sit like dumb listeners. You need to get them involved. When I was asked to conduct a leadership presentation to a group of high-school teenagers, naturally I wanted them to retain the information long term. To help them remember my main points, I used the acronym LEAD. For each point, I had them scream the acronym back to me. To invite a little competition, I split them up into two groups, and I'd ask them, "So, let's see which group is the most energetic group. Group A, say, 'LEAD.'" Group A shouted, "LEAD!" I responded, "Well, that sounds great—but what do you think, Group B?" Of course, Group B shouted, "LEAD!" even louder. And so on. Finally, at the end of the presentation, I had the audience repeat each of the four main points after me, following the LEAD acronym.

This technique is also called "anchoring the point to the audience." Although the audience may think it's simply an entertaining game, it actually helps them remember it. Months later, in the local mall I saw one of the young men who attended the presentation. He stopped me and recited the four major points from the presentation seamlessly.

When I say it, they're my words. When the audience says it, they becomes their words and their belief.

Another way to use the callback strategy for retention is to call back to known characters in your presentation. For example, in one of my presentations I used the acronym DREAM to structure my main points. To increase retention, I referred back to a figure everyone knew. I said, "Martin Luther King Jr. had a dream. What is *your* dream?"

Finally, you can increase long-term retention by using an activity people are familiar with and link it to your main point. I have seen my good friend Craig Valentine use this technique with good effect. He told the audience (my paraphrase), "We're going to play the grown-up version of Simon Says. Look directly at me and do what I say. Extend your hand. Touch your nose." Craig gave the audience a series of simple commands, and each time he also followed the command. Then he gave one more command: "Good—now, touch your cheek." This time Craig touched his chin—as did most people in the audience.

Craig also knew that when you lead an activity like this, it's important not to tell your audience the meaning outright. After the activity, he asked them, "What was the meaning of that activity?" After some reflection, they responded, "People do what you do, not what you say." This approach not only makes the activity more fun, but the point more memorable, because the audience figured it out themselves.

Whether creating rapport at the beginning of your presentation, memorable moments to sustain that connection during your presentation, or long-term retention after your presentation has ended, using callbacks is an easy, versatile, and powerful strategy for connecting with your audience. You'll never have to resort to tired jokes or talking about the weather again.

Wade Randolph is a leadership and productivity strategist who works with managers and directors to improve their employee's performance, productivity, and efficiency. He specializes in leadership, teamwork, communication, and motivation. He resides in Midlothian, Virginia, with his wife Alice. Wade can be reached at <u>*wade@themoreguy.com*</u> *or* <u>*www.randolphunlimited.net*</u>.

8

Create a
Compelling Scene
David Chase

People won't remember what you say as much as they will remember what they see when you say it.

—**Patricia Fripp**, executive speech coach, CSP, CPAE

reating a vivid scene is a powerful way to connect emotionally with your audience, enable them to remember your message, and persuade them to take action. In this chapter you will gain an understanding of:

- why clear, effective scenes are so important
- what to put in your scenes to draw in your audience
- how to deliver the scenes to keep your audience engaged

Story Is the Heart of World Class Speaking

Bill Gove, the first president of the National Speakers Association, summed up public speaking as: "tell a story, make a point." To be a World Class speaker, however, you want to go beyond simply telling the story. You must take the audience on a memorable, emotional journey. This is because they will be much more likely to remember the story. And if they remember your story, they are more likely to remember—and act on—your point. When you craft a clear scene that your audience can relate to, in effect you paint a picture your audience can become part of—that touches their world experiences.

Consider this example: *"Once when I was in the Navy, I had the awful job of Jack of the Dust."* So far, not a very interesting story. That's because you are not likely to have any point of reference or similar experience to relate to. Now let's set the scene: *"Imagine crawling to the bottom of a tiny storage compartment, crammed full of cartons of canned food threatening with every unexpected roll of the ship to come crashing down on your head. Somewhere in that dim, dusty space is a carton of lima beans the ship's cook has ordered you to retrieve. It was the worst job I ever had. I was Jack of the Dust."*

Is that better? Do you feel more connected? Even though you may not have the specific experience, you can likely see, feel, hear, and perhaps even smell the situation. By creating a scene you can relate to, I have invited you along on my journey. In World Class Speaking, this is known as "Tap and Transport"—tap into the audience's world and transport them to the world of your story (and message).

What to Put in Your Scenes

As illustrated in the example above, the goal of an effective scene is to create an emotional setting that the audience will find relatable. Throughout this process a critical element is to connect with the senses of the audience. In World Class Speaking, this is referred to as "Checking the VAKS." VAKS stands for visual, auditory, kinesthetic, and smell. When describing any of the elements of the scene, include a variety of these sensory elements. In this section we will focus on three components of an effective scene:[1]

- Circumstances: where are we?
- Characters: who's involved?
- Conflict: what's the problem?

Circumstances

Our first task in creating a scene is to describe, using the VAKS sensory descriptors, the setting of the story—everything the audience needs to know to put themselves

---

1   Of course there's more to a compelling story than these factors, but our focus here is on setting the scene. For a more thorough guide to telling a powerful story, I recommend Craig Valentine's six-CD program *The Edge of Their Seats Storytelling Home-Study Course for Speakers!*

in the scene. Where are we? What is the physical setting? What is the weather like? What time of day is it? A word of caution here, however. Anton Chekhov, the classic Russian novelist and playwright, offered writers this advice: "Remove everything that has no relevance to the story. If you say in the first chapter that there is a rifle hanging on the wall, in the second or third chapter it absolutely must go off. If it's not going to be fired, it shouldn't be hanging there."

Too many details, especially if they aren't relevant to your point, can distract your audience or, worse, bore them. The question to ask is what is the value of each particular detail for the audience? Will it help them understand the situation or get the point? If not, leave it out. For example, your audience may neither care nor need to know that you took the bus to work the day you were fired. Just because it happened that way doesn't mean you have to include that detail—unless of course it's relevant to the point of the story.

> *Too many details, especially if they aren't relevant to your point, can distract your audience or, worse, bore them.*

Characters

Strong scenes have memorable characters that the audience can relate to. This can be accomplished by providing not only a physical description but also a psychological (or emotional) description—how does the character think or feel about the situation.

As with details in the circumstances, too many characters can confuse your audience. Every story has a protagonist—who the story is about. In most cases the audience should like the protagonist and want him or her to succeed. We tend to like people who are in some way like us—they share our fears, loves, or aspirations. Introduce the protagonist so we can quickly get to know them.

Depending on its nature, your story may have an antagonist, or the source of the challenge or roadblock facing your protagonist. Once again a physical and emotional description will help the audience understand the nature of the conflict. They might also begin to anticipate what the protagonist must do to overcome the challenge.

Other characters may appear in your stories. For example, there could be a "guru" who teaches the protagonist a valuable lesson, or a confidant with whom the protagonist can share important ideas or thoughts (such as Sherlock Holmes's

Dr. Watson). Such characters can be introduced early in the setting of the scene or evolve as the story develops. In either case the audience will benefit from at least some physical description and explanation of the relationship to the protagonist.

Conflict

Conflict brings a story to life. In his book *Story*, screenwriting expert Robert McKee puts forth a Law of Conflict: Nothing moves forward in a story except through conflict. Without conflict that engages the emotions a scene will quickly lose its appeal. This is when your audience begins to check their email—not good. The earlier you can introduce the conflict, the better your audience will respond.

> *The earlier you can introduce the conflict,*
> *the better your audience will respond.*

"Ah, yes," you say, "but I need to give some background so my audience will understand the conflict." Fine, I get it. Your goal, however, is to get the audience thinking as quickly as possible *What's going to happen next?* Hollywood often does this with ominous music (think *Jaws*). As a speaker, you may not have that option, but you can still foreshadow what the conflict is going to be. One way to accomplish this is through delivery, which will be discussed in the next section. The words you use can also evoke an emotional reaction in anticipation of the conflict.

Here is an example: *"My friend Ed and I had just raised the mainsail on Steve's boat as we headed back up the Potomac River. Congratulating ourselves on a successful outing, we settled in for the sail home. Perhaps it was the celebratory cold beer that made us miss the menacing dark cloud fast approaching from the South."* [Cue the music…it's about to storm.]

Hollywood screenwriters have a maxim: enter the scene late and leave early. What this means for speakers is that the sooner you can get to the conflict—the dramatic event—the more engaged your audience will be.

How to Deliver a Scene for Impact

Delivery is key to selling a scene. Everything you do can either amplify and clarify what you say, or it can contradict and confuse your point. The difference comes down to how consistently you commit to the scene. In other words, when you are in the scene be completely immersed in the circumstances, characters, and conflict you have created. This will draw the audience into the scene with you. A clear vision of the scene in your mind will translate to a similar vision in the minds of your audience. In this section you will pick up three delivery techniques that will result in powerful, memorable scenes:[2]

- Provide visual cues to match the verbal details.
- React to the environment you have created.
- Make your movements matter.

Visual Cues

While your words can convey clear pictures in the minds of your audience, some details can be communicated more powerfully through nonverbal means. This is especially true of emotions. It also applies to shapes and spatial relationships. Providing strong visual cues of the size, shape, and relative location of objects in your scene will help the audience picture the scene. This is done with realistic gestures as if the imagined object were there.

As an example, suppose your story involves a first-grader learning to write in school. Where would you place the desk? Probably high on the chest, unless your character is a very tall first-grader.

Remember this: your audience will remember the visual scene you put in their minds. Once you have clearly identified where everyone and everything necessary is in your scene, keep everything in its place unless the plot makes it clear why someone or something has moved. Otherwise your audience will be distracted or confused, thinking *Did I miss something? Wasn't the hyena over there?*

React to the Environment

Once you have built the scene through consistent verbal and visual details, your characters' actions and reactions have to respect the imagined physical and environmental reality you have created for the audience. For example, if you put a table in the middle of the scene, your characters must walk around that table. Otherwise the audience will wonder where the table went rather than following the

---

2   More details of powerful delivery techniques are provided in other chapters of this book. See also Craig Valentine's *Dynamic Delivery Devices* DVD product.

rest of the story. If your characters are in a tight space, they should stand or move in a way that is consistent with the audience's mental picture of that space.

Similarly, if you tell the audience it is cold, your characters should act cold. Or if the scene is on a sunny beach, the characters should squint.

This is especially true of the emotional environment. World Class speakers don't retell stories, they relive them—showing the emotions of the moment. The primary tool for expressing emotions is your face. Human facial expressions of fear, anger, happiness, sadness, surprise, contempt, and disgust are recognizable across a wide range of cultures; some experts believe they are universal. If your characters are feeling any of these emotions, show it in your face.

Make Movement Matter

People are very alert to movement. We notice movement and quickly try to assess its meaning. At some point in our evolutionary past this was a survival mechanism. For the most part we don't need to identify predators today, but the capability remains. The point is that the audience will notice movement and attach meaning to it. This makes movement a potent part of your process. That movement should match the circumstances of the scene. If the action of the story implies the characters are moving—move. If not, don't.

Remember the sailboat and looming storm I described earlier? Suppose when the winds pick up, one of the characters goes forward to take down a sail. Go forward—quickly. Later when the characters are huddled in the cabin waiting for the wind to die down (stay with me...imagine that's the plot here), stay put—in the cabin.

One final word on movement: this relates to movement in and out of the scene. Characters in your scene react to each other and the environment you have created. As a character in the scene, you cannot engage the audience. That would disengage your audience, jolting them out of the scene. In acting this is known as breaking the fourth wall—the one between the actors and the audience. The same principle applies to speaking. If you need to interact with the audience, step out of the scene. This could be a literal step out—moving to a different space on the stage. Or it could be as subtle as a clear change in posture and voice, from character to speaker.

Next Action Steps

Creating a memorable, emotion-packed scene takes thoughtful planning and diligent practice. There are many questions involved. At what point should the scene begin?

End? What details matter to the audience? What is the emotional meaning of the scene? How do I convey that emotion? What does the audience need to know? How does the scene make my point? Thinking through all the questions will pay off in a well-structured scene that is both engaging and memorable.

Many of these questions won't have clear answers—there's not one right way to create a scene. There are choices to be made. Try different approaches, preferably in front of an audience that can give you feedback. Toastmasters International is one option for such an audience. If you are not already a member, find a club nearby.

Keep in mind, however, that not every audience is qualified to give you specific feedback on ways to improve your structure, content, and especially delivery. Reading books like this one can provide valuable guidance, but at some point you may want to engage a qualified coach. Every chapter in this book was written by a certified World Class Speaking coach, trained in the principles and techniques described in this book. Feel free to contact one in your area to see how coaching could benefit you.

David Chase is a certified World Class Speaking coach. He is founder of David Chase Presents, a firm that helps individuals and organizations maximize their influence through more powerful communication. You can find more information about his coaching and other training products at www.davidchasepresents.com.

9

Closing with Impact:
Leave Your Audience on a High

Robert Gordyn

Imagine you're delivering a forty-minute keynote speech with your audience's undivided attention. So far your message has been well assimilated and acknowledged. By combining fundamental delivery techniques with a significant and well-structured message, you've made a strong connection with your audience. And now you've reached the closing. At this point you must be on guard against your own complacency, for your speech is not yet over.

Regardless of how successful your speech has been up to these final few moments, without a *meaningful* and *memorable* closing your prior success will be for naught. Your audience will leave the lecture hall feeling deflated. In this chapter you'll learn six specific strategies to close your speech effectively. Used either alone or in combination with each other, these strategies will have you closing your speeches with impact and leaving your audience with a positive and unforgettable impression of your speech, your message, and you.

This chapter will describe why the closing is so important and present some dos and don'ts to remember during the final part of your speech. Additionally, it will outline the following six closing strategies:

1. Quotations
2. Poems
3. Call to Action
4. Letting Them Speak
5. A Question
6. Circling Back

A final note will illustrate the how and why of summarizing your speech effectively.

Why Is the Closing So Important?

With a favorite book or movie, chances are you can easily recall both its beginning and end. This is due to our tendency to remember most what we hear or see first and last of any event or piece of work. This applies to speeches as well. And in terms of the closing, as Hall of Fame speaker Patricia Fripp emphasizes, "Your last words linger." This refers to the final words you utter as you end your speech, for these are the words that will stick in the minds of your audience. There are three other reasons your closing needs special consideration:

- "Your close is the reason and the reinforcement to everything you've told your audience," says professional speaker Darren LaCroix. "Therefore, you are looking to craft your close to have it both summarize and enhance your message."
- Your message should never be left dangling, nor should your audience. The message needs to be summarized neatly.
- There exists an all-too-familiar and oft-used closing that should be avoided. This takes the form of "Thank you for your attention. Are there any questions?" This energy-sapping close is not creative and not what you want your audience to remember most from your speech.

Dos and Don'ts When Closing Your Speech

Don't:
- introduce any new points, as you won't have time to develop them.
- end with a Q&A session. This will just about guarantee a low-energy closing to your speech. You'll lose control of your speech, and the questions may be long-winded, irrelevant, and/or unanswerable at that moment.

Do:

- let your audience know you are about to close your speech; they'll pay attention to your final words.
- designate about 10 percent of your speech to the closing. For instance, a forty-minute keynote would include a three- to four-minute closing.

Let's now move on to the six speech-closing strategies and how to use them effectively.

Quotations

Using the compelling words and phrases of well-known individuals to help you deliver your message adds weight and credibility to your speech, especially when used at the close. There are a great many creative and thought-provoking quotations to choose from that will lend themselves to any topic.

For example, in a speech about success and the vital role of taking action, I quote Henry David Thoreau, who says, "Success usually comes to those who are too busy to be looking for it." This reinforces the main point of my talk, which is the need to take action and work hard in achieving one's goals.

Another speech that deals with the desire either for a career change or for embarking on a different path later in life has me quoting the Turkish proverb "No matter how far you have gone on a wrong road, turn back"—thus reinforcing the stages of my own personal journey where I took a sudden, dramatic, and successful turn in my career later in life.

Where to Find Quotations

I keep a book called *The Book of Positive Quotations*, arranged by John Cook, on my desk. It is a great resource for quotations on a wide variety of topics by persons from an equally wide range of backgrounds, professions, and ideologies. I highly recommend that any public speaker acquire a copy. Quotations don't necessarily have to be from famous people. Expressive and thought-provoking statements can be acquired from many other sources such as your friends, family, and acquaintances, as well as from the literature you read.

Tips for Using Quotations

1. Be careful with overly familiar quotations that have become clichéd through excessive use. Bear in mind that if you know them well, chances are your audience does too. An alternative would be to use lesser-known quotes from people who are nonetheless famous.
2. Select quotations that are brief, encompassing a single statement. It is their brevity that makes them retainable.
3. Ensure that the quotation is relevant to and encapsulates your message.

Carefully selected quotations add zest to your closure. Having audience members leave the room with a fresh quote resounding in their minds renders your message indelible.

Poems

People generally enjoy hearing well-crafted and image-provoking words. In this regard, poetry can be used effectively as a speech-closing strategy. One stanza of poetry can summarize and emphasize your main message in a lyrical fashion. You can be joined onstage, figuratively speaking, by famous poets who will aid in the delivery of your message.

For example, in a motivational talk I might close with a stanza from the poem "Still I Rise" by Maya Angelou:

> *Does my sassiness upset you?*
> *Why are you beset with gloom?*
> *'Cause I walk like I've got oil wells*
> *Pumping in my living room.*

This stanza reinforces the role confidence plays in achieving personal success. A carefully selected passage of poetry to close your speech will give the audience a memorable lift.

Tips for Using Poetry

*   Make sure your chosen poem is relevant to your topic.
*   Be certain that it contributes to your summary.

- Keep it to one short stanza of about four or five lines.
- As much as possible, select pieces that rhyme as these can be readily remembered.
- Be eclectic in your selections. For example, check out rap songs if you're speaking to a younger crowd. Browse through traditional sources for more senior groups.

A Call to Action

In many of your speeches, you will call upon your audience to take some kind of transformative action. This requires a specific call to action at the close of the speech. There are two reasons to consider employing this type of closing strategy:

1. The action will benefit those in the audience.
2. The action will legitimize and support, in a real and practical way, the arguments you've presented in your speech.

> *A call to action will legitimize and support, in a real and practical way, the arguments you've presented in your speech.*

When you've delivered your message convincingly, your audience will be eager to apply it in a follow-up action. And your call to action gives them the practical means to do that.

For instance, in my keynote on change, part of my closing includes a request that my audience meet new people. This involves stepping out of one's regular social circles and comfort zones and trying something different. This might include joining a Kiwanis Club, a Toastmasters Club, or a local Chamber of Commerce. Those who act upon my request support their belief in my message that meeting new people from different walks of life helps generate new ideas and perspectives.

A call to action imparts your speech with the substance that takes your audience from theory to practice. When they act upon this call, they discover that your closing request brings them benefits. And with this result, they experience directly the message embedded in your speech.

Letting Them Speak

Audiences love to be heard, and by being heard within the framework of the speech, they actively contribute to its success. You can give them numerous opportunities to participate throughout your speech, including at the close. By having them help you close your speech, they generate the repetition and reinforcement necessary to remember your message. One way to let them speak is to have them assist you in your summary.

For example, in my introductory seminar on speaking skills, I take my audience through the basic categories of public speaking competence: content, structure, and delivery. To review and reinforce these, I'll provide an example of a category we have reviewed and have them identify it. For instance, I'll say, "The words you use are part of the category of…" and they'll respond with "content." I'll then continue with "The organization of that content is from the category of…" and they should respond with "structure." Finally I'll say, "And the way you use the words and apply structure onstage is all about…" and they'll finish it off with "delivery."

When you encourage your audience to speak during your closing, they leave on a high because of the active review they've helped provide.

A Question

Posing a question is an effective way to begin a speech. It is an equally effective strategy for closing your speech. A well-structured and relevant question that brings your speech to a close gives your audience the opportunity to contemplate their possible response and combine what they've learned in your talk with their personal views.

For example, in one of Craig Valentine's keynotes, he closes by asking "Are you too good to be great?" This generates a great deal of reflection because it forces the listeners to consider whether their current comfort level is keeping them from achieving more in life.

In another example, at the end of my talk on leadership, when I have established the link between good speaking skills and effective leadership abilities,

I close with a simple three-word question: "Who are you?" This has them leaving the lecture hall contemplating their own leadership characteristics.

Tips on Closing with Questions

- For the most part, use open-ended "wh" questions, as these require thought and analysis. However, the occasional yes/no question can be effective if it is particularly thought provoking.
- Keep your questions short. This gives them clarity and makes them memorable.
- Ensure that all queries are closely tied to your main point.

Relevant and thought-provoking questions will leave your audience with something significant to ponder as they exit the lecture hall.

> *Relevant and thought-provoking questions will leave your audience with something significant to ponder as they exit the lecture hall.*

Circling Back

A most effective tool for closing your speech with impact involves circling back to your opening. By doing this, you provide a closing that highlights and revisits the opening ideas of the speech.

Some of the closing strategies discussed in this chapter can also be used for your opening, such as inserting a quote, a poem, or posing a question, each of which is then rounded off at the close. For instance, a speech that begins with a story can end with the conclusion of that story. Like what lies within the pages of a great novel, circling back is the binding agent that holds your speech together in the hearts and minds of your audience. Let's look at a few examples.

After having opened a speech with Sigmund Freud's suggestion that "every dream is a wish," I would close by rephrasing that statement in this way: "Maybe dreams aren't wishes, as Freud argues; perhaps they are portals in time...." I could then summarize my main points to support my rewording of Freud's idea.

Another example: in an introductory talk on public speaking, I could begin by asking the audience, "What do you think most people identify as their number one fear?" The response here is "speaking in public." The subsequent information presented in my seminar would serve to neutralize this fear. I could therefore close by revisiting the opening question: "You now know what most people don't: fear of public speaking can be overcome."

By using the circling back strategy, not only is your talk neatly packaged, it also affords you the opportunity to reinforce your message through the repetition needed to make it memorable.

A Final Note: Be Sure to Summarize

Along with employing the six closing strategies outlined in this chapter, do make time for summarizing the key points of your talk. Whether your talk is structured using numbers (1, 2, 3…), with an acronym (e.g. TALL, as Craig Valentine uses for Think, Act, Laugh, Learn), letters (e.g. The 3 Es of Speaking: Educate, Encourage, Entertain), or some other structural tool, build in the time you need in your closing to review each main point. Summarizing enhances the audience's retention of the main points of your speech.

Conclusion

In this chapter you've learned six strategies for closing your speech with impact:

1. Quotations
2. Poems
3. Call to Action
4. Letting Them Speak
5. A Question
6. Circling Back

You have also learned the necessity of including a summary at the close of your speech. To *circle back* to the opening line of this chapter, imagine you're delivering a forty-minute keynote speech that is well received. Imagine also the level of success you are going to attain with a closing that is memorable, meaningful, and leaves your audience on a high.

Robert Gordyn, MA, MPhil, is a speech trainer, keynote speaker, and certified World Class Speaking coach. He is the founder of Speech Training International and can be reached at www.speechtraininginternational.com.

Part 3

CREATING WORLD CLASS CONTENT

10

Be Diligent and Your Audience Will Be Delighted

Mohamed Isa

There is no feeling like leaving the stage knowing you have delighted your audience! You feel enchanted, elated, and elevated. In the following pages you will discover how to create a lasting positive impression with any audience. This chapter has a simple premise. To delight your audience you must...

- know who they are
- engage your audience beforehand
- let them laugh
- inspire your audience into action
- test new techniques all the time
- leave nothing to chance

To help you remember the steps of this process, I've devised an acrostic using the word DELIGHT:

- **D—Do** your homework. Research your client's requirements and the audience mix.
- **E—Engage** your audience before the speech begins. Greet them. Talk to them.
- **L—Laugh** at yourself and the audience will surely laugh with you.
- **I—Inspire** your audience into action by sharing with them easy-to-implement tips.
- **G—Get** it right. Do not leave anything to chance.
- **H—Harness** the energy of the audience by applying a variety of speaking tools.
- **T—Test** new contents and delivery techniques to continue delighting your audience!

I will share some of my firsthand experiences as well as my observations from a few World Class speakers. As you read you will pick up a number of tried and tested techniques to leave a positive impression with any audience you will ever face in your career.

Are you ready to *delight* your audience? Let's go for it!

Know Who They Are

In March 2013 I served as the chairman of a conference, and before the program the master of ceremonies asked me if I could go through her remarks. She had a joke against men. I told her: "Remove this or you will lose more than 70 percent of the audience." She was upset because she wanted to make the women in the audience laugh. "Just make them feel good if you can't replace this joke," I advised. "By the way, how did you get this role in the conference?" It turned out that her father knew the event organizer and asked him if he could help his daughter get some experience and exposure.

I gave her a suggestion that worked very well with the audience. As she took the microphone she said, "Whenever I speak in public I have butterflies in my stomach, but today is different. Today the butterflies flew away because my dad is sitting over there. Thank you, Dad, for being here for me."

What do you think happened that day? There was a thunderous round of applause and she received a standing ovation from the entire delegation, including the minister of defense. Compare this reaction to the possible scenario if she had told her joke about the man who could not change a light bulb!

Once I was invited to speak to a large group of health professionals at a military hospital. I conducted my research and customized my speech to meet their requirements as specified by the training officer. Three days before the speech, I called the officer to see if my audio/video needs were arranged, and luckily I asked him this question: "Tell me, do they like to laugh?" And this was his answer: "No, no, no. No jokes at all!"

This question saved me from trying to be funny with an audience that does not easily laugh given the nature of their strict military culture. And true to his words, there was not a single laugh for the entire ninety-minute speech. Had I not known about their "no laughter" culture, the speech delivery would have drained my energy and made me feel like I bombed.

Takeaway: *Get the audience right and you will be all right!*

Engage Your Audience Beforehand

Meet and greet your audience before your speech. I always make it a point to arrive early to the speaking venue to meet audience members either at the gate of the venue or by walking around the hall. In recent events I took this to a higher level. I started using subtle influencing techniques on the audience to shape their expectations about my speech. For example, after greeting the delegates sitting around the tables, I would tell them: "I have a feeling you will laugh a lot today. I can sense it right now. You like to have fun, right?" And their answer is almost guaranteed: "Of course! Who doesn't?"

My champion for applying this technique is Ron Kaufman, who is an expert in customer service. He engages the audience before, during, and after his events whether they are speeches, seminars, or book-signing events. When I met him in Bahrain in October 2012, I told him, "I'm so delighted to be at your event today. I wanted to attend this seminar since 2001 and my workload never allowed me to do so. This is a dream come true." He gave me a bear hug! I never missed a word from his talk. I was hooked, I was engaged, and I was deeply connected.

World Class speakers employ a variety of techniques to engage with their audience. For example, they send out written messages to the audience telling them the benefits of attending their talks, and a more recent trend is to send out video messages to get them excited about the event. What are you doing to engage your audience beforehand?

Takeaway: *Engage your audience early on or else they will move on!*

Engage your audience early on or else they will move on!

Let Them Laugh

I'm blessed to be bald and I'm making the best of it. Whenever I face a new audience, I always poke fun at my baldness and talk about my favorite shampoo: Head & Shoulders! The audience loves it and it works all the time. I get a few loud laughs every time I use this icebreaker, and what a way to start your speech by having the audience laughing.

If you are not comfortable using self-deprecating humor, try sharing some funny anecdotes or stories from your life. I'm sure you have many. Recently I spoke at a talent management conference and began my speech this way: "I'm blessed with two talented kids, Dana and Abdulla. Dana is talented in making us get angry whereas Abdulla is talented at…breaking things. So far he broke three iPads, two iPhones, and one forty-six inch TV!" The audience laughed for a few seconds and then I moved on to my speech.

In addition, heed the advice of "master of humor" David Glickman. He recommends that you build punch-lines into your introduction to get the audience laughing even before you take the stage. This helps set the mood for your engagement. For example, I use this line in my speaker introduction: "Mohamed is happily married with two kids—Dana and Abdulla—who are very calm and cool…until they wake up!" And since almost all people connect with kids because kids are all around us, the audience laughs every time. Reconsider the way you write your speaker introduction; make it fun and different to delight your audience.

Takeaway: *Remember, laughter is what people are after!*

Inspire Your Audience into Action

What is the greatest reward you received from a past speech? I don't know about you, but my greatest reward is when I meet an audience member and hear him or her say,

"I started applying some of your techniques in our company, and I'm seeing positive results." In my opinion, this only happens when you have delighted your audience by sharing with them *easy-to-implement tips and techniques.*

In November 2013 I had the privilege to work with Doug Lipp, who speaks about leadership and customer service using his experience at Disney University. His seminar was filled with easy-to-implement tips and techniques. One of the most powerful models he shared with us was the *Start–Stop–Continue Model.* You could use this model on a personal or a business level. What are the things you need to *Start, Stop,* and *Continue* to be more successful in business and life? Write them down and act upon them. Simple, yet so powerful.

In my keynote speech titled "The 3 R's to Employee Engagement," I give the audience an easy-to-follow formula to increase the engagement level at their organization by *recognizing* and *rewarding* their employees and by creating a fun corporate culture through *recreational* activities. Look again at the contents of your speeches. Can you make them tighter and easier to follow by creating formulas, models, or acronyms built throughout the speech?

Takeaway: *If your speech is too loose, you will lose!*

Test New Techniques All the Time

I started working with a large business group on a motivational speech for its top management team. I spoke with the event organizer, the training manager, the human resources director, and finally the general manager. One recurring theme came up in our conversations: they like to have fun (unlike our friends in the military hospital!). And guess what, I love having fun.

Since this was a local business based in Bahrain, I used the country's pearl-diving heritage to have fun with the audience. I used the chorus of a famous pearling song consisting of two parts: "hoob" and "hay." I introduced the concept to the audience by briefing them about the pearl-diving song and then the way we would have fun with it. I said "hoob" and the audience shouted back "hay" throughout the speech to recognize their participation whether in response to questions or comments. The technique worked very well, and the audience continued singing "Hoob Hay" until they left the parking lot! I have tried the "Hoob Hay" technique at different events and it always works. Why? Because the audience loves fresh and creative ideas.

Go beyond the pre-event questionnaire and interviews. Research the culture and heritage of your audience with the aim of creating an "audience energizer" to keep them connected with you. If they are having fun you will have fun too, and you will create a lasting positive impression.

Takeaway: *Be different or be forgotten in no time!*

> *If they are having fun you will have fun too,*
> *and you will create a lasting positive impression.*

Leave Nothing to Chance

Whenever I speak, I run through my checklist to avoid any surprises that may ruin my speech. For example, I will carry two slides clickers, spare batteries, memory sticks with a backup copy of the slides, and of course my own laptop. In the past I used to rely on the laptops or desktops of the organizers to project my slides until it happened: my client had a Mac, and I never used Keynote, the Mac version of PowerPoint. I struggled.

On another occasion I struggled even more. It was a French client, and their laptop was not English enabled. I almost cried. Since the menus were in French, I could not make important amendments to my slides. In French, this engagement was an *échec* (or failure)!

And now to my worst experience: I conducted a three-month public speaking program to a group of senior officials from a ministry in Bahrain. Everything went fine until that fateful day, October 23, 2013. I arrived thirty minutes early to check the venue only to find that the hall was not arranged to my requirements. Worst of all, there was a big steel structure on the stage, and dangling from it were Donald Duck, Spiderman, Superman, Batman, Mickey Mouse, Dora, Popeye, Pink Panther, and of course Tom and Jerry—the remains of a big birthday party held the night before. We could not remove the structure because we didn't have spinach for breakfast that day! Thank God we found another hall to save the day.

As a speaker, you are bound to face challenging situations regardless of your level of preparation. The key is to remain calm and be ready with a comeback. The late Steve Jobs, who was a master communicator, once encountered a technical failure during one of his keynotes. In the middle of his talk the slides clicker did not work so he picked up his spare one, which again did not work. He calmly announced that his clickers were not working, and he told the audience a story while his technical team corrected the issue. They laughed at the story, and then he continued with his presentation when the clicker was fixed.

Takeaway: *To have a happy ending you must have a happy beginning!*

Remember, you are guaranteed to DELIGHT your audience if you:

- **D—Do** your homework. Research your client's requirements and the audience mix.
- **E—Engage** your audience before the speech begins. Greet them. Talk to them.
- **L—Laugh** at yourself and the audience will surely laugh with you.
- **I—Inspire** your audience into action by sharing with them easy-to-implement tips.
- **G—Get** it right. Do not leave anything to chance.
- **H—Harness** the energy of the audience by applying a variety of speaking tools.
- **T—Test** new contents and delivery techniques to continue delighting your audience!

Mohamed Isa is the founder of 3D Speaking, a firm specializing in providing speech coaching services to its clients to help them get laughs, applause, and their messages across. He is also a regular speaker at conferences in the Middle East. He can be reached at Mohamed@3d-speaking.com and www.3dspeaking.com.

11

The True Message
Behind the Story

Jennifer Leone

When Renna sat down to tell me her signature story it was in the same format of many signature stories of clients who had come before her—rags-to-riches stories that tell of tragedy to triumph and hopelessness to happiness. All these stories had challenges, struggles, and the realization that the person wanted more out of life; they wanted to conquer their negative past and redirect their life, resulting in their present-day success.

Renna's story was no different. I asked her what made her go into the business of making massage and lotion candles. Her answer was always the same: "I've loved making candles since the age of fifteen. What started as a hobby is now a multimillion-dollar business." However, she knew that was not the whole reason, the full story, but she didn't know how to articulate the real reason.

The missing link had never been identified, the link that made the connection from what happened to why it happened. My job as a World Class Speaking coach was to find the missing link in her story. It's the *why* of the story—why was she moved to make candles into a business? It had to be more than the "hobby."

To find the *why* I always take my clients through a "detective" process. In this chapter you'll learn how to do the same. The steps in this process are:

- Take me back to the moment when…
- Ask better questions.
- Never stop at the facts—play detective.

Take Me Back to the Moment When…

In any personal life story there is always a moment that defines who you are and why you did what you did, or who you are now because of it. To find out the true message behind their story, I tell my client, "Take me back to the moment when…." The client mentally travels back in time to the scenes in question.

> *In any personal life story there is always a moment that defines who you are and why you did what you did, or who you are now because of it.*

I asked Renna many questions as she reflected back on being fifteen. The *why* was found a few layers down in her story. In order to discover it, I asked her to

- return to the scene
- describe it in detail using all five senses (the sights, sounds, smells, textures, etc.; include both characters and circumstances)

When you ask these exploratory and reflective questions your client will be directed to recall even the smallest details.

Ask Better Questions

- What was she/he like?
- How did they/that make you feel?
- What drew you to her/him?

There is always one character in the story that holds the *why*.

When Renna revealed the character Katerina in her story, she shared that this gentle old lady was her friend who made her feel wanted and loved. She would go to see Katerina every time she visited her homeland.

I didn't just stop there. I asked her, "What was it about Katerina that made you feel wanted and loved?" and "What did Katerina do to make you feel so loved?" Renna told me that her own mother had never bonded with her and gave her away at birth to live with an aunt for three years! She had overlooked this part of the story, considering it too small to mention (Renna eventually returned to her mother).

These questions and answers brought me to the next layer. By asking another question the layer revealed the difference in relationship between Renna's mother and Katerina.

Because Katerina had no children of her own, she befriended Renna as if she were her own. Renna felt loved and wanted. The old woman taught Renna to cook and grow vegetables. One day she wanted Renna to learn how to make candles. This information was my cue to direct my questions to the next layer:

- "How did that feel?" Renna went on to tell me about that day she was allowed to make her own candle—a day she would never forget.
- "Take me back to the moment when you first lit your candle; describe it for me."

Renna said, "When I returned home, I could hear my parents having another argument again. I avoided them and went into my bedroom. I lit my floral-scented candle."

"Do you remember how that felt?" I asked.

"Yes. I was drawn to the flickering light and the warmth of the fire. It reminded me of the warmth of my friend Katerina. The scent of jasmine and roses and sweet pea reminded me of the very few times I went on a picnic in the summer as a family and my parents were happy.

"The scent of the candle made me feel loved and wanted, and Katerina believed in me—that I could do anything I put my heart to. She made me feel I was worthy and I mattered. The floral scent reminded me of the few happy times I once shared with my family."

At that moment Renna started to cry. I could see and sense her *why*, but even more importantly so could Renna.

Now I could begin to construct her true signature story.

Now Renna has a story that connects her emotionally to her product and creates the branding of her product. Customers smell her candles and instinctively are transported to a happy memory or moment in time. Her marketing plan has also changed. Her candles have a story and a purpose and most of all a *why*.

> **To find the point, message, and purpose**
> **(or the why) you need to play detective.**

Never Stop at the Facts—Play Detective

In the structure of a story you have series of facts, characters, plots, dialogue, narration, and circumstances—and in the midst of it a point, message, and purpose. When you look further the true message of why you do what you do and the effect it has on you and the people around you emerges. To find the point, message, and purpose (or the *why*) you need to play detective.

- Break it down into story segments.
- Get your client to describe their characters in detail: how they look, what they wore, and how they made you feel.
- Remind yourself how you felt in the storyline.
- As you explore the layers pay attention to what you really wanted to happen and why.
- Remember the scents in your story. The sense of smell is very powerful and can trigger your memory of smaller details.
- Recall the tones of voice of your characters. Again, this triggers your memory of the smaller details.
- The small details are the clues to the bigger picture.

Elizabeth shared her signature story of troubled teenage angst, expelled from seven schools to becoming the nanny for the second richest billionaire in Australia. With his encouragement she became a millionaire at age twenty-five and one of Australia's first female property developers.

The facts in her story are inspiring. Her experiences traveling the world in a $50 million Lear Jet are fascinating. I knew her audience members would be on the edge of their seats wanting to know more.

As her speech coach I knew that her audience would also want to know at what point she decided she would no longer drift through life without a purpose. Elizabeth had had enough of being a nobody, and the billionaire she worked for was her inspiration to a better life. But I believe that was not the point that helped her to decide. Again I played detective and asked better questions and deeper levels of questions.

Keep Asking and It Will Be Revealed

Elizabeth knew her story was filled with intrigue and inspiration. I believe her missing link was "what made her change from a constantly expelled student to a successful property developer."

She gave the obvious answer: "I had enough." I understood but I knew there was more to it.

I asked more questions of her, about her years as a student. I said, "How were you treated by your peers? What did they call you?" Again she gave the answers, but I knew there was more to her story.

Ask Better Questions

When you feel that a part of the story needs more clarity ask better questions. For me it was her last years as a student. I wanted to know the real reason why she changed her attitude after leaving school.

Elizabeth finally remembered a story that was not in her manuscript. On the night of her formal (prom), she got all dressed up and curled her hair. She felt pretty. That night the teachers presented awards to the high achievers and the most improved, and then the students had their own student presentation. The award for *Most Likely to End up in Jail* went to—Elizabeth. As she recalled the story, for the first time she realized her *why*. With tears streaming down her face, Elizabeth knew this was her aha moment. She is successful because that night she vowed she would prove them wrong one day. And she did.

That was her *why*, her turning point, which gave her the purpose to prove them wrong. It was her missing link that now connected her to her audience. When it made sense to her it became clearer to her audience. She could then better articulate to her audience how they can find their *why* and better define their purpose in life.

The Clues to Your Purpose Are Found in the Why of Your Story

I have shared with you my personal experience as a speech coach and how I play detective in finding my clients' real purpose in their signature stories. The process I use has always helped me find what truly matters to their stories and the purpose they have for sharing them. Let's recap some of the clues I use in my process.

- Don't settle for what you hear in your client's story. These are only the facts. Become the detective and take your client back in time.
- Get them to recall the scenes in detail. Ask them to close their eyes and picture that time in their life.
- What do they see, what do they smell, how do they feel, what do they hear?
- Ask better questions so that you trigger their memory of the smaller details.

As a speaker you have a story to tell. The process I have shared here produces the results to uncover your pure intent and the true message of your signature story.

The more you can remember about your own personal story the closer you will get to your *why*.

Audiences today hear many inspirational stories, but only a few will really move them to think about the core message long after they heard it. Stories that share the *why* leave you moved beyond words; they leave with you the insight to search for your own *why* and purpose.

Uncovering your true message is an emotional journey—one that is well worth the trip.

Jennifer Leone is Australia's first specialized signature story speech coach, helping speakers uncover the true intent and message in their stories. Whether it is through one-on-one coaching or Skype sessions, Jennifer gives her clients exactly what they are looking for in their stories. She can be reached at www.talktrainers.com.au or by email at jennifer.leone99.

12

Uncovering Your PARTS Formula

Rena Romano

Most speakers have great intentions of offering value to their audience. The challenge for many is that they try to offer too much content with very little substance, which only confuses their audience. Speakers may share touching stories but the stories have no correlation to their message, or they have no stories at all and simply bore the audience with facts and figures.

Some speakers spend their entire presentation pitching their product or service, offering no value at all. Audiences are seeking a message of hope, words of wisdom, and as speakers we should offer these with a specific action-step to help them better their lives.

A World Class Speaker knows that every audience will have the following thoughts on their minds: "So what! Who cares? What's in it for me?" We speak to create change in others, and whether you're a keynote speaker or business professional, incorporating at least four if not all five pieces of the PARTS formula will help you create compelling content, avoid data dumping, and offer value to your audience.

The PARTS formula is designed to help speakers:

- get their **Point** across
- **Anchor** their message
- create change through **Reflection**
- apply **Techniques** for calls to action
- Sell an idea, product, or service (**Sale**)

Many professionals (including you?) speak at civic clubs and associations to market their businesses in the community. Keep in mind that these venues are looking for educational, informative presentations, and the best way to create connections and increase sales is to offer value when speaking—not a sales pitch. Also, you may only have twenty to forty-five minutes to speak, so it is imperative that you get to the point. This is where the "ten to one rule" should be applied: for every ten minutes make one point.

Meeting with a client I will ask, "What do you want to talk about? What is your main message?" Many people have a difficult time getting to the point, and more often than not they don't even know the point of their speech. Conclusion: they have too many messages or topics they want to speak about.

> *Too many speakers try to get across too*
> *much information in too little time.*
> **—Craig Valentine**

Whether you're giving a keynote or speaking in your local market, if your only concern is pitching your product or service you're sure to alienate the audience. Offering a presentation that provides value will help build your credibility and increase sales effortlessly. Incorporating the PARTS formula in your presentation will help you create compelling content so you can connect with your audience and make a lasting impact.

Point

Speakers often have a difficult time getting their *point* across because they can't communicate it in a short sentence. A *foundational phrase* is designed to help you develop a short sentence and get your point across in fewer than ten words. It must be brief, clear, and concise, keeping you focused; if it's rhythmic that's even better. Your foundational phrase should be a memorable, repeatable gift your audience can take with them.

The following are sample foundational phrases I use to help get my point across.

- Developing a foundational phrase will help you be remembered and repeated: *"If you want praise, include a phrase"* (seven words).
- Public speaking isn't about being a perfect speaker; it's about being an effective speaker: *"Don't strive for perfection, strive for connections"* (seven words).
- Speaking in your local market will help you generate more leads, more customers, and more profits: *"People buy from people they know, like, and trust"* (nine words).
- Practicing your presentation before going live will help you present it as a polished professional: *"Practice doesn't make perfect, practice makes improvements"* (seven words).
- Try to avoid data dumping; real stories will help you connect with your audience: *"Statistics are boring, stories stop the snoring"* (seven words).
- Being authentic in your delivery is vital to help you achieve a real connection with your audience: *"Be true, be you, and have fun too"* (eight words).
- Don't sweat the small mistakes when presenting; so what who cares, no one is a perfect speaker: *"Life is about success not perfection"* (six words; Dr. Alan Weiss, author and speaker).
- To help you build credibility, preparation is crucial to achieve an effective presentation. Don't wing it: *"If you fail to prepare, be prepared to fail"* (nine words; credited to Benjamin Franklin).

If you have trouble developing a foundational phrase, use a short quote that reflects your message. Just be sure to acknowledge the author. When developing your foundational phrase enlist the help of colleagues, family, and friends. If they're repeating it you know you have a winner.

Your foundational phrase should tie into your anchor. If any of your content is not relevant to your foundational phrase it must be eliminated. *"When in doubt leave it out"* (six words; Craig Valentine, author and speaker).

Anchor

An *anchor* is anything that helps your audience remember your points, and there are four anchors to choose from. Stories are the number one favorite. If you incorporate the others as well you can have an effective presentation.

1. **Anecdote:** a story
2. **Analogy:** a comparison
3. **Acronym:** an abbreviation
4. **Activity:** an action

Example: A client, the clerk of the circuit court, was asked to speak for thirty minutes to the local Realtors Association. She knew the premise of her presentation would focus on change. Her office was converting to an electronic filing system, and she wanted to assure the community that the changes would benefit local businesses. She established her foundational phrase, which was *"Change is good and essential for your business."*

The best stories to use are personal stories; however, she was hard pressed to come up with any that would help get her point across. She did have facts, figures, and a chart that were essential to her speech, but to avoid data dumping and boring her audience she agreed that she must add an anchor. After hearing how one or more of the anchors could be used in a presentation, she mentioned that she recently viewed a documentary featuring Henry Ford and wondered if she could use it.

To demonstrate, the following is a brief summation of the story she used. The documentary focused on Ford's Model T, which was mass-produced for nineteen years with very few changes. Ford wanted to keep the Model T simple and affordable for the masses. He believed the Model T was the only type of car a person would ever need, and therefore change was not necessary. The Model T was a commercial success selling more than fifteen million cars from 1908 to 1927.

Eventually other companies started introducing more comfortable stylish cars at competitive prices. The Model T was losing its market share, but Ford still would not make any changes to the design. With declining sales he finally conceded that *change is good and essential for business.* In May 1927 the company ceased production of the Model T and began producing the Model A. That model proved to be Ford's second best success, and it came in a wide variety of styles and luxuries to meet the needs of every economic lifestyle.

My client's presentation was an enormous success. Even though she didn't use a personal story the audience was captivated by the story/analogy of Henry Ford. The anchor tied effortlessly to her foundational phrase, *"Change is good and essential for your business,"* and helped her get her point across. Just as an anchor holds a boat securely in place, anchors in your presentation will hold your audience captivated in their seats.

Reflection

World Class speakers speak to create change in others. Sharing stories and asking questions can help an audience reflect on their current situation and assist them in change. As Patricia Fripp has said, "With reflection comes wisdom."

Another example is a client who is a wealth management advisor and works with people who are retired or nearing retirement. She offers affordable financial solutions so they can maintain their wealth and remain in their own homes versus being financially forced to live in a nursing home. She speaks often in her local community. Unfortunately, her return-on-invest (ROI) was less than stellar and she feared losing her job. Another client who was having great success using the World Class Speaking program referred her to me. Witnessing firsthand his ROI from just one speech—the leads and new clients he generated—she called immediately.

During the first consultation I was thrilled to hear that she had a presentation the following day. Rearranging my calendar, and with video camera in tow, I attended her presentation. At the next session we would watch the video together for a formal evaluation. To sum it up briefly, she was personable and showed no fear of speaking. However, her presentation was full of facts and figures. There were no stories for the audience to relate to or questions to help them reflect on their own situation. It was forty-five minutes of pure data dumping.

Introducing the PARTS formula, she thought about the clients she was currently working with and how her program had changed their financial situation to meet their goals.

The deeper she dug, the more her success stories started flowing. She immediately had nine stories to choose from. She picked three that would relate to the audience she was speaking to the following week. Without using clients' names or other references to ensure confidentiality, she incorporated their stories using the Then/Now/How method (explained in greater detail in the following chapter). She eliminated unnecessary data and asked questions to help her audience reflect on their own situation. For example: "Would you rather live out your golden years in a nursing home or remain comfortably in your own home for the remainder of your life?"

Her ROI from that one speaking engagement was over 50 percent, and she continues to break her own goals every time she speaks.

Helping your audience reflect on their current situation can create change in them. What do you want them to think, feel, or do differently after your speech? What stories and questions can you incorporate that will assist you in connecting and creating a change in your audience? Be sure to pause and allow them time to reflect on their own situation. "If there is no reflection, there is no connection."

> ### *If there is no reflection, there is no connection.*

Techniques

Reflection helps an audience think or feel differently. A *technique* is the "do differently" to help them walk a different path. It is the what, or tangible specific action, to give your audience to do. Speakers often tell their audience what to do in a way that doesn't influence them. Instead it creates resistance. Don't you hate being told what to do? Do you resist when that happens to you? If you want to help your audience improve their lives, show them how to do it.

The following are examples of how to incorporate techniques in your presentations. One client who is a massage therapist will have a volunteer come forward and show the audience how to sit properly in a chair to avoid back pain when working at the computer. He also encourages taking breaks throughout the day and shows them simple stretching techniques. His foundational phrase is *"Proper posture prevents pain."* Using the technique formula, he gives his audience a tangible action they can use when they leave. Forgoing the sales pitch and adding a technique has increased his business by over 60 percent.

One technique I often use is to encourage the audience to document their story ideas by writing them down and keeping a story file. However, I found that most of my ideas come to me when I am driving or out for my daily walk, and it's not possible to write them down. To capture my thoughts on the spot I use the voice recorder on my smart phone, and I encourage audiences to do the same. When I return home I transcribe my thoughts and save them in my story file on my computer.

What would you like your audience to do differently? Do you have a technique they can use that would help you be remembered? If so, record your ideas so that you may incorporate them into your next presentation.

Sale

Every speech is *selling* something, but that doesn't mean it has to sound like a sales pitch. The cold hard truth is that people don't care what we do; they only care about what we can do for them. If you don't offer your audience any value through a new idea or give them something tangible that will create change in how they think, feel, or do, you are sure to fail.

Speaking is selling: selling an idea, service, or product. If you can show them or use examples of how your product or service has helped others, it will create a desire, create change in their thinking, and help you obtain sales without sounding like a sales pitch.

Take for instance the clerk of the circuit court. She used an *anchor*-story to sell her idea: *"Change is good and essential for your business."* The wealth management advisor told stories and asked questions to create a need and sell her services by having the audience *reflect* on their own situation. The massage therapist used the *technique* formula to sell his stretching techniques and how proper posture prevents pain. I also introduced an action step to capture your story ideas by writing them down or recording them on your smart phone. Using at least four, if not all five, of the PARTS formula in our presentations has helped us create compelling content to connect with our audience, and it can help you too.

Allow me to get to the *point*: *"If you want to get rich, ditch the pitch™"* and incorporate the PARTS formula in your presentations so you can create compelling content and offer value to your audience, which will increase your sales effortlessly.

Rena Romano is an author, award-winning speaker, presentation skills instructor, and certified speaking and leadership coach. She provides speaking and leadership training to corporations and nonprofit organizations through group training and individual coaching. rena@renaromano.com www.RenaRomano.com.

13

My Pain Is Your Gain: Leveraging the Then/Now/How Technique

Anna Perdriau

What was the most frustrating experience of your life? If you can recall, it could be the one story that allows you to bring value to your presentations. So don't bury it in the past along with bad hairdos and daggy clothes. Don't be ashamed about it or bury it away in the security vault of yesteryear. Celebrate it! Such cringe-worthy events can be your ticket to add value to the lives of your listeners, those you seek to move with your message.

During times of challenge and pain, we are offered life's greatest lessons for our growth. Growth then results in personal gain through wisdom. By sharing your *pain* you can help your audience achieve great *gain*.

In this chapter you will learn the *Then/Now/How* technique to bring your pain to your audience and allow them to use it for their gain. Stated simply, you will discover how to connect with your audience through *story*, *struggle*, and *solution*. Let's break it down:

1. **Then.** In my past, I behaved in such a way that there was a painful or unproductive impact (e.g., I did "abc," which produced a result of "xyz"). This is your *story*.

2. **Now**. I have learned from the way of my past and am much better for it (e.g., this is who I am "now" compared to "then"). This is the journey of your *struggle*.

3. **How**. The secret formula that I now share with you (my audience) so you can benefit too (e.g., the key tools and processes they will benefit from). This is your *solution*.

How to Find Your "Pain"

Can you remember a painfully frustrating experience in your life? An experience that, while not exactly fun, resulted in your greatest personal learning? Your greatest growth and development and realizations? A story that uniquely defines you?

Here are three examples of challenging scenarios:

1. when I was trying to change jobs/careers
2. when I was having conflict with a colleague in the workplace
3. when I pushed myself too hard and felt stressed

For presentation purposes, these experiences are worth their weight in gold. They allow you to bring to your audience immensely powerful tools and processes to fast-track their speaking development. This is achieved through use of the Then/Now/How formula.

Connect with your audience through story, struggle, and solution.

Like an easy recipe, this formula has three simple steps. And when used with the right quantities at the right time, it can result in magic. Allow me to offer you an example of a true cringe-worthy story of pain just to showcase this technique.

Step 1—Then

This is you in your most vulnerable, naïve, and unenlightened state. Think back to a time when you were making some mistakes, mistakes you wish to prevent your audience members from making. This step involves really baring the bad situation of "before." Not just revealing the pain but opening up the wound in all its gory detail. Here is an example of Then:

> *Have you ever set your sights on a goal that was so important to you that you would have done just about anything to achieve it? Some years ago, I did. While climbing the career ladder I became so focused on achieving that next promotion. It was to the point that I was obsessive about it. To me, becoming a director at a young age (back then!) was the pinnacle of the career mountain. Becoming a director would be like seeing Victoria Falls in Zimbabwe for the first time, experiencing a white Christmas in Paris, and breathing in the atmosphere of the 2000 Sydney Olympic Games with a million people around me, all in one. It was my version of winning the gold medal.*

Let Your Audience Know Your Internal Dialogue (What Were You Thinking at the Time?)

> *Winning that promotion was on my mind at all times. There was not an ounce of doubt in my mind that it was where I needed to be to achieve true success. It was so important to me that I believed once I achieved this goal, I would have "made it" in life. I ploughed forward with my goal and told everyone who would listen of my great human quest. Those around me were forever saying comments like "slow down," "what's the rush," and "why don't you go off and have kids?"*

Let Your Audience Know Your Frustration (What Was the Challenge You Faced Being in This Position?)

> *Of course, having goals is a healthy part of life and something to be encouraged, isn't it? Yes, of course it is! And it is important to keep your eye on your goals and not be distracted. So this side of the equation was fine. It was the notion that I had to achieve this goal at all costs that had become unhealthy. This concept manifested itself in my work habits. I insisted on being the first one in the office and the last one to leave. It was known that I could be relied upon. If there were issues, I would always be there to listen, help, and address. I even worked on weekends. I would spend my Saturdays in the office to demonstrate my unbridled dedication.*

Let Your Audience Know Your Pain

> *Time passed. Several months. I applied for the director roles. I knew I would be a frontrunner. To my surprise I didn't win. Not even an interview. There must have been a mistake. I sought feedback. I took it on board. "You need more experience," they said. More experience? Couldn't they see I was perfect for the role? Okay, back to working hard.*
>
> *More time passed. In fact it was years. I had been working so hard that one day I realized I had been working many more hours than my employment agreement required of me, in the order of 3-4 hours each day. I calculated that over the years I had in fact spent 1,920 extra hours in the office. That means I spent the equivalent of ONE WHOLE EXTRA YEAR in the office. Ouch!*
>
> *Not many people wish they could work more and more. I needed a wakeup call to get me freed from this "hard work" mindset I was trapped in.*

You can see that Step 1 is all about bringing in your audience and showing them the pain you endured. Let them feel it. Incite their curiosity of what "not to do"—not making the same mistakes you did.

In Step 2 we undertake some time travel to a new point in time—and definitely a new story!

Step 2—Now

This is where you bring your audience to the current day, the now. You have taken them back in time and shown them the depths of your despair, shared your pain. It's time to wrench them out of the murky waters of that place and travel to the bright and shiny now. Here you clearly show them the transformational results. Of course it may *or may not* be what they expected, but after sharing your pain they deserve to hear your happy (or at least *happier*) ending.

Let Your Audience Know Who You Are Today

> *Some years later (than planned), I reached my goal, my dream, of being a director. It came on the tail end of years and years of hard work—blood, sweat,*

and tears. The reward for my hard work was even more hard work. I relished the challenge that stood before me. I thrived in the environment that called upon me to step up to such responsibility. It was an honor not only to achieve this amazing milestone but to deliver upon the promise I made when accepting the challenge of directorship. I had achieved at a young age what it took most people decades to achieve. Success was sweet.

When I think back to that time I recall the joy I felt, but I also realize that I went beyond what I needed to do to achieve my dream. I could have taken a different approach and achieved the same result.

Let Your Audience Know Your Changed Perspective

My perspective now is entirely different. Now I value my time like that metaphorical gold medal. I am very conscious about where and with whom I spend it. You might be pleased to know I no longer spend my Saturdays sitting in a cold dark office surrounded by plastic plants! So how did I get to this point?

There was a turning point for me, a change. A change that taught me the most important lesson: how to separate *myself to gain perspective.*

Step 2 Summary

We visit the current point in time where the circumstances for you are so very different to how they were in the Step 1 period of time. Just as you let them feel the Step 1, so to let them feel the Step 2, the improved and better place to be.

In Step 3 we move into teaching our audience the How of moving forward in life.

Step 3—How

Here is where you can offer *value* to your audience on a gold platter. This step is all about the *practical application* of solving the challenge. In other words, it is your chance to reveal the secret to your success. This is done through revealing the method you used, which should be wrapped nicely in a memorable, easy-to-apply process.

Simplicity Is Key

This is where your techniques and methods are explained in a packaged and simplified manner. For example:

- *Six Tips for Keeping Your Audience on the Edge of Their Seats*
- *Three Keys to Remarkable Results*
- *Five Steps to SWEET Success*

This way your *tools* and *processes* can be made available to anyone straightaway. Instant application of these tools and processes will be the true *value* you can add to the lives of your listeners. If you can achieve this, you can make a person's life more meaningful and much easier.

Where to Start with Packaging Your Message?

Patricia Fripp says, "Wisdom comes from reflection." Through reflection your message and your process from your Then/Now/How story should become clearer. Think thoroughly about your experience. What did you learn? How could your wisdom help others? Can it be explained in a simple manner? At this point you may wish to reference tools such as Craig Valentine's "9 C's" to storytelling and techniques for building your foundational phrase—to sum up your key message in less than ten words.

Example of a foundational phrase: *"Find something SWEET in every defeat."*

From Transactional to Transformational Leadership

You may be wondering how I broke out of this trance-like existence that had me trapped. It was by way of a higher power. This higher power came in the form of a leader named Ivan. Ivan was the first leader who cared enough to let me know I didn't need to work so many hours because it was immaterial to the results I had produced. Ivan did this more with actions than words. Ivan taught me how to take my defeat and turn it into something SWEET! His integrity spoke to me so loudly that it screamed "what are you doing?"

Ivan did this by recognizing my talents and then harnessing them. My "then" had been like doing surgery in the dark. Ivan appeared and turned on the light. And he opened up the blinds. Ivan offered a new perspective in his leadership style and embraced the difference in others. He didn't expect everyone to be of the same mindset as him. Ivan valued difference. Ivan was a pioneer.

Ivan helped me realize that what I needed was some separation from the issues.

When you are too close to a challenge, often you can't think beyond your emotional frustration. Sometimes you need to *separate* yourself to gain perspective and look for the logic. Creative problem solving can then occur.

This need to separate became the first of a five-step process that led me to finding resilience and being able to overcome any challenging environment and find the "SWEET":

- **Separate.** Separate yourself from a challenge and your feelings and emotions about it.
- **Wisdom.** Find wisdom through your personal reflection and deeper thought.
- **Evaluate.** Draw from others' feedback, support, and advice through evaluation.
- **Energize.** Locate energy from sources you find most effective in life to rejuvenate.
- **Tenacity.** Be prepared to work through a situation and never lose focus.

I now use the SWEET process in all that I do in life, including helping others to reach their goals and to resolve conflict in their lives.

Serve Your Audience

As speakers and leaders, it is our greatest duty and joy to *serve* our audience. The best way we can do this is not to dictate the "what" but demonstrate the "how." This will empower your audience to go and *do* as well as to know and understand *why*.

> *As speakers the best way we can serve our audience is not to dictate the "what" but demonstrate the "how."*

You have a story. You have knowledge. If you can succinctly package your wisdom, you can reach audiences you never even dreamed of reaching.

Use the Then/Now/How formula to connect with your audience through story, struggle, and finally solution!

Anna Perdriau is one of the Australian Defence Organisation's youngest female civilians to direct a billion-dollar acquisition program. She is a Distinguished Toastmaster, a World Class Speaking coach, and holds an MBA and a BA in communications. As CEO and founder of Destination: Excellence! she is passionate about the SWEET methodology to help individuals achieve their personal leadership and resilience success. Reach her at anna@destinationexcellence.com.au or on the Web at www.destinationexcellence.com.au

14

Tell a
Technical Tale

Bob Goodyear

Have you ever sat in a presentation that felt like a "data dump"? You know what I mean: usually it's a technical presentation on a subject the presenter is considered to be very knowledgeable about or even an expert. The subject matter may be detailed and complex and could be completely unfamiliar to the audience.

When called on to do a technical presentation, many professionals simply do a data dump—little more than a stream of facts and bullet-point presentation slides, a "just the facts, ma'am" kind of approach. At the end, the audience may barely remember the speaker's name, much less the key points presented.

How can this be changed? By using an illustrative story to "tell a technical tale," a speaker can make his or her points more relatable and more easily remembered. The problem is that most technical presenters are hesitant to tell a story because it's *not* "just the facts." They believe that a good technical presentation should only include facts and that stories will make their information less credible. Thankfully, people such as Bill Nye, Steve Spangler, and Steve Jobs have shown that a technical presentation does not have to be boring. When asked what advice he would give to scientists who are trying to influence people, Malcolm Gladwell responded "Tell stories."

Since birth we have wanted to hear stories, and once we hear them we remember them. I have never heard my two-year-old granddaughter ask me, "Poppa, give me a PowerPoint presentation." When we were children we wanted to hear stories. In fact, the stories we remember the best are those that come from the personal life of the storyteller. I remember my Irish grandfather telling me stories about leprechauns and how one had stolen his lunch money when he was a small child.

In this chapter we will look at the three reasons to add stories into a technical presentation. They are:

1. to create interest
2. to keep interest
3. to get the audience to act on their interest

If you want to include stories in your presentation, how and where do you add them? There are three parts of a presentation where a story can be used most effectively:

*   opening the presentation
*   illustrating a point
*   closing the presentation

Let's look at each of these and see examples of how they can be used.

Opening with a Story

A World Class Speaking principle is to "Begin with a Bang," which means to create interest right at the beginning of the presentation. One way to do this is to use a story as a hook to immediately catch the audience's attention. For technical presenters this can be exceptionally effective as it allows the presenter to callback (another World Class Speaking principle) to the story to emphasize a point later in the presentation.

One story I have used effectively involves my first experience with a computer. In the opening of a presentation I give to new technical sales teams called "Challenges in Today's Data Center," I start with the following story:

I was seventeen years old when I walked through my first computer. You heard me right—I walked THROUGH my first computer. If you had been with me that day, you would have seen the vacuum tubes glowing a bright orange. You would have smelled the hot dust being blown through the computer to cool it down. We affectionately referred to the computer as Bessie, which stood for Binary Enumerating Statistical System.

Bessie was the size of a basketball court and she took up the entire data center. She could do four things really well: she could add, subtract, multiply, and divide. She was almost as powerful as the calculator app on your cell phone.

After this story, I tell the audience their customers' data centers don't have just one Bessie in them; they may have thousands of Bessies. I then explain that the purpose of the presentation is to teach them how today's data centers are architected and why they are done that way. I also describe the products that a sales team can sell to help their customers manage the "thousands of Bessies" in the data center.

Throughout the presentation I make references back to Bessie to get the audience to remember where data centers started. I can also use "Bessie" instead of the word "computer" or "server" to bring some humor into the presentation.

How effective is this story? Salespeople in our company still come up to me over a year later and tell me how much they like the "Bessie" story. They tell me they use it as a reference when talking about a customer's data center. While the rest of my presentation is very technical in nature, the audience remembers "Bessie" first.

Illustrating a Point

Another fundamental principle of World Class Speaking is to tell a story and make a point. This thought originally came from a former president of the National Speakers Association, Bill Gove.

The main portion of any presentation consists of the individual points the speaker wants to make. In a technical presentation these are the keys that the speaker wants the audience to understand. Many times this is where the presentation becomes a data dump, as the speaker expounds technical details one after the other to the audience.

> *Illustrating a technical point with a story helps the audience keep interest in the presentation. They become more engaged or re-engaged with a new story.*

Illustrating a technical point with a story helps the audience keep interest in the presentation. They become more engaged or re-engaged with a new story. The point is more readily remembered by following this formula:

- tell a story
- make a point
- call back to the story

One story I use illustrates several different technical points. It's a personal story that shows how my mistake teaches a lesson.

I was at my first job out of college. I had just finished a programming project and was cleaning up my work. I spent thirty minutes removing all of the unneeded data I had created in order to test it and then sat back in my black leather office chair and put my feet on top of my desk.

About five minutes later I heard one of my colleagues down the hall yell out "Hey, is the system down?" This was a common occurrence so I was even happier that I had just finished my cleanup. Another voice responded, "I think the system's up, but it's like the data has disappeared!" I quickly got out of my chair, closed my office door, and stayed quiet.

It became very clear that the data had been deleted. I decided to join the conversation in the hallway a little later, at which point I mentioned what I had been doing right before the failure. I realized that I had entered a series of wrong commands to the computer that had deleted ALL of our data.

We went to our backup tapes and found that a backup had not been done for five days. We ended up losing over a week's worth of work, including my own. Yes, it appears that I had become an earlier version of the Allstate Insurance character called Mayhem.

I use this story as an introduction to several technical topics such as daily backups and planning for disasters. I tell this story and then talk about some technical aspect of backup or disaster recovery. After I finish explaining the technical feature, I then callback to the story to remind my audience that if our company had been using the specific feature I just explained, the data loss would have been less significant. *"Mayhem existed long before Allstate created him!"*

Closing with a Story

The closing of any presentation is key because the speaker wants to leave the audience with a "call to action" as a result of hearing the information. This is another World Class Speaking principle.

I used to close all of my technical presentations with a question and answer (Q&A) session. I knew I was doing something wrong based on the indifferent reactions of my audiences. When presenting to my peers, I could see most of the audience's eyes glaze over as one detailed question after another was asked. When I was presenting to managers, I could tell that most of them didn't care about the questions being asked. In my technical conference sessions the attendees would just wander out of the meeting room as they became disinterested. No motivating energy was gained from the presentation that I had so meticulously crafted and presented.

At the end of most technical presentations, there is an expectation that the speaker will have a Q&A period. Most technical speakers finish their presentations as I did by asking if anyone has a question. Sometimes no questions are asked as the audience is just ready for the presentation to end. However, when questions are asked many times they are on a very specific point. The answer provokes even more detailed questions, and many times most of the audience loses interest. When this happens the presentation's effectiveness has been lost.

There is a better way to end a technical presentation. When I learned the World Class Speaking principle to never end a presentation with a Q&A session, my presentations began to have more impact. If a Q&A session is held, it should be before actually closing.

This is an uncommon technique for technical speakers. How does a speaker easily do the Q&A before the closing? The answer is actually very simple. Before opening the presentation up to questions, I say something like this: "I have one more story for you before I close. However, I'd first like to see if you have any questions on what we have talked about so far. "

After the Q&A session is done, I deliver the story. The audience is still interested because I promised them a story. The story content will vary depending on the purpose of the closing. For example, if I am speaking to a group of potential customers I use a customer success story. I talk about a problem that a customer was having, tell about how they resolved the problem using our product, and then ask the audience to consider looking into the product we have discussed in the presentation.

When I first started using this technique I was very uncomfortable because it was not something I had done before. I had never seen any technical speaker do it.

> *Since incorporating this technique into my presentations, I have witnessed a noticeable change in my audiences' reactions....I find them talking among themselves about the information they learned.*

Since incorporating this technique into my presentations, I have witnessed a noticeable change in my audiences' reactions. Instead of leaving the room with a lack of energy, I see them leave with enthusiasm and find them talking among themselves about the information they learned. My call to action in my closing is actually discussed and hopefully remembered.

Summary

Technical presentations by definition can be difficult to make. Detailed information about a subject is often very difficult to deliver in an interesting way. One way to make the information more interesting is to use stories during the presentation. Opening with a story that sets up the topic helps generate interest with the audience immediately. Including stories to illustrate points helps maintain the interest of the audience and helps them remember the points. Closing with a story helps the audience remember what you have talked about and act on the interest that was generated. "Telling a technical tale" does not discredit a technical presentation but rather adds interest to it.

Bob Goodyear is a veteran speaker on technology who is known as "A geek who speaks." He has spoken in seventeen different countries about technical subjects and currently works for Symantec in technical education. He also coaches technical speakers to be more interesting than a "data dump." You can find out more about him at www.ageekwhospeaks.com.

15

Using Activities for Engagement

Monika Sugiarto

Whenever I see a speaker or trainer engaging their audience successfully, I am awed and also a little bit jealous—especially if the entertainment looks like fun and helps the audience understand the point more effectively. An activity should flow easily and naturally, and the audience should respond to it enthusiastically without pressure. World Class speakers use games at the right time and make them fit perfectly with the substance of the presentation. On the other hand new and inexperienced speakers often ignore their listeners and concentrate too much on the material they need to deliver. This leads to a disconnect with the audience.

Once a presenter finally realizes they've lost the audience, they scramble to find an activity that helps them connect. Whether giving a keynote speech or training, as a World Class Speaker I always use our valuable PARTS formula. The *T* or what we call *Technique* intrigued me from the beginning, and it is this point I want to discuss with you in this chapter. Time is very precious, and when you are standing in front of an audience you want to do your best to give as much value as you can.

It's not difficult to find activities to engage your listeners. In my part of the world many people expect to have fun and be engaged physically at seminars; they call it the "icebreaker" and it can be anything—from leading an exercise or dance routine to a quick memory drill that pits one side of the room against the other in a fun way. Activities liven up an audience, especially after lunch. But I believe an activity should provide more than mere entertainment.

An activity needs to:

- suit your speaking style
- drive home the point you are making
- get your audience involved

An activity should also:

- be entertaining
- promote interactivity
- gain the audience's trust
- help listeners practice what they learn
- instill a sense of accomplishment and pride

Each of us has to discover our unique activities that help us become remembered and therefore recommended as speakers. Of course it's possible to find great games that fit you and your material in a book or from another speaker. However you choose to do it, make them your own. You have to be absolutely convinced that this is the only game you could play in this particular case. *You must be confident to be able to command the people in the room*. Once you project that confidence, expect them to comply willingly—maybe even eagerly.

Confidence Comes from Knowing What You Know

I am sitting across the table from my friend Rinaldi. He leans forward, a serious expression on his face: "Monika, my company is looking for a program that helps employees of an insurance company practice better presenting. They don't have the budget and time to coach each of them individually. I already promised them a great program, the one you are offering. I know you are a trainer who can connect with the audience, but how do you make a room full of people all practice presenting at the same time?"

Before I can answer, his face—and tone—turns desperate. "Monika, we need this client, they are huge; your training has to wow them." I realize he is really worried and has no clue how this challenge is going to be solved.

"Relax, Rinaldi," I say. "I have done trainings like this before and I know how to make it work. I promise I will not let you down."

On the morning of the training, I meet Rinaldi, his boss, and the human resources manager of the insurance company while having breakfast in a rustic mountain resort two hours from Jakarta, the capital of Indonesia. "Monika, you have forty junior managers, and by the end of the training we are expecting all of them to better understand the art of presenting and have had a chance to practice," Rinaldi says.

I smile and assure them: "I have prepared this special program tailored to your needs, and it will involve all of them."

As we are leaving the breakfast room, Rinaldi leans over and whispers "Do you mind if I come and have a look at how you handle this?"

My confidence has set the tone. Not only are the bosses intrigued, but soon forty junior managers will be too.

Get Them to Relax

When I walk into the good-sized hall, many of the trainees are already sitting in their chairs waiting to start. I hear a sigh of concern rush through the rows when they see me. I hear comments like: "Oh brother, we're going to be trained at public speaking in English. Look at the trainer; she's a foreigner!" I know very well that asking people to get up and speak is causing lots of stress in them; having to do this in a second language is absolute horror.

That is why I open my presentation with a question: "What is the biggest challenge you face when asked to speak?" I address them in their language, and immediately their body language shifts and they start relaxing. They realize they can get all their anxieties about this scary subject off their chest so they answer with a million reasons why speaking is so difficult.

Next I move on to my theoretical explanation and say, "At the end of today's training we shall discuss these issues again, and I promise that you will know how to solve them."

Practice What You Present

After an hour or so of the basics, the time for the *Technique* rolls around. Speaking needs to be practiced and experienced, like riding a bicycle or swimming. You cannot grasp it by just listening to somebody explain the does and don'ts, even if that includes stories and examples. You need to make mistakes and fall off the wheels or float freely to eventually find the correct balance, movement, and speed.

> *Speaking needs to be practiced and experienced, like riding a bicycle or swimming.*

The audience is already grouped around tables as I requested, and it is easy now to split them into specific groups. I give them clear instructions: "Prepare an introduction of yourself; tell your personal story, how you chose this job and career, and what your future plans are." My personal introduction of how I became a speaker and trainer serve as illustration and sample for their tale.

After some preparation time the activity part of this session starts; they have to practice. They are limited to five minutes of talking time per person. Somebody in the group is asked to keep track of time by using two sheets of paper, one green to be raised after four minutes and a red one after five minutes to show the speaker it's time to stop. I assign an evaluator to each of them by asking them to pass the evaluation form from their workbook to the person on their right. Each person will cast a vote for the best speaker of their table and also for the best evaluator. The best speaker and evaluator of each group will then have a chance to perform in front and will get a prize.

Some of the groups understand the instructions very well and immediately assign the first speaker. Others deliberate until I come around and make decisions for them. All of a sudden though at every table one person is standing and delivering their first speech. Their audience listens attentively, because even though the hall is quite big, several participants speaking at the same time makes a lot of distracting noise. I move from table to table to listen and take notes. I am pleased but not really surprised; I am able to make them all talk and listen. They all follow instructions—some more willingly than others, but they are all trying very hard.

While walking to the back I pass by Rinaldi, his boss, and the human resources manager observing the scene. They give me a nod of approval. "Well done, Monika; we didn't think you could pull it off."

It is actually quite simple. You do not need complicated gadgets; you just need confidence, a firm grasp on your subject, and a suitable room.

Prepare Meticulously

For a successful presentation with activities, you need to know…

- **What topics to present.** In the above example, I needed to know exactly why and how the participants would use public speaking in their jobs. I wanted them to practice something they knew and that helped them in their career since time was very limited.
- **Who is helping whom and how.** The next issue to think through is the technique of evaluation. Their workbook included an evaluation form. There they saw a list of positive things to look for:
  - smile
  - facial expression
  - confidence
  - voice
  - flow of speech or story
  - passionate about the subject
  - body language

I did not even give them the negatives. My instructions were: "As the evaluator you have to give an accurate picture of their speaking. Give them at least three points that they do well. Then discuss one matter you think needs improvement by saying: 'I think…' or 'I believe…' or 'I would…' And then end by congratulating him or her and mentioning more good stuff." It is very rewarding for me to observe their faces and body language after they have delivered their speech and received positive reinforcement. *They almost literally grow in stature.* When subsequent sessions are announced they approach them with much more confidence, and the results are even better than the first time around.

Every Presentation Must Come to an End

"Rinaldi, how about helping me count the votes?" I ask after everyone has practiced speaking. He anvd his boss immediately clear the table and help me with the list of champions. Of course I do not announce the winners; I ask the HRD manager, who is delighted to hand out the well-deserved rewards.

As promised, at the end of the day I always come back to my initial question: "What is the biggest challenge you face when asked to speak?" The faces looking back at me now are relaxed and much more confident than in the morning, and they agree they now know how to prepare, practice, and deliver a presentation that will be successful. For me this means: I achieved my goal!

> *My reward came when the CEO congratulated me and said he learned a lot from my training— and booked me again for his next event.*

I have done this kind of practice many times over the years. On this particular occasion, my reward came when the CEO who booked me stood in the middle of the room delivering his story to his fellow participants, his staff. At the end he congratulated me and said he learned a lot from my training—and booked me again for his next event.

My unique activities have earned me lots of satisfied customers! Why? Because of the benefits for the participants:

- practice what they learn immediately
- become more confident
- learn to listen to and respect at least one speaker
- learn to evaluate positively
- compare speakers
- learn how to manage their speaking time
- friendly competition among speakers
- help each other succeed
- practice being courteous

Activities Breathe Life into Your Speaking

A speaker I once saw made some of his audience stand up and read his slides overflowing with text while he stood in the back of the room observing and correcting. This is *not* a good way to interact with your audience. They will not remember you for your brilliant oration technique, nor for your slides, nor for what they learned, and definitely not for the fun they did not have.

For a successful activity, you need to be able to observe and assess your listeners' state of mind and react positively and actively to their needs.

- **Ask** the question that is on their mind to help diffuse their tension and get them ready to open up.
- **Practice** what they learn through activities that fit you like a glove and that you can confidently command your listeners to participate in.
- **Observe** them enjoying practicing the lesson you want them to learn.

And this is how you realize speaking or training goals with lots of rave reviews, because speaking is about the audience not the speaker. Find more games together with practical advice on my site www.your-public-speaking.com. Contact me there and let me help you develop your unique activity.

Monika Sugiarto has traveled the world and lived in many different countries. She realizes that miscommunication has very little to do with not understanding the language. It has a lot to do with people not communicating effectively and not being aware of the differences in culture. Find her insights on www.your-public-speaking.com.

16

How to Create Anchors That Captivate, Motivate, and Activate Your Audience

Dr. Richard C. Harris

Have you ever listened to a speech or sermon and couldn't remember the points the speaker was making just five minutes after the talk concluded? It's frustrating, isn't it? And it's just as frustrating for the speaker *if* they are aware of the problem. But that *is* the problem—most speakers don't know that people aren't remembering their points because the socially acceptable thing to say to a speaker after the talk is usually "Thank you so much for that talk," "Good sermon, Reverend," or "That was such a good presentation!" Then they go out to lunch and either never think about your speech again or discuss with their friends what a nice person you are. Not a good speaker but a nice person.

I don't know about you, but I want to be both a nice person and a great speaker. A memorable speaker. A speaker whose message they will be talking about for months or maybe even years to come. I want to give speeches that captivate, motivate, and activate my audience.

World Class speakers know that "what is loose is lost; what is tight stays in sight." You tighten up your speeches by tying your main teaching points to anchors because, after all, "If your audience can't remember your points, then your speech was pointless!"

You know what an anchor does. It keeps a boat from drifting aimlessly wherever the winds and waves will take it. An anchor keeps the boat in one place, solid, secure. And that's what anchors do for your speech. A speech anchor is anything that will help your audience remember the main points you present in your speech. What is the point of speaking if the audience walks away and can't remember anything you said? So you want your points to be "anchored" to something they will remember after your talk is over.

Although there are many types of anchors a speaker can use, World Class speakers have identified the top four you will want to consider as you put together your talk. For longer keynotes, it is advisable that you use all four types of anchors:

- Anecdote
- Analogy
- Acronym
- Activity

Take an informal poll after any speech or sermon and ask, "What do you remember about what you just heard? What stands out to you?" Invariably, most people will start talking about our first and most popular type of anchor. If you master the art of using this anchor, you'll be light-years ahead of other speakers in your field.

> *A speech anchor is anything that will help your audience remember the main points you present in your speech.*

Speech Anchor #1: Anecdote

An anecdote is a story. People love stories. People relate to stories. People remember stories. And if people remember your story, they are more likely to remember the teaching point you attached to that story. World Class speakers know that one of the most valuable tools a speaker can pick up is how to tell a story and sell a point.

Your stories need to be just that—*your* stories. Where do you find stories to tell? They need to *pour* forth from your life. They pour forth out of your experiences, your life events, your successes, your failures, your fears, and your frustrations. And POUR is a good acronym to help remember what kinds of stories to tell:

Personal. There are probably a lot of people who speak on the same topics you do. So what makes you different from them? Your stories. They don't have *your* stories. Only you do. Only you have your experiences, positive and negative. Your audience wants to get to know you, and they do that through your stories.

Original. Of course, when you tell your personal stories, you can rest assured that they are original. Wannabe speakers get their stories out of illustration books or from other speakers. The result? Stories that many in your audience have already heard. And what happens with those audience members? Two things: first they label you as unoriginal; second, they label you as boring because you're telling them stuff they've heard before. Bottom line: they tune you out.

Useful. Your stories need to connect to a main teaching point or foundational phrase that you want your audience to remember. I've got lots of really good entertaining stories in my repertoire that have never made it to the stage simply because I haven't yet developed any good point for the story to illustrate and be anchored to. Your time onstage is too precious to waste by telling stories that don't drive home the points you are trying to make in your speech.

Relevant. For your story to be useful it must also be relevant—relevant to your topic, your main points, and your audience. Computer software programmers probably won't relate that well to stories about farming, nor will senior citizens be all that interested in a story about the latest hip-hop moves. So ask yourself if the story is right for your topic, your points, and your audience.

While anecdotes are the most popular type of anchor to use, remember that variety is not only the spice of life it is also the spice of your speech. Instead of just adding story on top of story, this next type of anchor will not only help your audience retain your material it will also ensure they understand your material at a deeper level than most listeners.

> *Your time onstage is too precious to waste by telling stories that don't drive home the points you are trying to make in your speech.*

Speech Anchor #2: Analogy

An analogy compares one thing with another. A difficult-to-understand concept becomes easier to comprehend when it is compared to something that your audience has experienced before. One of my coaching clients has a keynote on reaching your goals in life. He asks for a volunteer from the audience and sets the scene on the stage as if they were in a soccer game. He wads up a piece of paper to use as a ball; the volunteer is the goalie and the speaker is trying to make a goal. Just as he begins to take the shot, he stops, looks at the audience, and asks, "Wouldn't it be much easier if this goalie weren't in my way trying to block my shot?" He moves back into the scene and takes the shot.

It doesn't really matter to his speech whether he makes the goal or it is blocked. He turns back to the audience and says, "That's what life is like. We set our goals, do everything we can to reach them, but there are always people and obstacles in our way. We have to learn how to deal with them. Sometimes we're successful, and sometimes we aren't." He then calls back to the soccer goal analogy throughout his talk as he walks the audience through a plan for success. What makes his analogy so memorable is that he demonstrates it visually as well as verbally. And he gets a member of the audience involved.

Have you ever listened to a speaker and gotten the feeling that somewhere along the way his mental train jumped the tracks and there was no telling where you would end up? This next anchor solves that problem not only by making the speech more memorable but also easier to navigate while your audience is listening to it.

Speech Anchor #3: Acronym

An acronym is a pronounceable word made up of the first letters or sounds of a series of words. Notice that I used the acronym POUR earlier in this chapter when discussing anecdotes. An acronym can be used to anchor one point in your speech or it can anchor the entire speech.

Acronyms are useful for providing an outline or roadmap of where your talk is going so the audience can follow along. It provides a structure that your audience will be able to remember long after your talk is finished.

A social media consultant I coach has a presentation she makes to small business owners wishing to break into social media to improve their customer base. Her acronym encouraging them to "A.C.T. on Social Media" spells out her three talking points—things they must consider before jumping into social media and what they need to know about each: audience, creativity, and time.

A keynote address I give on "Moving beyond Diversity" uses a close cousin to the acronym, alliteration, which doesn't spell out a word but rather utilizes the same letter or sound for each point. I ask my audience to "Challenge Your Information, Change Your Involvement, and Choose Your Intentions." If they can remember *information*, *involvement*, and *intentions*, they'll likely remember what I said about each one and be able to put them into action in their own lives.

Even with anecdotes, analogies, and acronyms, the best of speakers will start to lose an audience once in a while. But the difference between a World Class speaker and a wannabe speaker is that the first has a tool in their toolbox they can use to regain that audience connection. It's your fourth anchor, and if you use it in your speeches, you'll stand less of a chance of losing your audience in the first place.

Speech Anchor #4: Activity

Activities promote audience involvement and can be a speech saver if you're starting to lose their attention. An activity can be anything from asking your audience to close their eyes and imagine a scene as you describe it, to asking them to turn to their neighbor and briefly discuss something about your topic with them, to asking them to stand up and do something physically.

All of these are ways to get the audience involved with your speech. But a word of caution is in order before I give you a couple of examples: be careful not to ask too much of an audience too soon in your speech. You have to earn the right to ask them to do something out of the ordinary. That is why I usually don't start my speech off by asking my audience to do anything more physical than raising their hands in response to a question. As your speech goes on, you can build enough rapport by giving them quality content so that they are more likely to participate in whatever you ask them to do.

In a keynote speech on the benefits of laughter, one of my clients in the entertainment business uses an activity in his speech in which he invites his audience to play a simple game with him, "Laugh Till It Hits." He holds a piece of paper high in the air, drops it, and asks his audience to laugh out loud as the paper slowly floats to the ground. When it hits the ground, everyone has to stop laughing. He does it about three times, and by the third time everyone in the room is loosened up, smiling, and laughing. He then drives home the points that laughter helps them socially, mentally, and physically and talks to them about how that simple game they just experienced has already changed their attitude, attention, and activity level.

I have a fun activity I use in one of my keynotes on "Three Tools to Take You to the Top: Thinking, Speaking, and Persuading" that underscores the importance of focused thinking. I borrowed it from Dave Crenshaw's book *Multitasking Is a Myth*. I ask the audience to draw two parallel lines on a piece of paper. On the top line they write "Multitasking is worse than a lie." And on the bottom line they write the numbers 1 through 27. They do this twice. The first time they write the first letter, M, then switch to the bottom line and write the number 1. Then back to the top line for the second letter, U, then to the bottom line for the number 2 and so on until they have written the entire sentence and the numbers up to 27. They are timed while they do this.

On the second attempt they write the same sentence and numbers, but this time they focus on writing the entire sentence first then move on to write the 27 numbers in order. The time for the second attempt is usually less than half of what the first attempt was. And usually they make mistakes and have to correct them on the first attempt. I then talk about how our brains are not wired to multitask. They can switch tasks very quickly, but efficiency and effectiveness both suffer. The audience never forgets that activity and the value of focused thinking over distracted thinking.

Some Final Thoughts about Anchors

These four anchors (anecdote, analogy, acronym, and activity) aren't the only ones, but they are the most effective ones you will want to use in your speeches. When implemented, they will help you tap into the logical, rational brain of your audience as well as the emotional brain. When both are engaged, you will be able to captivate, motivate, and activate your listeners to give you their attention, get on board with your ideas, and move into action in response to your speech.

One of the saddest things I see in the speaking industry is when talented men and women present excellent, world-changing ideas but do it in such a poor way that their audiences leave the boardroom, the speech, or the conference uninspired, uninterested, and unchallenged. But that doesn't have to happen to your presentation. You never need to be boring or forgettable. If you pick up the tools for anchoring presented in this chapter and use them in every speech you give, you will see immediate results in the reactions of your audience. Maybe they'll even go to lunch after hearing your talk and say, "He's so nice . . . she's so nice . . . *and what a great speaker!*"

Dr. Richard C. Harris (www.ThinkSpeakandPersuade.com) is an award-winning author, certified World Class Speaking coach, and the lead speech professor at Southeastern University in Lakeland, Florida. In his earlier years he was the leader of the largest underground terrorist organization in the Midwestern United States. A keynote speaker audiences never forget, he anchors his keynotes with leadership lessons drawn from his experiences in the underworld.

17

Metaphors: Tuning into Your Audience's Understanding

Nate Dunlop

P retend you're listening to a radio program that starts to cackle with static. Your difficulty understanding the program increases as the radio frequency becomes lost in a storm of static. Without a clear transmission, you can't tell if you're on the same channel anymore.

Has your audience ever become out of tune with your speaking frequency because you transmitted the static of unfamiliar language to them? When you transmit a message your audience cannot receive, you put yourself on another channel that your audience isn't connected with. When that happens, your audience will tune you out and turn you off.

In this chapter you will learn how to stay on the audience's channel when you use metaphors. They will give you a clear frequency that will ensure the static of unfamiliar language doesn't disrupt your transmission to your audience. By the end of this static-free broadcast you will know:

- what metaphors are
- the magical properties of metaphors
- the alchemy to making metaphors
- marrying metaphors to your speech

What Are Metaphors?

The opening paragraph provided a metaphor about what happens when you speak with the static of unfamiliar language to your audience. As a speaker, consider metaphors as language symbolizing that one thing is something else. For example,

> *The power of determination is an arrow hitting its target in a hurricane.*
> *Life is the clay you can sculpt into whatever your head, heart, and hand desire.*
> *Failures in life are chapters in your book of experience that you can learn from.*

As you can see, the above examples follow the formula A is B, but the comparisons aren't literal. The use of symbolism in metaphors enriches the understanding of something and expands its meaning beyond a literal level. Metaphors should simplify complexity, transform abstraction to concreteness, and bridge the unknown to the known.

> *The use of symbolism in metaphors enriches the understanding of something and expands its meaning beyond a literal level.*

For example, the following excerpt on choosing your level of success in life lacks simplicity and concreteness:

You have the choice to determine what you want to make from life because of all the possibilities you have access to. Those possibilities are put together by your efforts to structure the level of success in your life. You have equal opportunity based on the probabilities given.

Did that tangle of technical twaddle make you confused on what I was talking about? Here's the metaphorical version.

You're given a deck of cards that represents your chance to play the game of life. You have access to a full deck of fifty-two cards to pick through and put together in any card combinations. The more work you put into arranging the cards determines the strength of your hand. Do you stop at a pair of fives or refuse to rest until you have a royal flush?

Did you notice that the metaphors cited above have two essential traits? Without these traits your metaphors will not live.

You could consider a metaphor a living organism with a heart and sensory organs. The heart of a metaphor is the prior knowledge your audience has of the world.

Without prior knowledge a metaphor wouldn't have a pulse. Using prior knowledge allows your audience to understand what you're talking about.

The sensory organs of a metaphor activate your audience's senses of taste, touch, smell, sound, and sight. Without sensory words, you would have ambiguous abstraction. Let's see another example.

Fear is a puppet master hiding behind the curtain. When it pulls the strings, you are fear's puppet—prevented from participating on the stage of life.

In the above example fear is compared to a puppet master. Although fear is an abstract and complex topic it has been put into a concrete framework. The metaphor uses prior knowledge of puppet masters, stage, strings, curtains, and puppets to represent what happens when fear takes over. The sensory language includes visual, aural, and tactile imagery. Could you feel the strings? Maybe you hear the puppet master call you or hear the sounds of a puppet polka as the puppet master yanks you back.

The Magical Properties of Metaphors

Would you rather read through a movie script or watch the movie? Metaphors are mental movies for your audience that connect with them both intellectually and emotionally. The magical properties of metaphors:

- convert lifeless language into living language
- make a stale perspective fresh
- allow you to convey more in less time
- present a compact, memorable, and meaningful message
- add an extra and unexpected dimension to your speech

The Alchemy of Making Metaphors

It's time to take all the elements discussed so far to the laboratory to put together a four-step spell that will allow you to make your own metaphors to improve the quality of your speeches.

1. Identifying Your Audience

If you were a paleontologist and pointed randomly to the grass to proclaim a dinosaur finding, you would spend a lot of time guessing what kind of dinosaur lay beneath the soil. A better method would be to dig up the soil and uncover the bones. The more definitive outline you start with, the more likelihood you have of identifying the dinosaur. As a speaker, the more you know about your audience the better chance you have to make a metaphor that identifies with them.

Who is your audience? Are they businessmen, architectural engineers, software designers, or a potluck audience? Some audiences will understand your message more than others. Knowing who they are will allow you to assess their understanding based on the material you present.

What do they know about your topic? What your audience knows will reflect their present understanding level. For example, a group of business executives will have a solid understanding of the language of implementing business plans, but a group of inexperienced entrepreneurs would have less understanding. It's your responsibility to make your message understandable to the audience. They cannot act upon what they don't understand.

Now that you have uncovered information about your audience, you can proceed to find comparisons that will become your metaphors.

2. Finding Comparisons

A metaphor is composed of taking the unknown, complex, and/or abstract components of what you want to say and comparing them with some known, simple, and/or concrete equivalent so that your audience can understand what you are saying. To know whether your comparisons will have meaning, you need to first ask two questions.

Is your comparison relevant to your message? Let's say you like classical music and want to use the violin as a symbol for tuning into the melody of life, but your speech is about workplace layoffs. At present you don't have relevant content for your message.

Is the comparison relevant to your audience? Imagine that you're a science-fiction fan. You want to make comparisons about the Star Wars movies. The problem is your audience may not care or even hate Star Wars. Also, the Star Wars universe has a lot of information that only followers understand.

If you have satisfactory answers to the above two questions, then you have comparisons that are meaningful. Here are the two ways to find comparisons.

Guaranteed comparisons. Common associations are a goldmine of available comparisons that your audience shares. Common associations group your audience together into one category. If your audience works in the same industry, you have found a common association. They will understand their industry, so that gives you known information to work with. What kinds of comparisons can you think of that relate to your audience's industry? For example, if you're speaking to hospital management you have many comparisons to pick from that could include anything from medicine, ambulances, and surgery to caring for sick patients, hospital equipment, and the emergency room.

> *Common associations are a goldmine of available comparisons that your audience shares.*

Known and concrete comparisons. If you're speaking on finance to a non-finance crowd the terms of subprime borrows, derivative instruments, and legacy securities might cause brain bewilderment because they aren't known. You should ask yourself,

- What does my topic relate to that the audience would understand?
- What comparison would require the least amount of explanation?

Once you have something that is known, ask yourself if it could pass the sensory Pictionary test: *What can my audience's senses detect? How concrete is my present example?*

3. Putting Your Metaphor Together
There are two aspects you need to know before you can put together your metaphor.

Does the metaphor match? If you have multiple comparisons you will want to categorize them so they will match; otherwise you'll have the undesirable mixed metaphor. Pick only the best comparisons as your objective is to give a metaphor, not a Shakespearean sonnet.

What images come to mind with a carpenter? Maybe a hardhat, tools, gloves, boots, an astronaut helmet, and a scuba suit. Did those last two stick out? They didn't belong with the uniform. When you stitch together multiple metaphors you make a mismatched quilt of confusion for your audience. The loose seams of mixed metaphors cause the illustrations you have created to fall apart. Here are mixed metaphor examples:

If you don't uproot the seeds of fear they will grow out of darkened waters into sea serpents.

Your checkmate will be my touchdown in the game of life.

Let's redress these metaphors in the proper clothes so they'll be in uniform.

In the second example land and sea get mixed. How about *If you don't uproot the seeds of fear they will grow into monstrous weeds.*

In the second example there should be one game not two (chess and football). *Check doesn't mean checkmate on the chessboard of life; other moves are always available.*

What do the metaphor parts represent? You must identify what the metaphor parts relate to and represent. Poetic language and statements aren't metaphors. The following example will sound choppy because the parts do not represent anything other than bowling terms.

On the bowling lane, take your bowling ball to the line and release it from your hand. You want to hit the pins, but if you miss you can take another shot to score.

Here's the completed version that compares what the metaphor parts represent.

On the lanes of life the bowling ball of destiny is in your hands; however, you can only score when you release the ball at the line that separates action from inaction. Even if you miss your target in life, you can always take another shot. You're always one pin closer to scoring on your goals.

Now that you know who your audience is, how to find comparisons, and how to put a metaphor together you can begin to insert metaphors into your speech.

Marrying Metaphors to Your Speech

Those metaphors you created can't remain single forever; you have to marry them to places in your speech. You can marry your metaphor to:

- your introduction or speech opening—reel in their attention from the beginning to set the framework for your speech.
- the "space" before your story—introduce a teaser trailer preview for a story. This adds curiosity before you begin and gives you an established callback to use.
- the body of your story—maybe the metaphor will be your message or used to reinforce your message. Another option is that your story could be intertwined with metaphorical elements throughout. Lastly, the metaphor and story run parallel and complement each other.

- a solo point—a metaphor that stands alone and needs no further explanation.
- an activity—this works especially well in a workshop setting. For example, *What is the importance of unity? On ancient ships, teams of galley oarsmen needed to have unity with their rowing. A mistake meant the ship would stop, oars could break, the ship could spin, and in times of battle an enemy ship could ram into and sink the ship that didn't have rowing unity. When a team doesn't have unity it brings consequences. How has disunity affected you in the workplace? Break into your groups and...*
- material that is difficult to understand—consider the content of your speech a spool of thread, and let your audience's ability to understand represent a needle eye. A knot of difficult-to-understand content won't pass through the needle eye of your audience's understanding. You need to unknot the difficulty so it can pass through. You can find knots in the content that need metaphors. TIE your metaphor to your speech with these three steps: *time, interrogate, experiment.*

TIE Your Metaphor

Time. Mentally travel back to a time before you became an expert on your speech topic. How did someone else explain your material so you could understand it? If you were hearing or reading the material for the first time and didn't know anything about the topic, what would make you uncertain? Recollect the feedbacks. Review the archives of past commentary given on your speech. What prior feedback has your audience given you on difficult material? If you had a Q&A, what questions came up that showed a lack of understanding about what you said? Did they have any difficulty understanding your message? What kinds of questions were voiced in terms of understanding?

Interrogate your speech. Get out your brass pen and pummel your speech with scrutiny. Ask yourself: How are my points anchored in my speech? Does sensory language support my main points? What parts of my speech have presupposed knowledge that the audience may not understand? Are there any abstractions that need to be replaced with concreteness? Does sensory language support my main points?

Experiment. Your metaphor crystallizes through experimentation. Here is what you can do.

1. Give the speech to people who should know what you're talking about. If they don't understand, you need to make changes before testing with the second group.
2. Give the speech to people outside your field of expertise. Get feedback on what isn't clear and ask them to explain it back so they demonstrate their understanding of your material.

You have now learned:

*   what metaphors are
*   the magical properties of metaphors
*   the alchemy to making metaphors
*   how to marry metaphors to your speech

In your next speech, remember to use metaphors so that you are speaking on a frequency that is on the audience's channel of understanding.

Nate Dunlop is a keynote speaker, corporate trainer, metaphor mastery maestro, and certified World Class Speaking coach who started www.yourspeakingsolutions.com. He can be reached at nate@yourspeakingsolutions.com.

18

How to Uncover Humor in Your Speech

Kimberly Myers

P icture this: you are onstage, and the audience is laughing and smiling, embracing your message. You know that finding the humor in your message helped engage the audience. As you walk off the stage, members of the audience stop you and praise you for delivering a serious topic with a touch of humor.

Many speakers believe they need to deliver one-liners or do a comedy act to help the audience laugh. They try hard to add humor to the speech rather than uncover the layers of the speech to find the humor. Bill Cosby, a genius at finding humor in the everyday, says, "You can turn painful situations around through laughter. If you can find humor in anything, even poverty, you can survive it."

You will never be Bill Cosby, but you can learn to find humor in every situation. This chapter will help you uncover the humor in almost all situations. You will discover:

- why humor is important in almost every speech
- how to share one of the 4 F's
- how to use personal stories to uncover humor in your content

- three World Class delivery tools to help you uncover the humor
- a word of caution about using humor

Why Humor Is Important

The Mayo Clinic says that laughter has many medical benefits: reducing stress, lowering blood pressure, reducing pain, and even improving your immune system. It's no surprise then to understand why we enjoy humor in our presentations. Some speeches are just funny, but often a speech is serious in nature. As humans we need a break, a release, a stress reliever. Humor also allows the speaker to connect with the audience because humor makes the speaker human.

When a speaker tries to *add* humor rather than find the humor within the speech, the result may be laughter, but the value of the speech is reduced if the humor does not relate to or reinforce the message of the speech. So how do we find the humor in our speech? The answer is in the stories we use in our speeches.

Studies at the Mayo Clinic indicate that those who find humor in the worst of circumstances live longer. Dramatic television shows often have characters that are deeply flawed in a humorous way. This leads to uncovering the humor hidden in the characters and their dialogue. In the same way we can find the humor buried in our topic—and even in ourselves—to help put the audience at ease. This is especially important when we're speaking on serious topics because our senses need the laughter to reduce the stress.

How to Share One of the 4 F's

One of the best methods to uncover humor in your speech is to analyze your 4 F's:

1. Failures
2. First
3. Flaw
4. Frustration

We've all had a failure or a "first" that did not work out the way we expected. Most of us have a story about our first date, our first time driving, or a first day on the job. Sometimes that first is also a huge failure. Ordinarily we would not think this is something to share, but 4 F stories provide a perfect opportunity to uncover humor. Audiences love self-deprecating stories. They make us normal.

> *Audiences love self-deprecating stories. They make us normal.*

Flaws and frustration are a bit different because they are not something that has happened to us, they are part of us. These can also help us uncover humor and connect with our listeners.

To identify your 4 F's, write a list for each of them. For instance, I am very tall and a bit paranoid about it. I use a reference to my size in my "Throwaway Children" keynote. In the story, I am meeting my new son's biological mom at my front door for the first time. I am truly defensive…

"Hello, may I help you?"

The tiny, curly-haired woman says, "I'm Cameron's mom. I heard he lives here and is going to school. May I see him?"

I am a big woman. I feel myself expanding to fill the doorway just like a dog with their hair standing on end.

Naturally, I spread my shoulders and plant my feet to emphasize the point, but between the words and the filling space, I always get laughs.

Use Personal Stories to Uncover Humor

Stories are the best place in a speech to uncover humor. Now that you have the perfect story, one that reinforces the message of your speech, it is time to gently peel open the layers of the story to find the humor in it. If the story includes one of the 4 F's, uncovering those layers is easy. Finding the humor in our lives is universal. How often have you been mortified by something you did or said, but as you relived the story it became funnier?

Stories allow the speaker to be authentic. While the story may be abridged for clarity's sake, we must tell the emotional truth. As we refine the story, places for humor pop out of it.

Three World Class Delivery Tools to Help You Uncover the Humor

The following tools are sure to help you uncover humor in your speech: *Look before the Line, Stop on a Dime,* and *Dialogue Duty.*

Look before the Line

When you *Look before the Line*, you are analyzing the dialogue between your characters. Conversations include both verbal and nonverbal communication. Speakers usually ignore nonverbal communication as a source of humor. *Look before the Line* forces the speaker to think about the reaction of the characters. What is the emotion? The most humorous stories are when one of the characters is confused or embarrassed.

I have a story in my keynote "Prejudgment" in which I am in a taxi with a driver who is very serious and I am very tired.

> *My young colleague and I are returning to our hotel after a long day at a conference. We finally find a taxi. Ten minutes into the drive, we hear music coming from somewhere in the car.*
>
> *"Do you hear that?" I say. "Where is it coming from?"*
>
> *The driver checks the radio, which by law is off, and we all check our phones. Nothing. We continue hearing the music. I check my purse and pull out my iPad. It has turned itself on to a Nine Inch Nails song?*
>
> *The driver reaches into his seat. "Is this the album?" he asks, showing me a CD. I look on my iPad and the album cover is the same.*
>
> *As he pulls into the hotel, he says, "Lady, any lady your age who has Nine Inch Nails on her iPad is my kind of lady. No charge." To my colleague Jason, he says, "She has great taste in music." And he refuses to take a tip too.*

In this story the look between each sentence helps to tell the story:

• The confusion on our faces as we search for the mysterious music
• My embarrassment at finding my iPad has turned on
• The driver's reaction to my music
• My reaction to the free ride

Each reaction to the dialogue adds to the humor of the situation. Ask yourself: *what was I thinking, feeling, or doing* (after the line of dialogue)? Then relive that emotion.

Stop on a Dime

Stopping on a dime is another delivery tool in your World Class Speaking arsenal. This is adding a twist into the story. Often a story will set up an expectation for the audience. They are lulled into thinking that something will happen, but you turn their perception. You set them up to believe something then twist the response. In the taxi story, the audience believes that Jason will be the character playing the music—not the fifty-year-old.

This can also be used in delivering a single line. Comedians use this often. Judy Carter calls it the *List of Three*. The first two in the list are related. The last item in the list is not really related but has relevance to the previous two. Since we listen in threes, do not add more to the list just because you can. Keep to three.

As a speech and debate coach, I am honored to teach my students to speak with authority, win or lose with grace—and to twirl their pens. (When I say twirl their pens, I demonstrate.)

Dialogue Duty

By now you realize that dialogue versus narration is critical for a successful story. Take the time to refine the dialogue and to uncover the humor in it. The best practice is done in front of a video camera and a live audience. Refinement is key to uncovering humor. As speakers we are often too close to our material. Comedians practice their skits in front of a live audience. As speakers we should emulate their practice.

> *Comedians practice their skits in front of a live audience.*
> *As speakers we should emulate their practice.*

I was working with my speaker coach refining a story. In the story I am a nine-year-old who's angry with my parents because they are focusing on my very sick brother. At one point my dad is in the kitchen rinsing my head in the kitchen sink.

"Kimmy Lynne," my dad says, *"I know you are frustrated and angry, but we need to be a cohesive family unit."*

After that line, my coach stood up and asked, "Did your dad really talk that way?"

"He was a nuclear engineer," I said.

"Well, then tell us that!"

We decided to leave the dialogue, but I stepped forward on the stage and in an exaggerated whisper told the audience, "You see, my dad is a nuclear engineer." It gets laughs every time!

As you refine your dialogue, think about interesting words that are visual. Words like *slick*, *smelly*, and *smart* carry an image. When they are matched up to the actions of the speaker, they are humorous.

A Caution to Using Humor

Speakers who add humor because they are told to add humor find audience members rapidly losing interest in them. Added humor is often not relevant to the message of the speech. Audience members may laugh, but they are intelligent and can sense that it is artificial. The humor needs to be authentic.

I invite you to uncover humor in each and every speech you give. Find the failures, firsts, frustrations, and flaws that apply to your presentation and you will relate better to your audience. They will remember the speech more if you are authentic and uncover the humor within your stories. Don't forget, we love funny stories even with a serious topic. Remember, humorous stories are "sticky"—they stay with us long after we hear them.

Kimberly Myers, DTM, is a keynote speaker and certified World Class Speaking coach. Her specialty is helping women in technology find their voice. Visit her website at www.yourlegacyspeaks.org.

Part 4

WORLD CLASS
SPEAKING DELIVERY

19

Upholding the Grand Bargain: Why You Must Connect Emotionally with Your Audience

David P. Otey

If you are only worried about not making a mistake, then you will communicate nothing. You will have missed the point of making music, which is to make people feel something....It's all about making people care what happens next.

—Yo-Yo Ma

Substitute the word "speaking" for the phrase "making music" and this quote by the world-renowned cellist applies equally to speakers as it does to musicians. Throughout this section of the book, you will pick up invaluable tools for making people *feel* something. World Class speakers use these tools to build a stronger audience connection than you may ever have thought possible. But the tools will be wasted if you are not motivated to use them.

"*Why* do I have to connect emotionally with my audience?" is a question I often hear when coaching speakers—especially those in quantitative, technical, or scientific pursuits. "Isn't it enough to present compelling information?"

I always answer that question with one or more of these questions:

- Do you want your information to be remembered?
- Do you want your message to make a difference?
- Do you want to be invited back to speak again?

If you answer yes to any of these questions, you need to master the art of making an emotional connection. The rest of this chapter is dedicated to convincing you of the truth of that claim. The chapters that follow will tell you *how* to do that; for now we will focus on *why*.

It All Starts with Purpose

The starting point for every World Class speech is a clear statement of *specific purpose*. What do you want your listeners to think, do, or feel differently once they have heard you? Notice that this question is all about making a difference. The purpose of any World Class Speaker is always to make a difference to his or her audience. If you are not there to make a difference, you ought not to be speaking.

For you to make a difference requires that the audience do at least three things:

1. accept what you have to say
2. remember it
3. act on it

In other words, each listener has to make a series of decisions: Will I allow this new information to displace what I already know or think? Will I commit it to memory? Will I take action as a result?

What we now know about decision making—thanks to new advances in neuroscience—is that it always takes place in the emotional part of the brain. We may weigh the merits of an argument in our rational brain, but ultimately the decision is made and owned by the emotional brain. What that means for you is that no matter how compelling your information is, it will not make a difference in the lives of your listeners unless you connect with the emotional, decision-making part of their minds. In short, you must connect emotionally if you want to accomplish your purpose.

> *You must connect emotionally if you*
> *want to accomplish your purpose.*

The Grand Bargain Controls the Best Payment of All

Do you get paid to speak? Regardless of whether a meeting planner hands you a check as you take the platform, or eager audience members line up at your table to purchase products when you're done, there is one type of payment every speaker wants. We all want audiences to pay *attention*! That simple fact brings us to the second point about connecting emotionally. If you want audiences to pay attention, you must uphold your end of the Grand Bargain.

What is the Grand Bargain, and how does one uphold it? Simply put, the Grand Bargain is the deal the speaker makes in return for the audience's attention. Now I know what you are probably thinking: audience members willingly give the speaker their attention in return for the information being delivered, right? Not necessarily.

If you are just trading information for attention, the audience is getting a lousy deal. The average English speaker speaks at a rate of 125-150 words per minute. The average adult reading speed is twice that. That means if you were to write down your 30-minute keynote and hand it to me, I could probably read it in 15 minutes or less. Not only could I consume the information in half the time, but once you have handed it to me I can read it in any 15 minutes of my own choosing, instead of having to work my schedule around yours.

But let's say you didn't write it down. Let us assume that you are delivering it live and I am in your audience. You are giving me what amounts to fifteen minutes' worth of information (if we take the written version as our yardstick) and taking thirty minutes of my time in return. If you want me to accept that deal, you must "bring something else to the table" as the saying goes. That is the Grand Bargain, and you ignore it at your peril.

So what do you bring to the table? You should bring everything an information-filled piece of paper doesn't bring. You bring the awareness that people connect with the spoken word at a different level than they do the written word. You bring emotional engagement. You bring the ability to draw your listeners into your stories so completely they feel what your characters feel. When you do that, they will eagerly trade their attention, not for the information, but for the feelings you are giving them. You see, if you want to get paid you have to earn it. Even if all they are paying is attention.

> *You see, if you want to get paid you have to earn it.*
> *Even if all they are paying is attention.*

I have seen the truth of this time and again, not only in my own speaking but also in my coaching. I have worked with a two-time Olympian who later coached an athletic team to a national championship. Her stories range from athletic nail-biters to personal triumph over huge setbacks. She came to me because she wanted to use those experiences as the basis to pursue professional motivational speaking.

The problem was that initially her stories all sounded as if she was delivering them from the sidelines of a hard-fought college basketball game. Her intensity was scary. I would not have wanted to be one of her players!

As we worked together, she learned many of the World Class Speaking techniques of storytelling that you will pick up in subsequent chapters. As she developed a wider range of delivery skills, her intensity softened and came under her control. She learned there was as much value in the way she told a story as there was in the story itself. After a recent successful speaking event, she told me she was amazed at "the number of people who came up to me and told me they felt like they were right in the middle of the story with me—that it impacted them to a different degree because they *felt* the story and didn't just hear it."

That is emotional engagement. That is World Class Speaking. That is upholding her end of the bargain.

Emotions Lead the Way

We have seen that emotional engagement is key to making a difference as a speaker and that honoring this fact in your speaking is essential to gaining audience goodwill. But is it all a one-way street? Ultimately, are you connecting with your audience or encouraging the audience to connect with you? Does it really matter? The important thing is that a connection is made at a personal emotional level, not merely at an informational level.

Several years ago I learned a powerful lesson on the importance of looking beyond the informational level when communicating. I was tasked with creating a training program that would reach thousands of technicians in hundreds of TV stations across the United States. The training covered the use of a new digital generation of the technology used in news vans and helicopters. Like the other engineers involved in the project, at first I believed we needed a slick way to present this highly technical information about the differences between the new and old generations of technology.

Then the project took an unexpected turn. As I spent time in the field with some of the people we would be training, I came to understand their needs better. "I don't care how it works. I just don't want the producer yelling at me because my live shot failed in the middle of the newscast!" was a typical comment.

Sure, some of these people were curious about the technical details. But most of them weren't concerned about lack of information; they were concerned about lack of a job! They feared for their job security as they perceived their skills becoming obsolete. The problem our training needed to solve was not lack of information. It was fear.

Once I understood my audience's needs better, my team changed our whole approach to the training design. Although we never said "We are here to ease your fears," that became our unstated purpose. We refocused the training experience around guiding participants to discover for themselves that using the new equipment was not much different—and in many ways was easier—than doing their jobs the old way. You could almost hear their concerns melt away as they completed each virtual workshop. During the three-year run of this program, we successfully trained more than ten thousand individuals in over nine hundred locations using distance-learning technology.

What I learned from this experience is that the emotional needs of an audience cannot be ignored if any speaker or trainer is to be successful, no matter how technical the topic. What does this mean for you as a World Class Speaker? It means you must be prepared to use the techniques in the following chapters not simply as "tricks" for connecting with an audience but as a means of allowing your audience to connect with *you* at an emotional level.

Key Takeaways

- Decisions and memories are both made in the emotional brain. If you want your message to be accepted and remembered, you must meet your audience at an emotional level.

- Your audience does not owe you their attention. They *pay* it to you only when you earn it.

- When you move your audience from *hearing* your stories to *feeling* them, you will make a difference. And that is why you speak.

- To uphold your end of the Grand Bargain, you must connect with your audience emotionally. It will pay off every time.

David P. Otey is a former broadcasting engineer turned inspirational speaker and speaking coach. He helps technical presenters master the art of storytelling and shows companies how developing leadership is as much about listening as it is about learning to speak persuasively. He can be reached at www.davidoteysos.com.

20

Using the CLAP Formula to Engage Your Audience

Lewis Roth

D o you want to be the kind of speaker who consistently engages and transforms your audience—and gets invited back time and time again?

By the end of this chapter, you will know that when your audience *claps* at the end of your speech, it isn't just because they're being polite. It's because you had them on the edge of their seats, and they want you back. It's because you engaged them through the formula called CLAP:

- Conflict
- Laughs and humor
- Activities
- Participation

Conflict

The greatest enemy of the speaker is being boring, and conflict is the cure. While conflict is one of the most critical tools in speaking, it is also one of the most underused.

> *The greatest enemy of the speaker is
> being boring, and conflict is the cure.*

How Conflict Hooks Our Audience

1. **Conflict creates tension in our scenes.** Movie directors know how important it is to create a sense of tension to hook the audience from the very beginning. For almost the first hour of the 2013 movie *Searching for Mr. Banks*, the audience is pulled between scenes of the present and flashbacks from the past of the life of P.L. Travers. Throughout we are kept wondering what happened in her past that had made this woman so bitter, cynical, and unhappy in the present.

2. **Rising conflict creates powerful suspense.** As conflict rises, like stretching a rubber band to the breaking point, we know that something will have to give. We need an answer, and we're waiting for it at the edge of our seats.

3. **Conflict puts our characters into a struggle.** As your characters engage in a battle of wills, your audience is not only engaged because they are wondering how things will turn out for the characters, but because they are connecting the character's struggle with a struggle in their own lives.

As you're crafting conflict in your speech, also remember two important tools that can heighten its impact: *curiosity* and *contrast*.

Create Curiosity

Curiosity sets the stage of your conflict—for example, my speech "Fear Wears the Greatest Disguise" tells the story of how I pursued my dream to become an airplane pilot. Here is a scene that occurs just after I had begun training with Chuckie, my seventh instructor and my best friend.

> *So we're doing one takeoff and landing after another, and each time I do a takeoff and landing, I feel like I am getting better and better. And suddenly we come down to our final landing, and we stop, and Chuckie looks at me and says, "Lewis—bye!"*

Here the audience is wondering, *Why did Chuckie say "bye?" Had he perhaps given up on Lewis, as all the other instructors had?* Curiosity is created when we don't reveal why everything is happening as it happens.

Create Contrast

It's human nature to become bored of the "usual," and it's no different in speaking. When speakers use the same tone and style, whether high-energy and loud or low-key and monotonous, the audience will eventually tune them out. When we contrast *emotions* in our speeches—shifting meaningfully from high energy to quiet and reflective—we take our audience on a roller coaster ride that keeps them on the edge of their seats.

Remember: where there is conflict, there is emotion. Look for the natural emotional/energy shifts and relive them for your audience.

We also need to create contrast with the *scenes* of our story. If every story in your speech is between you and your mother, or you and your wife, the audience will eventually get bored. This is why great movie directors won't go too long without changing the setting, place, and characters within their scenes. Take a cue from Hollywood and contrast the scenes in your speech.

The Climax: Where It All Comes Together

The conflict typically reaches the breaking point in what is called the *climax*, or the apex of the conflict in the scene.

For example, the climax in "Fear Wears the Greatest Disguise" occurs after my instructor and friend Chuckie tells me I'm ready for my first solo flight, and I start listing all these excuses about why I'm not ready. Suddenly Chuckie goes into a two-minute rant:

> *Lewis, I am going to tell you something that I never wanted to tell you. You are afraid, and you always have been. I know you, Lewis.*
>
> *Remember when you were playing the drums at all those events, and you told me that you never had the time to step out from behind the drums to meet people? Lewis, that wasn't a legitimate excuse; that was fear.*
>
> *And what about the time you were going after all those computer certifications and kept telling me, " I just need to get one more certification, Chuckie, and then*

I will get a job," but you never did! That wasn't a valid reason, Lewis—that was fear.

And don't let me get started on Rachel. Remember breaking up with Rachel, even though she was perfect for you? You said that your relationship hit a brick wall. Lewis, that wasn't a brick wall you hit; that was fear.

Lewis, you are all out of excuses, but you are filled up with fear. Lewis, you are an afraidaholic!

At that point, just before I delivered my impact line, I dropped all the energy, paused for three seconds, silence took over, and anticipation filled the air (emotional contrast). If you were sitting in the audience, you would've felt that something had to give. *What was Lewis going to do now? Was he going to chicken out again, or was he going to triumph?*

So if your story has no conflict, no tension, no battle of wills, it won't captivate. Either add elements of conflict to the story, or find another story that does have conflict to support your message.

Laughs and Humor

It's been said that you shouldn't include humor in your speaking—unless you want to get paid! Meeting planners know that humor is the ultimate magnet that pulls an audience back to the speaker. Regardless of whether you're looking to get hired as a speaker, humor is a great way to recharge the batteries of your audience.

One way you can create humor in your speaking is through *dialogue with your audience*. Laughs are created when you cause your audience to experience a snap shift in their thought process. They think they are going in one direction and expect to continue in that direction, but then suddenly they are shifted in another direction where they experience a sense of unexpected resolution, and you get a laugh. For example, take a look at the following example from "Fear Wears the Greatest Disguise":

So, at the age of 26, I drove down to Sparta Aviation in Teterboro, New Jersey, and I started to take flight lessons. Now, it usually takes about 40 hours for someone to get their pilot's license. Oh no, not me. You see for me, it took 150! [Laughs]

Do you see the twist here? With my body language and cocky enthusiasm, I have the audience thinking that I am a hotshot pilot, and it took me much less than forty hours to get my pilot's license. The laugh comes from their realization that I wasn't a hot shot after all, and I was actually a terrible pilot. (By the way, an audience also loves it when you humorously self-deprecate.)

Another way is to create humor in the *dialogue between characters in your story*. If you're working on your speech, wondering, "How can I insert humor here?"—you're asking the wrong question. What you should instead be asking is, "How can I *uncover* humor here?" One place to look is within the character dialogue of your stories. Here's an example that comes towards the end of "Fear Wears the Greatest Disguise":

And finally, after several bounces, I came to a halt, and I caught my breath and rubbed my brow, and I said, "Boy, did I lick that landing—I am good!" [Audience laughs from self-deprecating.] "I think I am going to take this baby up for another spin" [more laughs].

Suddenly Chuckie comes running out of the hanger, and he runs up to me and says, "Lewis, don't go just yet. I gotta tell you, the other pilots and I were watching you, and I gotta be honest with you, we were taking bets [laughs from the twist]. Not only to see if you would make it, but to see how many times you would bounce [laughs]. I won—I had you down for seven" [laughs].

Activities

While stories emotionally anchor your points to your audience, *activities* kinesthetically anchor them. Unfortunately many speakers use activities simply to involve their audience without anchoring their points, or even worse, they use an activity only to fill space and pass time.

When constructing an activity to anchor your points, remember these three rules.

1. Balance the Length of Your Activities with Your Content

The length of any activity will be relative to the length of your speech. If you are conducting a full-day program, doing two or three 10-15 minute activities spread out through the day will fit well. However, doing a 15-minute activity in a 25-minute speech will not. Remember that the purpose of an activity is to anchor a point, not just take up air time.

2. Never Start Your Speech with an Activity

Before you ask your audience to do anything, they need to get to know you, like you, and trust you first. A few years ago, I attended a three-day Millionaire Mind seminar with T. Harv Eker, where all participants were asked upon registration, quite mysteriously, to bring a 100 dollar bill in an envelope.

On the second day of the program, we found out why. We were divided into groups, where each group had a leader with a lighter. We were asked to chant a mantra—"I rule money; money doesn't rule"—and then line up to burn our 100-dollar bill to demonstrate our belief in this mantra. As soon as the first person in line was ready to burn their 100-dollar bill, the leader called off the activity and explained the point: whoever was ready to burn their 100-dollar bill clearly did not respect the value of money and had issues with money management.

If this activity was done on the first day of the program, what percentage of the 500 people in attendance do you think would have stepped up to the plate and voluntarily burned up their money? The answer is probably zero. This high-stakes exercise needed a lot of buy-in and trust, which is why it was done at the end of the second day of the program.

3. Always Test Your Activity before Taking It Prime Time

At that same Harv Eker Millionaire Mind seminar, there was another activity I can almost guarantee was never tested before taking it to prime time, because it totally flopped.

The seminar leader began the activity by asking everyone to close their eyes and imagine a time in their life when they were bullied, mocked, or laughed at.

Within seconds, the sounds of people laughing started coming out of the loudspeakers. The idea was to mimic real sounds of people laughing, in order to enhance the experience of the exercise. It backfired! The seminar leaders did not realize that the laughter would be contagious. Soon everyone in the room was laughing, and the exercise had to be stopped in its tracks.

Most likely the seminar leaders never tested this out with smaller test groups before implementing it in a big way. Always test out your activity with smaller audiences first before taking it to the big stage.

Participation

Most speakers never invite participation from their audience. But speakers who just stand up on stage and spew forth content, without ever checking in with their audience, will eventually lose them. No matter how great your story is, *if you don't check in, they will check out.* On the other hand, speakers who actively engage with their audience, stepping in and out of their stories to check in with them, will keep their audience hooked.

> *No matter how great your story is,*
> *if you don't check in, they will check out.*

Throughout your speech, you should be asking questions that get your audience to think and reflect, either internally or overtly.

Whenever your audience is nodding their heads in agreement or murmuring *mmhhh, yeah, ahhh,* etc., you've established *internal* reflection. Here is an example of a reflective question from "Fear Wears the Greatest Disguise":

When it comes to taking your life off to another level—when it comes to realizing your dreams—if you're not living it, is there anything holding you back? Is there something in the way, like a legitimate excuse, a valid reason, or insurmountable obstacle that tends to show up?

With every question, the audience got a chance to reflect on their own lives internally, and I could see it in their body language and facial expression.

Overt reflection is established when you've asked your audience a question that requires an actual response. For example, here is an excerpt from a great speech delivered by Nick Vujicic, where he's talking to an audience of high school kids about bullying:

I want to ask you today, do you think I'm cool enough to be your friend? [Audience: "Yeah."] But I don't swear. I don't use the F- bomb. Am I still cool enough to be your friend? [Audience: "Yeah."] But I don't tease people. Am I still cool enough to be your friend? [Audience: "Yeah."] But I have no arms, no legs. Seriously . . .

[pause with lowered voice] you would be my friend, even though I have no arms and no legs? [Audience: "Yeah."]

As each "yeah" from the audience gets louder and louder, with more and more conviction, Nick then throws his most powerful punch.

So you're telling me that it actually doesn't matter, right? If it actually doesn't matter how we look, then why do we tease each other for how we look—if it actually doesn't matter?

Asking questions that require a response from your audience not only gets them involved, it also causes them to reflect on their own lives.

Putting It All Together

Your goal as a speaker is to strive to use all the elements of CLAP within your speech, but the key is to use them in the right balance. Your audience won't always be riveted by conflict, bound by curiosity, or feel hooked during every moment of your speech. So you might need to check in with them, or perhaps do a quick activity to anchor your point. At the same time, if you spend too much time doing an activity, you could lose your audience. If your audience has spent considerable time reflecting, humor can wake them up and reel them in again. The art is in the mix.

Note: If you want to see how a person with no arms and legs puts together all the elements of CLAP and delivers an impassioned and moving speech to one of the toughest possible audiences (high school kids), I invite you to view Nick Vujicic's twenty-minute speech on bullying delivered at Southwest High in Elcentro, California, in February 2013. On YouTube, search on "Nick Vujicic Bully Talk" to find the clip.

If you can incorporate and balance all the elements of CLAP throughout your speech, you will not only keep your audience on the edge of their seats, but you will also get invited back!

Lewis Roth is a certified World Class speech coach, award-winning speaker, and presentation skills instructor. He is the author of 52 Presentation Tips (www.52presentationtips.com). You can learn more about Lewis at www.HighTouchSpeaking.com.

21

Human Neurobiology:
The Science of Speaking Success

John K. Bates

I f you were making a big mistake you'd want to know about it, right? I made mistakes for years and never knew it, and this practice got in the way of my success on every level: speaking, managing, fundraising, you name it. It is also something that bedevils many of my most brilliant clients, be they corporate leaders or TED and TEDx speakers. The good news is that once you know more about how our brains are wired you'll be set up for World Class Speaking success like never before.

In this chapter you'll learn about

- the three-part human brain
- how to connect with and move people
- the evolutionary power of storytelling
- using nonverbal communication

Once you understand some of the evolutionary and neurological underpinnings of World Class Speaking in action you will be better equipped to genuinely, deeply move your audiences and be a far more effective communicator.

Stories Sway Us

You, like me, were probably under the impression that emotions, stories, anecdotes, and entertainment are somehow less important than logic and reason. That may be true with computers, but I have news for you. Unless you're working on Area 51 stuff, everyone you communicate with is a human being. Underneath our cultural and genetic differences we are all wired with some very important commonalities. Surprisingly, much of effective communication has little to do with logic or reason—and that was my big mistake: thinking that logic is more important than emotional connection.

When you look at a cross-section of a human brain you can see that our brains have three basic parts: the brainstem, the midbrain, and the cerebral cortex. Together the brainstem and midbrain make up the paleomammalian brain, also called the limbic system, or simply the emotional brain. Wrapped around the emotional brain is the cerebral cortex, a later evolutionary development, which handles logic, reasoning, and language among other things.

The emotional brain does *not* have access to language, logic, or reason. It communicates with you by giving you "gut feelings" and is dialed into your surroundings: smells, sounds, people's body language—things the conscious brain doesn't notice. The emotional brain is constantly paying attention on a profoundly deep level and is the part that makes decisions. It's what Simon Sinek is talking about in his wildly popular TED Talk "How Great Leaders Inspire Action—Start with Why."

If I were to put you into a functional magnetic resonance imaging (fMRI) machine and then give you a decision to make, I would see your emotional brain fire first, followed almost immediately by your cerebral cortex. The emotional brain *makes the decision* while the logical cerebral cortex agrees or disagrees, but it does *not* make the decision. In his fascinating book *Blink*, Malcolm Gladwell delves into this topic at length.

In my sales calls I've had experiences like this:

> John: "Do you like the product?"
> Customer: "Oh, I love the product."
> John: "Do you think it's the right price?"
> Customer: "Oh, yeah, I think it's the right price; it's a really great price."
> John: "Do you think it would make a difference for you to have this product?"

Customer: "Oh, yeah, yeah."

John: "Well, do you want to sign on the dotted line so we can start delivery?"

Customer: "No, no…I'm not ready. I want to think about it a little more."

Whoa! What happened? What happened is that the cerebral cortex, the logical part of the brain, was saying "yes-yes-yes" to the first three questions. Logically, the person wanted the product. But because I didn't connect with their emotional brain, they said "no" to actually buying. I couldn't get them to take action because I didn't connect with their emotional brain.

Have you ever had an experience like that? Well, it's the same with your audiences. Win over their emotional brain and they'll write the check—they'll take action! Connect with them emotionally from the beginning, or, as Bert Decker, author of *You've Got to Be Believed to Be Heard*, might say, be *believed* before you dump all your facts, figures, and features on them, and you will succeed.

> ***Connect with your audience emotionally from the beginning and you will succeed.***

A great way to connect with the emotional brain is through storytelling, a key aspect of World Class Speaking. But many people say storytelling seems unimportant, certainly not as important as the facts and figures. Let me assure you, there is a deep importance to storytelling and tremendous scientific evidence (facts and figures) demonstrating the power of storytelling in any human communication.

Imagine you and me together in a time long before the printing press. How do we share our information? Orally; oral tradition! That's right. But it isn't just long lists we blurt out at one another. Oral tradition means *stories*. Throughout history everything from how to build the pyramids, brew beer, grow crops and more was passed on in the form of a story. That is the only way we human beings could remember the many things that went into life and civilization. Therefore our brains evolved to *value stories*.

When I put you into that fMRI machine again and say "Let me tell you a story," the part of your brain that lights up is the same part that lights up when you expect to get a *reward*. Well told stories are like *rewards* for your audience! I have a friend named Jim Tenuto of the San Diego Renaissance Executive Forums, and *he tells great stories*. It's no wonder that I love spending time with him, as does everyone who meets him. Being with him is like getting little presents in the form of stories, every time we talk.

Using Mnemonic Devices

A very simple example is the use of mnemonics when you speak. Mnemonics are devices akin to tiny stories—such as songs, sentences, or words—that help people remember something. It means more to you when I share the saying "Memory Needs Every Method of Nurturing Its Capacity" as a mnemonic for how to spell "mnemonic," and it reminds you of what a mnemonic is too. From mnemonics to stories, that's how our brains work.

World Class Speaking says: "Don't restate your story. Relive it and invite your audience into your re-living room." When you tell stories that way you activate the entire brain of your audience members, delivering your message more deeply and memorably. Typical language processing, whether written, sign language, or vocal, happens in a relatively small part of the brain called the Wernicke region. However, when you use active storytelling, you engage the entire brain.

Ann Murphy Paul (*New York Times*, March 17, 2012) wrote about several studies that used fMRI machines to study the brains of readers. The interesting results support the use of stories filled with rich, descriptive words that fully engage the audience and have them remember. "[When] subjects in their laboratory read a metaphor involving texture, the sensory cortex, responsible for perceiving texture through touch, became active. Metaphors like 'The singer had a velvet voice' and 'He had leathery hands' roused the sensory cortex, while phrases matched for meaning, like 'The singer had a pleasing voice' and 'He had strong hands,' did not."

Similar research shows that active words such as *grasped, threw,* or *kicked* activate the motor cortex of the brain. So telling stories filled with descriptive words, metaphors, and similes activates regions beyond merely the language processing areas; it activates what I call "experience processing" regions. People don't just hear you talk—they feel like they've *lived an experience* with you. "I stormed out the door like an angry river breaching a dam. Across the green, freshly mown grass I flew. Jumping into my robin-egg-blue Ford Fiesta, I slammed the tinny door and sped away."

That's the beginning of the story I tell about running away from home with my rock band. It employs the kind of description that activates your whole brain.

Months and years later people remember the color of my car and smell the grass because I activated their whole brain.

Another World Class bonus: beginning your speeches with a story connects with the emotional brain, gets people's attention, paves the way for your facts and figures to matter to them, and results in people being far more likely to take action on what you share as well.

Suggestion: Use stories to illustrate your points, and make sure they activate the whole brain with descriptive words, colors, smells, dialogue, similes, and metaphors.

Exercise: Go through the stories in one of your current speeches and build at least two senses into every story you tell. Include dialogue wherever possible.

Body Language—Louder Than Words

It's not just your words that communicate. Research suggests nonverbal communication is at *least* two-thirds of all communication. Nonverbal communication is ancient and deeply programmed. World Class speakers build trust, confidence, and engagement using body language. As a speaker, you must master what you're saying with your body, your gestures, and your expression just as surely as you master what you're saying with your words. In my coaching work the three most common mistakes I see people make involve *speed of delivery*, *movement onstage*, and *eye contact*.

> *In my coaching work the three most common mistakes I see people make involve speed of delivery, movement onstage, and eye contact.*

World Class speakers use vocal variety and vary their *speed of delivery* to appeal to different types of learners; visual learners like a rapid pace while kinesthetic learners prefer a slower pace. And there is a little known scientific secret of which you need to be aware. As an undergraduate in sociology/social psychology I had the opportunity to take a number of truly fascinating classes. In one we read about a well-controlled study examining speakers' presentation speeds. The researchers found that those who spoke rapidly were consistently rated as not knowing what they were talking about, trying to pull one over on the audience, being untrustworthy, and being low-status. This reminds me of what my father often says: "Slow down! I don't hear that fast!"

In contrast, speakers who spoke more slowly were rated as being experts, being dependable, being trustworthy, and being high-status. I explain it like this: the lion is the high-status King of the Jungle. And lions don't hurry for anything if they don't feel like it. Be the lion!

Suggestion: Use vocal variety, but overall, slow down!

Exercise: Record yourself giving a talk on the faster side, and then record yourself giving the same talk more slowly. You'll be amazed by what an expert you sound like when you slow down.

Movement while onstage is another big nonverbal cue. Purposeful movement is powerful. However, if you pace from one side of the stage to another, switch your weight from one foot to the other, or make movements with your hands not directly related to what you're saying, people will quickly tune out. Your nonverbal message will crush your verbal message like a steamroller.

In high school I had a coach who was at the top of the international ranking of speaking coaches. He had me practice standing stock-still with my arms hanging at my sides for hours and hours. This exercise gave me amazing control over my movement. Try it. It feels really weird. Now try it while looking in the mirror. It doesn't *look* weird, it just *feels* weird. It is actually a very vulnerable position. Standing in front of a group of humans with your arms at your sides is risky. What if one of them goes for your throat? You laugh, but that's the evolutionary basis!

Exercise: Practice giving your speech with your arms at your sides until you can deliver your speech moving nothing but your head. Then bring back hand gestures and finally bring back purposeful movement.

Finally, there's *eye contact*. Uniquely, as primates we have whites in our eyes. Research suggests that is so we can see where others are looking, better empathize, and better know what others are thinking. Our eyes communicate powerfully. Here's the good news: whatever size your audiences, you can make eye contact and speak to one audience member at a time. World Class speakers scan and stop, scan and stop. That takes your experience of the audience from being a large, threatening, amorphous group to being an intimate one-on-one conversation with this person and then this person and then this person.

President Clinton gets very high marks as a speaker. People consistently say, "I felt like he was talking directly to me!" That's because he uses this technique. Next time you speak, scan and stop, scan and stop. Scan to find an audience member and look into their eyes while you communicate a few sentences, then scan to another part of the room and look into another person's eyes as you communicate another few sentences, and so on throughout the whole talk. Remember to include audience members from the entire room: right, left, front, and back. Your unconscious facial expressions and body language will say, "I'm talking directly to you."

Suggestion: So that you can do this when the lights are bright and you can't see the audience, practice talking to the wall. Picture different people as you speak, and scan and stop from one part of the wall to another. Picture actual people in your mind and speak directly to them. You will generate the same nonverbal messages you would if you were actually seeing people.

Close Your Speech the World Class Way

Finally, World Class speakers close their speeches powerfully. One of the best ways to do this is by telling a story. In his TED Talk "The Riddle of Experience vs. Memory," Nobel laureate Daniel Kahneman explains why the closing is so important. Kahneman contrasts the "experiencing self" with the "remembering self" and in several different experiments demonstrates that even a wonderful experience that ends badly will be remembered as bad, even if the vast majority was sublime. And how we *remember* it is how it *was*!

Knowing how human beings are wired is a great advantage in having your communication—both verbal and nonverbal—achieve the things you want it to achieve. Being remembered, connecting with your audience, and moving them to action all become far less mysterious once you understand we're all wired for stories. As important as your facts and figures are, they'll never get as far on their own as they will when packaged and delivered in ways that human beings can understand.

Key Takeaways

- Include the emotional brain so people care about your facts and figures, remember what you say, and are more likely to take action.
- Use storytelling that includes sensory, active, descriptive language, which engages the whole brain, to captivate the audience and have them remember you.
- Master your nonverbal communication by
  - Slowing down for believability and status.
  - Controlling your movement so it is purposeful and not distracting.

o   Scanning and stopping; making eye contact with individuals in the audience so the entire audience feels seen by you and connected to you.

John K. Bates is an international keynote and motivational speaker, executive coach, and trainer. He is a leading authority on using human evolutionary biology and human neurophysiology to make his clients stand out from the crowd, be remembered, and lose their fear and anxiety around public speaking. John speaks, trains, and coaches TED and TEDx speakers, along with top-level executives and speakers all over the world.

22

World Class
Body Language

Hayward Suggs

I bet you didn't know that when you are giving a speech, there are actually two of *you* speaking. There is the verbal you, the one your audience will hear. And there is the nonverbal you, the one your audience sees and feels.

The trick is to be sure the audience doesn't get two different messages from the twin "yous." Your goal as a World Class Speaker is to establish congruence and alignment between what you say verbally (your words) and how you say it physically (your body).

Your body language works to amplify your spoken word. When your amplifier is firing on full current, you eliminate distortion, produce a clear, clean sound, and maximize the impact of your speech. Your audience experiences the fullness of your presence and the richness of your words and is able to connect with you meaningfully.

World Class speakers know how to combine verbal and nonverbal messages effectively to boost speaking impact. Some speakers understand how to use body language intuitively; others have to work at it. As with any skill, with the right knowledge and abundant practice you can improve significantly. Of course, there may be aspects you struggle with, but that's part of the joy in growing and developing.

In this chapter you will learn the keys to ensuring congruence with your body and voice. Fair warning: you will likely still only receive one paycheck, but with your body language and verbal skills properly aligned, your speaking fees may actually double. Here are the topics we will cover:

- the importance of body language
- the use of hand gestures
- inviting eyes
- using motion and stances
- maximizing comportment

On the following pages you will also find several exercises to help improve your body language skills. To accelerate your own development and possibly spark someone else's, I highly recommend you teach the exercise techniques to another person who can serve as your accountability partner. Nothing adds velocity to learning new soft skills like teaching them to other people.

Mitch Meyerson and Craig Valentine have totally sold me on the value of an accountability partner, and soft-skill building is a great use for one. An accountability partner can give you feedback on your skill development and serve as a sounding board as you test new techniques.

The Importance of Body Language: What Does Science Say?

You may be thinking, *I have spent so much time learning how to write and deliver a speech. How important could body language be?* Dr. Albert Mehrabian, researcher and author of the groundbreaking book *Silent Messages*, found that only 7 percent of a message is conveyed through words, 38 percent through other vocals, and a whopping 55 percent through nonverbal communication.

Kevin Hogan, noted influence expert, says that understanding body language is a vital component to any person or business interested in forging stronger relationships and communicating effectively with customers or staff.

Body language, technically known as kinesics, includes but is not limited to gestures, proxemics (use of space), facial expressions, vocalics (non-word verbal utterances), positioning, movements, and manipulation of objects. And while we may challenge the numerical breakout of Dr. Mehrabian's research efforts, there is no denying that the communication impact of body language is real.

And if the science weren't enough to convince us, the real-world success of speakers such as Les Brown, Patricia Fripp, Darren Lacroix, Ed Tate, and Craig Valentine serves as a powerful commercial for the impact of body language in public speaking. Your body language matters.

> ## *The most important thing in communication is hearing what isn't said.*
> ## —Peter Drucker

Use of Hand Gestures

Keep your hands visible and active in the context of your speech. You don't want your audience to be distracted from your speech by wondering what your hands are doing. If you are using a podium or lectern it's important to keep gestures unobstructed. In fact, unless it's truly needed, come out from behind the podium for parts if not all of your presentation.

As a general rule, maintain your hand gestures just below your chin area, above your waist, and within the width of your shoulders. You don't want to block your facial features or bring undue attention to your nether regions. The larger your audience, the bigger your gestures will need to be to be visible and believable. Conversely, a small audience rarely calls for overly exaggerated, sweeping gestures. Your physical movements should amplify your words without distortion or distraction.

You may find it helpful to match your gestures with the corresponding audience sizes:

- individual
- small
- medium
- large
- extra large

Finally, be cognizant of any overused or default hand gestures. These can easily become distracting and redundant. I receive frequent ribbing from colleagues about my overreliance on what has become known as my signature hand gesture. I am working on it—for real this time.

Inviting Eyes

The eyes are your way of inviting your audience into your speech. When you make eye contact you extend an invitation to connect and the audience does as well. It's your opportunity to bond with each other and share your emotions. Emotions are an essential currency in the effective exchange of ideas.

Maintain eye contact with an audience member long enough to convey a point, and then move to another point with a different audience member. Do this consistently throughout your speech. Be careful not to break off eye contact too abruptly or stare down your audience. You always want your invitation to connect to be well received.

Using Motion and Stances

Some years ago a valued and trusted colleague, the late Charlene King, gave me some feedback after one of my management team speeches. She said, "Hayward, I really enjoyed your talk, great message. But I got kind of dizzy trying to follow you all around the room." We laughed about it and I told her I would work on it for the next time. But I never did.

Over the years the same feedback would come to me every now and then from other audience members. I never really addressed it. Then one day I had the opportunity to see myself on video. Whoa daddy! That feedback got my attention and helped to reshape my behavior. Charlene King was right on point, and dizzying was a generous understatement.

Moving around too much can be a major distraction for your audience. Practice your movements; if they don't add value to your speech, get rid of them. Nervous prancing and non-purposeful movement have limited the impact of many speeches—as mentioned, even a few of my own. My advice: get a video camera.

Be sure to maintain an open posture. Make certain your body center line is unobstructed. Beware of crossing your feet or standing in an unbalanced position. Crosses and imbalances can make you feel awkward and look clumsy. Pay close attention to lower body crosses when you are feeling nervous. The farther our body parts are from our brain, the more honest they tend to be.

The legs and feet are notoriously accurate.

Move with poise and certainty; own the whole stage. Find the areas that best highlight your voice and visibility, and stay in them. But don't become rooted. Just ensure that your movement is purposeful and adds to your speech.

Maximizing Comportment

Comportment is how we link our appearance, behavior, and presence together. Comportment is essentially how we carry ourselves. You have taken the time to write a World Class speech; now it's time to get your appearance, moves, voice, eyes, hands, and entire body working together to amplify your desired message. Your presentation starts the minute you exit your car in the host site parking lot.

Walk with confidence, upright, shoulders strong. Step with purpose, as if you have somewhere to be (you do!). Don't appear harried or rushed; be smooth and graceful.

Greet anyone who meets you with a smile and firm handshake. Establish good eye contact. You have no idea whether it's a potential audience member or the person signing your check. But your presence in this brief exchange can help make people comfortable and interested in whatever you have to say.

How you walk from the parking lot, on the site grounds, and through the building will speak volumes to anyone watching. It will also help send a calming and positive message to yourself. Imagine that cameras are broadcasting your entry to millions across the globe. Your body language will say to you and anyone watching that you are a World Class Speaker. You will feel like one too.

When you walk to the stage, extend your hand to the host with supreme confidence and move about the stage with purpose and poise. How you enter the speaking area sets the tone for your presentation. Your speaking audience will decide how they feel about you in about thirty seconds. Give them only two choices: like you or love you.

Take a confident stance onstage, make strong eye contact while making your points, and use your hands and other body movements to complement your words naturally. Flash that winning smile where appropriate, and remember your goal is to get all the moving parts going in the same direction as your words.

How to Use Nonverbal Cues to Gauge Audience Feedback

For most speakers, applause and laughter in response to intended humor are the feedback they most enjoy and rely on. But other forms of audience feedback are also very revealing:

- the nodding head as a sign of affirmation and alignment
- the patting foot that may be anxious about the content

- the fidgeting body appearing restless or bored
- the lean forward, toward you, that says edge-of-the-seat connection
- the upper torso that faces you while the foot points toward the door, signaling it's exit time

These and many others can be valuable clues from your audience letting you know if you are doing well or if you still have some work to do. Speaking of clues, it's important not to use just one clue or cue to gauge how well you and the audience are connecting. Instead, look for clusters of cues in the context of your speaking effort and consider the overall audience response. After all, an audience member may actually be on the edge of their seat because of the call of nature.

> *What you do speaks so loud that I cannot hear what you say.*
> —**Ralph Waldo Emerson**

In short, being in tune with your audience's body language response is a great way to stay connected and help ensure a world-class speaking delivery.

World Class Credibility

A few years back, I had a coaching client who had a speaking credibility problem. Whenever he addressed his leadership team, people had serious doubts about whatever he said. They had major concerns about his sincerity and didn't mind telling him so.

When I first heard him speak I really didn't know what the fuss was about. He actually sounded knowledgeable and passionate and overall did a good job. But after the speech, when I observed him walking around the room, the problem became very apparent. His comportment said it all. He was two different people: the man who led a team and the man who gave speeches.

The one who gave speeches was upbeat, vibrant, and forward thinking, standing tall with great physical presence. The team leader was low-key, monotone, hesitant, and slump-shouldered, almost disappearing into the background. His motivational speeches were fine, but his day-to-day speaking lacked genuineness and authenticity, and everyone who worked there knew it.

The negative, downtrodden leader he presented on a daily basis made it impossible for his team to take him seriously as a speaker. He mistakenly thought motivational speaking was an event. As noted consultant Alan Weiss says, all speaking should be motivational; otherwise what's the point?

To improve his speaking credibility our coaching work focused on his day-to-day comportment and beliefs, not his event-driven speeches. He thought being World Class was something he could put on. It has to be in you.

Be sure that your gestures, vocalities, and words are the genuine you. Learning new skills requires belief and practice to truly make them your own. Once you possess them, they become your authentic tools for separating yourself from other speakers. They can help you have World Class body language.

Here are a few skill-building exercises.

Skill Building Tip One: Voice Tone/Inflection

Repeat this classic sentence (I heard the late great Zig Ziglar use it) eight times:

"I did not say she beat her man." Each time you say the sentence, place voice tone/inflection emphasis on the next word in the sentence until you have highlighted each word. Done correctly, you should now have one sentence with eight different meanings.

Now that's just one eight-word sentence. Imagine what you could do with eight different sentences. The possibilities are endless when you, the world-class speaker, determine the point of emphasis through voice tone and inflection. Your audience will be mesmerized.

Skill Building Tip Two: Appearance

Your appearance should convey professionalism and not speak louder than your performance.

Video yourself in three different outfits and give the same short speech each time (two to four minutes). Deliver your speech in jeans, a business casual look, and in something really dressy. Does your speech look and sound the same?

Odds are each look will feel distinct and convey a different message. Use the video to help you determine which look best transmits the message you want your audience to receive. Your speaking attire should match or be one level above your audience, never a level below.

Skill Building Tip Three: Hand Gestures

Try giving a short speech using only your hands. Yes, it will feel a tad silly at first. But use your hand gestures to convey the concepts of distance, size, direction, speed, weight, and temperature consecutively. Next, convey various emotions like anger, frustration, happiness, and relief. Try to find gestures you are comfortable with that get the message across and that you look good executing.

Now add in some words. The goal is to use hand gestures to complement your spoken words. Use a mirror to see how you are doing; a video camera is even better. If you still have doubts about the impact of hand gestures, try giving a few lines of your speech with your hands planted firmly by your side. Ugh!

Sometimes my coaching clients believe that by mastering new vocal or body language skills they will somehow lose the authentic version of themselves. Simply not true. In fact, think of your newly acquired soft skills as a software upgrade or YOU 2.0.

When it comes to building soft skills, the following quote sums up my thoughts on the matter: "Whatever you do, don't let who you are get in the way of who you could be."

Hayward Suggs, MS, MBA, adds velocity to business and personal success through soft skills coaching. He is a Toastmasters district champ in table topics (impromptu speaking) and speech evaluation and finished in the top one hundred in the World Championship of Public Speaking, twice. Contact Hayward through info@commonquest.org. Learn more at softskillsthatwow.com.

23

Using Visuals the World Class Way

Hiba Hamdan

As a World Class speaker, your presentation is intended to create a transformational experience that leaves your audience excited, fired-up, and inspired. So how could a PowerPoint presentation support this World Class experience when it's crowded with a 10-point font and small graphics? It can't!

Congested slides do not stimulate the creativity of your audience and will not help you communicate your visionary ideas.

How can you use visuals to grab your audience's attention and keep them listening and engaged? How can visuals make your message more memorable?

In this chapter you will learn an eight-step process that will show you how to:

- know your audience
- plan in pen and paper
- sketch your compelling story
- prepare your captivating visuals
- rehearse and perfect
- have a backup plan

- look over the location
- deliver a memorable experience

Garr Reynolds, author of *Presentation Zen*, says there's a limit to a person's ability to process new information efficiently and effectively: "Understanding can be hard enough without the excessive and nonessential bombardment by our visuals."

I sure hadn't heard of Reynolds's advice when I first started using PowerPoint (PPT) for work to report on system issues or to show improved performance. I was marveled by this amazing tool!

I'd open the PPT software, plug in data charts and graphics I had prepared using other software, add a lot of text to explain the content, and then decorate my slides with clip-art the PPT software generously provided as templates.

Once I was satisfied with the piece of art I'd created, I did the math: if I had fifteen minutes to present thirty slides; that meant two slides per minute. But then I'd remember, *Oh, I should leave some time for questions and answers at the end. Okay, then I'll try to squeeze in three slides per minute—that's ten minutes, which leaves five minutes for Q&A. Voila!*

No wonder I had to place hundreds of calls and arrange for dozens of more meetings to re-explain what I had already presented before I got the results I was hoping for!

Rick Justice, former executive vice president of Cisco Systems, says that presenting is not "simply about aesthetics or making things pretty; it's about creating meaning. It's about being present. I need to ensure that every person in the audience believes I'm having an individual conversation with them. That is my goal."

How can you use visuals to engage your audience and create meaning? Let's take a look at the eight steps that will show you how.

1. Know Your Audience

Before choosing your visuals or preparing your content, you first need to answer the following questions to help you know your audience:

- What are they like? Their age, likes and dislikes, different cultures?
- Why are they here? Why did they come to hear you?
- Where are they now? How much do they already know about your topic? You need to meet them where they are.

- How can you solve their problem? How are you going to make their lives better?
- What do you want them to do? What's your call to action?
- How might they resist adopting your message or carrying your call to action?
- What's the best way to reach them (which visuals to choose, how to set up the room)?

Your presentation needs to appeal to all three types of learners in your audience: *visual*, learns by seeing (the majority of people are in this category); *auditory*, learns by listening; *kinesthetic*, learns by feeling and touching.

> *Your presentation needs to appeal to all three types of learners in your audience: visual, auditory, and kinesthetic.*

2. Plan in Pen and Paper (PPP your PPT)

Before you even open the presentation software (e.g. PowerPoint) or choose any other visuals, research your topic and script in the old-fashioned tradition of pen and paper:

- Outline your ideas.
- Draw a roadmap.
- Create Twitter-like headlines.

Garr Reynolds says, "There is just something about paper and pen and sketching out rough ideas in the 'analog world'—in the early stages—that seems to lead to more clarity and better, more creative results."

3. Sketch Your Compelling Story

It's the story not the slides that will capture the imagination of your audience.

I discovered the power of stories—by coincidence—back when I was working in the airlines industry for SITA (*Société Internationale de Télécommunications Aéronautiques*). At the time, I considered the stories as simple examples to illustrate a case.

To highlight the importance of our satellite telecommunication service to a prospective airline customer (in the nineties), I gave the example of an Air France aircraft that was trapped in a no-fly zone suddenly imposed over Bosnia. When all direct communication links with the ground were cut, the captain was able to communicate via satellite with the airline's operations in France to get instructions on how to redirect the plane. That crucial action saved the plane and its passengers from being shot down.

Even though I didn't know at the time how to tell my story in a compelling (World Class) way, I still remember how these simple "examples" grabbed people's attention.

Stories work to get your message through. Use visuals to support your simple yet powerful story that brings your point home.

In his book *The Presentation Secrets of Steve Jobs*, Carmine Gallo says: "A Steve Jobs presentation unleashes a rush of dopamine into the brains of his audience.... Each presentation tells a story, and every slide reveals a scene."

How can you sketch your story? Simply use the basic "5-C" elements:

- Characters: Hero, antagonist
- Conflict: Problem
- Cure: Solution
- Change: How your characters changed after implementing the solution
- Carry-out: The memorable message you want to leave with your audience

Your hero offers a better way of doing something or inspires people to change for the better.

The 5 Cs in my airline story: 1. Captain (hero), 2. No-fly zone (problem), 3. Use satellite (solution), 4. Plane was saved (change), and 5. Save passengers and crew by installing the satellite system (carry-out message).

If you watch Steve Jobs's video "2007 iPhone Presentation (Part 1 of 2)" on YouTube (http://youtu.be/Etyt4osHgX0), you'll be able to identify the 5 Cs:

- Carry-out message: "Today Apple is going to reinvent the phone."—*Slide* with the words "iPhone" (large font) and "Apple reinvents the phone" (underneath, small font).
- Hero: iPhone

- Antagonist(s): "Here's four smart phones, the usual 'suspects.'"—*Slide* with images of Motorola-Q, BlackBerry, Palm-Treo, and NokiaE62.
- Conflict: "The problem with them is in the bottom forty....They all have these keyboards that are there whether you need them or not."—*Same slide*, the top half of each image fades away leaving just the keyboard.
- Solution: "We're going to use the best pointing device in the world; a pointing device that we're all born with....We'll use our fingers."—*Slide* with image of index finger appears next to iPhone.
- Change: "We've invented a new technology called multi-touch, which is phenomenal!"—*Same slide*, finger fades away and "Multi-Touch" words appear.

With very few words and no bullet points, the late Steve Jobs transformed the boring technical slideshow into a theatrical event, filled with stunning sceneries. He told a story.

4. Prepare Your Captivating Visuals

Visuals help people better understand and remember complex and abstract ideas. In fact, information presented visually is processed by the brain faster than a verbal message.

At TED 2008, neuroanatomist Jill Bolte-Taylor described her experience of suffering a stroke. She used only a few slides and a memorable prop: a real human brain.

To create a visually engaging presentation, you need to select the right visuals for your *audience*, your *topic*, and your *location*:

1. digital visuals like PowerPoint: for large and small audiences
2. flipcharts for small-group training and brainstorming sessions
3. whiteboards for small audiences (allow you to display simple diagrams and write audience responses)
4. props (like a rare object or funny costume) help you drive your point home

To be effective, keep your visuals simple and consistent. Consistent fonts, colors, and artwork will make your visuals more pleasing to the eye.

You may use different types of visuals in your presentation. Variety adds interest. But as Guy Kawasaki, author of *The Macintosh Way*, says: "The goal is to show the audience enough to get them tantalized, but not so much that they get bewildered."

> *The goal is to show the audience enough to get them tantalized, but not so much that they get bewildered.*
> **—Guy Kawasaki**

Guidelines for Designing Your PowerPoint Slides

Slides are intended to reinforce the content visually rather than create a distraction.

"To succeed as a presenter, you must think like a designer," says Nancy Duarte, author of *Slide:ology*. "The arrangement, visual elements, and movement of a slide, function either as a signal, delivering information clearly and directly, or as a noise, interfering with the message and causing the viewer to tune out."

Slide Arrangement

How slides are arranged has the most impact on whether a slideshow's message is visually clear.

To create meaning, Duarte recommends using design tools such as:

- contrast: to identify the main point quickly through size and color
- hierarchy: to highlight the relationship between the elements
- white space: to give your audience visual breathing room

Your last slide needs to present a compelling call to action, a powerful image that recalls your message, or a memorable statement. As professional speech coach and sales presentation expert Patricia Fripp says, "Your last words linger."

Text

Remember that your presentation is like a billboard displayed on the freeway. People have just three seconds to glance at it and process it while driving past.

Design your text as Twitter-like headlines.

Comedian Jerry Seinfeld says, "I'll spend an hour reducing an eight-word sentence to five words because the joke will be funnier." The same applies to designing powerful slides: use fewer words!

When choosing fonts, it's best to:

- not combine more than two fonts per presentation
- not go smaller than 28 pt, especially for keynotes
- choose the font that best fits your personality (serious or playful, bold or humble, etc.)

Colors

Colors add interest, improve retention, and communicate the type of journey you will be taking your audience on. Ask yourself:

- Who is my target audience? What colors appeal to them? (Avoid too many colors.)
- What industry am I in? (Choose colors to help you stand out from your competitors.)
- Who am I? (Pick colors that represent your personality and brand.)

Images

Images translate, words don't. Choose images that:

- reflect the audience's culture or ethnicity
- are context-appropriate
- represent your industry, customer experience, and real-life situations

Displaying Data

Data slides are not really about the data. They are about the meaning of the data. How do you present data in the clearest way?

- Get to the point: articulate the conclusions, then present your data.
- Pick the right tool: pie charts (show large differences in proportion or percentages) or bar charts (accommodate larger data sets). Sometimes the best chart is no chart at all.
- Keep it simple (data can be confusing).

5. Rehearse and Perfect

It's easy to get impatient, but you need to invest enough time to prepare, rehearse, and refine in order to develop a great presentation. Carmine Gallo describes a Steve Jobs "insanely great" presentation as "a finely crafted and *well-rehearsed* performance that informs, entertains, and inspires."

6. Have a Backup Plan

With digital visuals, be prepared for technical failures (of laptop, projector, etc.).

Have a copy of your presentation and any supporting files on a thumb drive, and have paper copies of your slides ready to distribute to the audience.

7. Look over the Location

Check the room to make sure the audience at all sides, and at the back of the room, can have a clear view. Test your equipment before the audience members arrive. Don't waste the audience's time trying to fix any failed equipment.

8. Deliver a Memorable Experience

"In most cases, I've got a few thousand people in the audience; and just *one chance* to capture their imaginations by showing them something they've never seen before, while ensuring the content is relevant and inspiring to them," says Rick Justice, former executive vice president of Cisco Systems.

Take that "one chance" to make your presentation a memorable experience for your audience. Remember, visuals complement your presentation; they are not your presentation!

Here are five important points to consider while delivering your presentation:

- Display the visual for a few seconds before you start talking about it. This will give your audience time to comprehend it.
- When displaying slides, don't read from the screen. Your slides are not a cheat-sheet, and you don't want to turn your back on your audience!
- If you're using a flipchart, don't write as you speak.
- Avoid blocking the screen (or any other visual). Stand to the left side, and use your left hand or a pointer.
- When you don't need your slides, turn the screen off (black) by either using the remote control or by pressing the "B" button on the keyboard. You need

your audience to focus on you, not your slides, especially when you're telling a story or closing the presentation with your call to action or memorable statement.

When speaking, the most important thing to do is *listen*. Pay attention to what you say, how you say it, and how your audience reacts when you say it. This will help you refine your materials and elevate your future presentations to a greater level.

Presentation design expert Nancy Duarte, who transformed Al Gore's 35mm slides into the Academy Award-winning documentary *An Inconvenient Truth*, says, "World Class presentations require time and focus."

Take the time to understand your audience, refine your message to fit that audience, and express yourself through visuals tailored to your audience and your message. Only then will you be able to deliver a spectacular presentation that transforms your audience.

To your success!

World Class Speaking Coach Hiba Hamdan helps her clients skyrocket their success by creating brilliant presentations. An electrical engineer and senior project management professional who speaks four languages, Hiba has worked for three of the largest international telecommunications companies, where she managed large-scale complex projects for global customers and provided training in Europe, Asia, and North America. In 2008 she founded her own consulting and coaching business in Redondo Beach, California. Find her at www.hibahamdan.com.

24

Elevate Your Visuals from Boring to Breakthrough with the 3C Compass

Manley Feinberg

Ready to attend another boring presentation today? Or are you preparing to give one?

It is estimated that more than 30 million PowerPoint presentations are delivered every day. The good news? The vast majority of them are beyond boring, which creates an incredible opportunity for you to stand out from the crowd, and elevate your speaking to the World Class level.

In this chapter you will learn a fast and effective process to build World Class Visual Anchors that engage your audience and get the results you want.

> *"Keep in mind that a slide's value is determined not by the amount of information it contains, but by how clearly it communicates its message."*
> —**Nancy Duarte**, *Slide:ology*

All visual aids you leverage during your presentation ultimately have one essential purpose—to support your message. But most speakers lead their audience into the graveyard of presentations by making three critical mistakes:

1. They use their slides as a tool to support their delivery—teleprompter style—and undermine the *clarity* of their message.
2. They hide behind their slides because they are often underprepared or uncomfortable with speaking, preventing them from *connecting* with their audience.
3. They develop their slides to also serve as a handout. This approach fails to effectively *communicate* their message during the presentation, and their slides also fall short as a handout reference.

Whether your intent is to inform, influence, or inspire, the point of any visual support is to deliver your message and supporting data with maximum *clarity*, drive a deeper *connection* with your audience, and keep your audience engaged by dynamically *communicating* your content. In this chapter you will learn how to address these essential needs with the 3C Compass of World Class Visuals, and take your visuals from *boring* to *breakthrough*.

Clarity: Crystal Clear Clarity Will Set You *and* Your Audience Free

To ensure your visual aids are crystal clear, ask yourself two questions:

1. Is this slide as visually *clean* and *simple* as possible?
2. What can I *remove* to increase the *clarity*?

Create Clarity by Cleaning Your Canvas

Start with a blank canvas by bagging the default templates in your presentation software.[3] This will immediately free you from falling into the Title, Bullet Point, Bullet Point march.

Next, you will want to establish your background style. Simple backgrounds with minimal if any texture or artwork are best to ensure they do not distract from your actual content.

---

3   Unfortunately, Microsoft has not made the steps above easy to accomplish in PowerPoint. To make it easy and fast, I have created a step-by-step visual guide with World Class examples that you can access for free: www.WorldClassPowerPoint.com.

Yin or Yang?

When in doubt, keep your background simple and go black or white. Remember that the background is your canvas and serves as a foundation to build your visual support upon. Many World Class presenters use a simple solid black or very dark background. Here are some advantages and disadvantages to consider as you choose the best background color:

Dark background advantages:

- very professional, formal look and feel
- more effective in darker rooms; does not affect ambient light
- spotlights individual items well, allowing for dramatic placement and contrast if needed

Dark background disadvantages:

- does not print well (which is not an issue if you create a separate handout document or do a mass color conversion)
- limits 3D shadow effects

White background advantages:

- text more legible in brightly lit rooms
- does not spotlight individual objects on slides as much
- shows 3D shadow effects well

White background disadvantages:

- easy to convert to a handout if needed (caution: slides are typically ineffective as handouts!)
- can create distracting back light for speaker

Connect: Select a Strategic Structure Style That Drives a Deeper Connection with Your Audience

To ensure you connect with your audience, ask yourself the following two questions:

1. Does each slide *connect* with my audience in a relevant way? (See Hiba Hamdan's seven questions from chapter 23 to ensure you know your audience.)
2. Does it *connect* with my audience *emotionally?*

After years of research on effective visual presentation styles, I have uncovered 3 effective approaches to help you connect with your audience through your visuals. These three approaches are slightly different ways to put into practice the same basic principles: First, they encourage you to minimize text and use proven structures that increase retention and action. Second, to make a deeper emotional connection in the hearts and heads of your audience, they encourage you to strategically leverage visual images. It has been scientifically proven that our brain links information and emotionally charged memories to visual images in our brains.

Say It/Show It Style

This strategy was developed by Michael Alley, a professor and leading researcher on the effectiveness of presentation slide design. Through years of study, Alley and his colleagues have proven that audience engagement and retention is much higher if you structure your visual support with what they call the Assertion Evidence Structure. It has two components:

1. *Say It* with a single sentence, or "assertion," at the top of the slide. As with World Class Foundational Phrases, you want this statement to be concise and memorable. Ten words or less is a good target. The key difference between the *Say It/Show It* approach and typical slide design is what you *say*, aka the assertion, is a statement or simple sentence, rather than a title to the slide. For maximum influence, include the result or benefit. As an example, instead of "Our boring new process," say "Our Improved Process Saves You 30 Minutes a Day"
2. *Show It* with a visual anchor that supports what you *say*. This is the key difference in the body of the slide: it is filled with your visual evidence, such as an image, chart, or illustration, but never overloaded with the bullet-pointed text most presenters fill the space with.

Note that while the standard *Show It* structure establishes the assertion first at the top of the slide, it can also be very powerful to present the visual evidence first, drive curiosity and interaction as you reveal its meaning, and then animate your assertion last.

Visual Verbal Style

With this approach, you avoid text completely on the screen and rely on visual images to support your presentation, while delivering your content verbally. Seth Godin, among other noted speakers, have used this style with incredible results. Note that it can be very powerful to "leverage the B key," or build in blank black slides, for a segment of your presentation to ensure the focus is on you and your verbal delivery.

Steve Jobs Style

Finally, we have what I call the Steve Jobs Style. Jobs's presentation style is so well regarded that many consider him one of the most effective corporate speakers ever, and multiple articles (and even a book) have been written on his presentation approach. The structure of his visual support encompasses a mix of the two styles above, while consistently leveraging the following principles:

- no bullet points, minimal words on each slide (when possible, Steve would use a single word on a slide)
- heavy use of visual images, which are proven to increase retention
- focus on one idea per slide

See WorldClassPowerPoint.com for examples of each of these strategic structure styles.

By using any of these strategies or combining them, you will connect more effectively with your audience and stand out from the crowd.

Communicate: Multiple Slides Multiply Your Impact

To keep your audience engaged as you communicate, ask yourself the following questions:

1. Does each slide *communicate* your content as a single message, idea, or supporting point?

2. Can your audience *get it* in three seconds or less? Does it pass the billboard test?

3. Does it *communicate* your content at the appropriate *technical* level?

Avoid packing each slide with too many details. Each slide should support a single idea or point. Spread multiple ideas across multiple slides. For example, instead of five bullet points, create five separate slides. It is also desirable to leverage multiple slides to support a single point.

Multiple slides multiply your impact.

Before you design any visual content, it is critical that you establish the key point of each slide in a single word or sentence first. Once you have crystal clear clarity on the single point, you can then leverage the power of visual imagery to help inform, influence, or inspire your audience.

Increase Impact with Images

Countless studies have proven that visual images dramatically improve the retention and comprehension of information. Regardless of which structure strategy you choose, you will want to leverage the power of images. If you're looking for relevant images, I have found CanStockPhoto.com to be a great resource for four reasons: it is more affordable than most, the images are high quality, you don't have to worry about copyright infringement, and it is much faster than creating the images yourself. When using the Visual Verbal strategy, you will typically want to maximize the photo to the full size of the slide. Here the black background can be helpful: if your photo doesn't scale perfectly to the slide size, it can seamlessly be placed anywhere on the black background.

With the Say It/Show It or Steve Jobs structure, the following five-step process will help optimize image placement on your visual canvas:

1. **Evaluate the horizontal thirds.** When you break the slide into three equal horizontal bands, decide if you want the image to occupy the lower two

thirds and reserve the upper section for your key text. This is the standard Say It/Show It layout, but it is not required.

2. **Evaluate the vertical thirds.** When you break the slide into three equal vertical bands, decide if you want the image to be more heavily weighted to one side. In this layout, you would most commonly place your image on the left two thirds of the slide and place supporting text on the right third.

3. **Evaluate eye flow.** Consider the fact that in Western culture, your eye typically scans as you read from the top left, across to the right, and down the slide. When placing smaller images, you can use eye flow and placement to establish sequence or a desired future state. As an example, you could place an image representing a goal in the lower right third of the slide and then bring in supporting text from the top left to illustrate a process.

4. **Visually scan for balance and symmetry, or intentional asymmetry.** Does the image center with any other key items, or if using asymmetry, does it have the intended effect? Asymmetry can be a powerful visual technique to subconsciously imply an undesirable, unbalanced state.

5. **Compare to previous slides: Consistency is king.** For a series of related content, be consistent with your placement of images based on the four steps above, and move between the previous slides and the current slide to confirm the general layout is consistent, and that key anchors do not unintentionally jump around on your visual canvas.

See www.WorldClassPowerPoint.com for visual examples.

Six Concepts to Help Communicate Your Data Content

While images are considered to be the most powerful visual support, many presentations can be strengthened with visual data. As in text support, most presenters fail their audiences by making three common mistakes. They overload their audience with too much detail, they never clearly illustrate the meaning of the data, and they fail to match the technical level of the data to the audience. Staying on course with the 3C Compass when creating data slides is critical. The following six concepts will help you transform your slides into exceptionally powerful communication tools that will inform and influence your audience.

1. **Ask, "What does all this mean?"** The *meaning* of the data is more important than all the data. Bottom line, what are you trying to illustrate with the data?

2. **Simple sells.** Summarize complex data into a few select elements that support your primary point of each slide.
   - Use three to four elements, and seven maximum: i.e., no more than seven pieces of pie, bars, etc.
   - Highlight the most important segments or features of the data.
   - Convert PowerPoint bullet points to Smart Art.[4]

3. **Contrasting color clarifies.** Two or three key colors that sit opposite on the color wheel will help clarify data in your charts.

4. **Fly it in to keep them connected with animations.**
   - Put a fact or chart up, *interactively quiz the audience* on the statistic or data elements, and then animate the answer in.
   - Use a chart and animate in key data elements one by one as you address them verbally.
   - Since animations are guaranteed to grab your audience's attention, keep them simple and avoid speaking during the animation.

5. **If a picture is worth a thousand words, it's worth a million numbers.** A visually compelling and clean chart beats a text table nearly every time.

6. **The right tool at the right time.** Hand out detailed data as a Word or pdf document, preferably after the presentation. Avoid the temptation of bloating your visual support with content that will muddy your message in the minds of your audience. You can let them know more detailed data is available if needed.

From Awareness to Your Advantage: World Class Visuals in Action

Old habits die hard. If you are like most people, just becoming *aware* of the World Class strategies will still leave you short of having a true *advantage* in your presentations. As you create every slide in your presentation, intentionally check your 3C Compass and actively evaluate your efforts with the following checklist. When you use the 3C Compass throughout your presentation design process, you will elevate the quality of your visual support to stand well beyond the masses.

---

4   See WorldClassPowerPoint.com for examples of effective data slides and step by step visual guides.

Your 3C Compass of World Class Visuals Checklist

Clarity

- Is this slide as visually *clean* and simple as possible?
- What can I *remove* to increase the *clarity*?

Connect

- Does it *connect* with my audience in a *relevant* way?
- Does it *connect* with my audience *emotionally?*

Communicate

- Does it *communicate* a single message, idea, or supporting point?
- Can my audience *get it* in three seconds or less? Does it pass the billboard test?
- Does it *communicate* my content at the appropriate *technical* level?

Next Steps

See WorldClassPowerPoint.com for downloadable examples, step-by-step tutorials, and more World Class Visual tips and techniques.

After 18 years of business leadership, adventures around the world, and professional speaking, Manley is ready to help you reach your next summit. He is recognized as an award-winning speaker and information technology leader, business expert and author, executive coach, and communication consultant. Manley works with organizations that want to get out of their comfort zones, develop World Class communication skills, build momentum, and get what's important done. Get On Belay at VerticalLessons.com.

25

Staging Your Presentation
Bob Mohl

"All the world's a stage" according to Shakespeare. He knew how to use his stage for maximum effect. Do you? World Class speakers move with purpose when they speak. They use their movements to add structure and meaning. They avoid thoughtless movements that distract their audiences.

In this chapter you'll pick up tools to add impact and "memorability" to your presentations. You'll benefit from tips and examples to:

- Stage the Page (how to go from offstage to onstage)
- Stage Your Structure (how to move with purpose)
- Stage Your Meaning (how to gesture for meaning)
- Go Backstage (how to deconstruct a speech)

Stage the Page

David Brooks, Toastmasters 1990 World Champion, says, "Good speeches come from good writing and good writing comes from good editing."

Many of us write out our speeches in detail or at least write out notes. But written text on a page is very different from words delivered by voice. Think about the differences:

Writing	Speaking
Punctuation—. ! ? , " " ...	Pauses, inflection, gesture, facial expression
Font *style*, font size	Intonation, volume
Paragraph breaks, chapter breaks, page titles, bullet points, etc.	Pauses, physical movement, visual aids
Length = pages	Length = minutes
Nonlinear experience. Pace and focus controlled by the reader.	Linear experience. Pace and focus controlled by the speaker.
No interaction between writer and reader.	Interaction between speaker and listener: eye contact, laughter, applause, questions, activities, etc.

The book you're reading is a good example of the typical elements used in writing to make structure and meaning clearer: chapter headings, subtitles, bullet lists, paragraph breaks, punctuation, font styles, etc. None of these devices is available in speech (except with "Phonetic Punctuation" invented by comedian Victor Borge; Google it on YouTube for a good laugh). On the other hand, speech has its own powerful devices to add meaning and structure: volume, pitch, intonation, rate, and of course the all-powerful...pause. There's another one you may not have considered. There's another one you may not have considered. Repeating a phrase is totally bizarre in text but can be very powerful in speech.

Okay, there's a big difference in the rules for writing and the rules for speaking—so what? What are the takeaways?

- Write for the ear, not for the eye (everything else follows from this one).
- Use words that are easy to understand.
- Use short simple sentences.
- Even incomplete sentences
- Feel free to use repetition.
- Put *time tags* at the beginning of sentences and *punch words* at the end.

That last point, which I learned from Patricia Fripp, may need elaboration. Time references are seldom the most important part of a spoken sentence. "Clinton was re-elected last night" works well in journalism, where you lead with what's most important, but in speech last words linger. So it has more impact on the ear if you say, "Last night Clinton was re-elected." World Class speakers put the punch phrase at the end so they finish their sentences with power.

Try saying: "Our fathers brought forth on this continent, a new nation, conceived in liberty, and dedicated to the proposition that all men are created equal, four score and seven years ago." See how the time tag ruins the punch? Lincoln actually had three punch phrases in that sentence—*new nation, liberty, all men are created equal*—and the punctuation shows that he paused after each one. Lincoln understood how to write for the ear, not the eye.

> *Good presentations benefit from good staging*
> *and good staging begins with good writing.*

To paraphrase David Brooks, "Good presentations benefit from good staging and good staging begins with good writing." After you Stage the Page, you're ready to go onstage.

Stage the Structure

Unless you're stuck behind a lectern, you have an opportunity to move around in front of your audience. Many speakers move to reach different sides of the audience, to appear more dynamic, and to use their feet to release nervous energy. These are the reasons I moved when I started speaking onstage. If you'd seen me, you would have thought you were at the zoo watching a caged tiger pace back and forth. I wasn't moving with purpose.

The key to Staging your Structure is to move with purpose. It's simple but it takes planning. In the previous section we listed the devices written text uses to convey structure. Onstage, movement is one of the simplest and most effective ways to help the audience follow *and remember* the structure of your speech.

What is the structure of your speech? If you don't know, you haven't Staged the Page. If you don't understand your structure, the audience certainly won't.

Okay, you've got your structure. Let's say it's really complicated:

- Opening
- Point 1
- Point 2
- Point 3
- Closing

Did I say *complicated*? I meant *common*. Many speeches have this structure (and many more *should!*). This was pretty much my structure when I gave my seven-minute Toastmasters speech about "Changing Perspective." Once I learned to stop pacing and start moving with purpose, my speech became much clearer and more memorable.

Opening—Center Stage
My opening was delivered center stage.

Point 1—Stage Left
I launched my first story stage left where I pointed up at the twinkling Eiffel Tower. The world's tallest birthday candle saved me because I'd forgotten to bring candles to little Tobi's birthday party.

Point 2—Center Stage
As a result Grandma Peggy gave me some life-changing advice. That dialogue took place center stage.

Point 3—Stage Right
My final story took place on Christmas Eve, when little Sasha led me into the living room, conveniently located stage right, to see the stockings hung above the fireplace.

Closing—Center Stage
Back to center stage for the closing.

Okay, this is not rocket science, but mapping the structure of the speech onto the stage did accomplish three valuable things:

- It made it easier for the audience to follow and *remember* my speech.
- It made it easier for *me* to remember my speech. (Ancient orators used the *Method of Loci* as a memory aid by mentally distributing elements of their speech along a visualized path.)
- In my closing I was able to callback to the three points of my speech by simply pointing to the three scene locations on the stage. This is an incredibly powerful and efficient device.

Further Nuances

1. How to Move out of the Story to Address the Audience

When I want to leave a story to address the audience directly with a comment or question, I step forward out of the story space.

> *And the frog turned into a prince. He married the princess. They had three little tadpoles, and they all lived happily ever after.*
> <step forward>
> *Is there a frog inside of you waiting to turn into a prince? Will you set him free and let him live happily ever after?*

Who cares? This is silly, but notice that I stepped forward out of the story to address the audience. Of course you can even walk *into* the audience to engage more fully.

2. Remember Where You Put Things

Darren Lacroix refers to the virtual people, objects, and scenes you create onstage as holograms. At one of Darren's World Champ workshops a student gave an emotional speech about his uncle who had passed away. He described the funeral and had the casket at a particular spot on the stage. Later in the story, this speaker placed a family picnic in the same spot—on the casket! Remember where you put your holograms because the audience will (even unconsciously).

3. How to Structure Time

Since Western audiences read from left to right, it's a convention to show timeline chronology from left to right—for the audience. If you're staging events that go from the distant past to more recent past or to the present or future, try sequencing them from left to right for the audience (if you can without making your staging awkward).

4. Think Backwards

Left to right for the *audience* is *backwards* for you as speaker. Just follow in the footsteps of Ginger Rogers—she had to match every dance move of Fred Astaire, only she had to do it backwards. In one of my first speeches I had a fake meat cleaver prop, which I hid onstage. It wasn't until the time came to retrieve the meat cleaver that I realized I'd put it on the wrong side of the stage. So I had to make an inopportune trek back and forth, all because I forgot to think backwards!

Stage the Meaning

Gestures

Ever watch people gesturing while they speak on the phone? Their gestures are only for themselves with no practical meaning. That may be okay on the phone, but not in front of an audience. Moving your arms onstage should follow the same rule as moving your feet—move with purpose. And the purpose is to enhance meaning for the audience.

Just like revisiting different parts of the stage to callback to earlier parts of your speech, you can repeat memorable gestures to callback to earlier meaning. In "Lessons from Fat Dad," World Champion Randy Harvey used a different strong gesture to punctuate each of the three stories of his speech. In his closing, he recapped his message by calling back those three gestures.

Like many speakers, I started off using symmetrical double-handed gestures, arms bent at the elbows, hands waving in unison—you know, the *chicken wing* gesture. Meaningless, except maybe to a chicken.

Once I learned to use single one-handed gestures, my effectiveness increased enormously. My gestures became more natural and more meaningful. But it took an adjustment to stand in front of an audience with my hands at my sides, raising only one arm or the other to make a meaningful gesture. There's an irony to standing with your arms down. The audience sees you as more confident, and yet it probably makes you feel less confident—until you get the hang of it.

The key is to establish your base stance, become comfortable with it, and let your gestures rise naturally from there. If your base stance is the *chicken wing*, your gestures have almost nowhere to go to become meaningful, so you just keep waving your hands. If your base stance is lowered arms, your gestures are more likely to rise for deliberate meaning.

The one simple step that helped cure me of bad gestures was videotaping my speeches. Actually there are two simple steps: 1) record yourself, 2) watch the video. Step two is the hard part.

By the way, watch the video four ways to learn the most:

- normal
- audio only
- video only (if the gestures *seem meaningful* without sound, you're on the right track)
- fast speed (the easiest way to spot meaningless repetition)

Dialogue

This is one time when speakers often move with too much purpose. Like many amateurs I thought that when switching between characters in dialogue, I needed to take a couple of steps and turn around. That usually becomes quite awkward and interrupts the flow. To keep the flow, I'd have the first character finish speaking, or the second character start, while I was moving into position. That was even worse! By watching World Class speakers, you'll see the solution is simple. Often simply a turn of the head and maybe a slight shift in upper body between characters will work just fine. By the way, don't turn a full 180 degrees from profile to profile. Minimize the angle, the way actors do. And of course it's good to use other devices to help distinguish between your characters: different postures, gestures, facial expressions, voices, etc.

> *The key to creating structure and meaning with impact is to look at your presentation through the eyes, ears, and minds of your audience.*

Backstage

We started Offstage looking at the Page; we went Onstage looking at Structure and Meaning; now we go Backstage to look at how to deconstruct a speech after the fact.

There's so much to learn from deconstructing successful speeches—and even more from speeches, or parts of speeches, that didn't work so well.

Deconstructing the Page

When I became Toastmasters European Champion in 2008, I was wholly unprepared to compete against the top eighty-one Toastmasters speakers in the world at the next level. I was a complete novice, having only presented the minimum six speeches required to even enter the club contest. To make matters worse, I looked at Randy Harvey's winning speech from 2004, "Lessons from Fat Dad," and was totally intimidated. However, I went from intimidation to inspiration to improvement once I deconstructed how Randy Staged the Structure and Meaning of his speech. (You can see the text here: http://www.fatsheep.org/articles/true/fatdad.php). It wasn't complicated:

Story 1, stage left (being trapped by dogs as a child).
> Message 1: Rescue or be rescued with love.
> Transition (and foreshadowing setup): four generations of "Fat Dad"

Story 2, stage right (wrecking his first car)
> Message 2: Loved ones are irreplaceable.
> Transition: from cars to girls

Story 3, stage center (teenage bravado vs. mature love)
> Message: Love for a lifetime.
> Transition: first Father's Day without Fat Dad

Closing:
> Recap of three messages about love
> Callback to the new generation of Fat Dad

Deconstructing the Impact

In 2011 Olivia Schofield was Toastmasters European Champion. I was proud to be her coach as she advanced to the next round. The first thing I did was deconstruct the impact of her speech by analyzing which parts the audience remembered. Then I created an animated graph that played in sync with the video of her speech, showing the audience reaction to each moment. See: http://www.youtube.com/watch?v=hNozCgP-7og

As a result of this analysis we learned exactly where to strengthen the structure and where to eliminate distractions. She took her speech from good to great, becoming the first European to win semifinals and advance to the World Championship finals, where she blew the audience away with a spectacular speech.

Curtain Call

To Stage your Presentation, start with the Page, move on the Stage, deconstruct Backstage. The key to creating structure and meaning with impact is to look at your presentation through the eyes, ears, and minds of your audience. Once you understand how to stage the audience experience, you'll find yourself invited to give your presentations on bigger and bigger stages in front of larger and larger audiences. Make the world your stage!

Takeaways

- Write for the ear, not the eye. Create structure that will translate to the stage.
- Map the structure of your presentation onto the physical space of the stage.
- Move with purpose. Change positions to reinforce structure. Use gestures to enhance meaning.
- Deconstruct speeches after the fact to understand why they work well or why they don't.

Bob Mohl, Toastmasters 2008 European Champion, has coached many successful speakers including three European champions and one finalist at the World Championships. He has been invited to give public speaking workshops, creativity training, TEDx talks, and keynotes in fourteen countries. He is a professor, consultant, and multimedia designer with several award-winning titles to his credit. "Captain Bob" lives on a houseboat on the Seine in Paris, where he hosts a monthly Full Moon Picnic. He can be contacted at bobmohl@gmail.com or www.bobmohl.com.

26

Using Emotion to Enhance the Motion of Your Message

Tim Juda

Y ou have a great story to tell, you deliver it in a dynamic way without error, and you leave feeling pretty good about yourself, only to find out that your audience left feeling...*nothing!* The message of the speech didn't resonate with the audience because there was one missing ingredient: *emotion*.

Have you ever avoided talking about a person, story, or belief because you didn't think you could get through the speech without being overwhelmed with emotion—and that such emotion was inappropriate? Or perhaps you declined to give a eulogy because you knew you couldn't get through it?

You will leave lasting memories with your audience and have the confidence to utilize emotions effectively in your speeches by using the simple techniques presented in this chapter, which will explain:

- why using emotion in speaking is not optional
- how to connect emotionally with your audience using the VIP Method
- three tips for keeping the audience emotionally connected to your speech
- four tools to control your emotions with preparation and practice

194

Why Using Emotion in Speaking Is Not Optional

The goal of a speaker is to make the audience think or act differently after hearing the speech. The message needs to resonate with the audience for the speech to leave a lasting impression. When you elicit emotions from the audience, they will remember the speech longer and therefore your message too.

Scientific research has shown that without emotion there can be no effective long-term memory. If information fails to elicit an emotional response, it will not be viewed as important and will have little chance of being stored in your memory.

> *Without emotion, there can be no effective long-term memory.*

Think back to moments in your life that you can recall quickly, even as far back as to when you were a child. You are able to recall these memories because they had some sort of emotional impact on your life. The stronger the emotion, the stronger the memory.

How to Connect Emotionally with Your Audience Using the VIP Method

A World Class speaker learns to use storytelling tools to deliver their message and connect with the audience. The beginning of the story is where the speaker should introduce characters and describe the circumstance. The more descriptive the speaker is with characters and the circumstance, the more emotional connections they can make with the audience. You will connect with your audience and keep their attention by incorporating the VIP Method into your speech and delivery. The VIP Method will:

- enable your audience to *visualize*
- encourage your audience to *imagine* and *reflect*
- utilize your *passion* for your subject matter and message

V—Visualize

Help your audience *visualize* the *characters* and *circumstance* of the story. Failing to build up the characters and circumstance at the beginning of the story can leave your audience emotionally disconnected when conflict or change happens later in the story. Describing physical characteristics and personality traits will help the audience build a vision of the characters as you speak.

In one of my keynote speeches titled "Swing" I tell a story about watching my son, Joseph, play Little League baseball at the age of six. While watching him play, I noticed one of the boys on the other team had some physical limitations. In the story, I show how the boy succeeds by living up to his own expectations and not the expectations of others.

To make the story and message memorable, I needed to find a way to quickly endear the little boy to the audience and emotionally connect them to his character. Toward the beginning of the speech I describe the little boy by saying: *"He had many challenges the other children didn't have to face that day. He was born with limitations in one arm and one leg, and when he ran, he had to run sideways around the bases."*

To help the audience build a clearer image of the little boy, I physically demonstrated how he ran as I finished the second sentence. Some audience members connected to the little boy just by knowing he had limitations. Their emotional connection grew stronger by having a clear mental image of the little boy running.

Once the audience creates a vision of the characters and the circumstance of the story, we can add another emotional hook by enabling them to *imagine* and *reflect* on how they relate to this character or situation.

I—Imagine/Reflect

You can build on emotional connections by getting the audience to look at your point or circumstance from their own perspective. How can you get the audience to think about their own situation as related to your point? What kind of scenario are your audience members likely to find themselves in down the line that's related to this point? What questions can you ask the audience members to allow them to imagine and reflect?

If you do use questions, even as a rhetorical device, make sure to let your audience sort through their own emotions before moving on to your next sentence. Pause and let the emotion sink in. Let the audience sort through how they feel at the moment. If you don't give them time to reflect, you lose an opportunity to make an impact.

You can also encourage the audience to reflect on your point by the way you provide the details of your story. The media is clever in keeping interest by continually adding ways their reading or viewing audience can connect to the story.

Read through the following progression of sentences relating to a tragic event in our history, the bombing at the Boston Marathon. Pause after reading each sentence to see how you connect emotionally:

> *There was a bombing at the Boston Marathon.*
> *There was a bombing at the Boston Marathon and three people were killed.*
> *There was a bombing at the Boston Marathon. Three people were killed, and hundreds more were injured. One of the three victims was an 8-year-old child.*
> *There was a bombing at the Boston Marathon. Three people were killed, and hundreds more were injured. One of the three victims was an 8-year-old boy who was standing close to one of the explosions. Just seconds earlier he was peering through the crowd, eating ice cream, waiting to see his dad pass by and finish the race.*

As you read from section to section, did your emotions change? Did you find another way to connect to the story? How did each section relate to you? Not everyone gets emotionally connected at the same level. Even though the first line is powerful, describing a horrific event, it may not be enough to connect the audience at an emotional level.

As more details get added, the audience finds their own connection as they reflect. In this example, the audience can connect from many different levels: as runners, Bostonians, Americans, parents or grandparents, or even as themselves remembering back to a time when they were young.

You connected the audience with a strong visual image and provided ways to imagine how they personally connected to the story. How can you add impact to your story? Use your passion!

P—Passion

Use your *passion* to move your audience. The audience needs to know you are being sincere and believable. When you are passionate about a subject matter or cause, the audience will pick up on your energy, authenticity, and sincerity. Your emotions will be natural, and building rapport with the audience will become easier.

The opposite effect materializes when your audience picks up that your emotions are more rehearsed and insincere. Have you ever heard a speech and thought *Sure, that sounded good, but they don't seem sincere in their message*? The audience may tune out for the rest of the speech and question whether the speaker believes in their subject matter and message. Passion helps you *show* emotion, not just *go through* the motions.

> **Passion helps you show emotion, not just go through the motions.**

In August 2010 I had the pleasure of competing in the semifinals of the World Championships of Public Speaking and a few days later being in the audience at the finals to hear David Henderson, the eventual world champion, deliver a heartfelt, emotional speech. He told a story of losing a childhood friend to sickle cell anemia. It was a passionate story with a message he was passionate about telling: "We all fall down, but love will lift you up."

David was visually emotional during his speech. His heart raced and tears streamed down both cheeks as he delivered the parts of the speech that touched him the most. But because he was exceptional in developing his characters and circumstance at the beginning, the audience didn't care. They were along for the ride and felt the conflict right along with him.

The audience felt like they knew the character, Jackie, and they understood completely why David lost some control of his emotions. He brought the audience to the same emotional level. Most importantly, he kept the speech moving. Even though he lost some control of his *emotions*, he stayed in control of the *speech.*

David Henderson helped the audience to *visualize, imagine,* and feel the *passion* in his speech. He had the audience emotionally connected to his story and, more importantly, to his message. Because the three powerful elements of the VIP Method were included in his speech, the audience was emotionally connected and will remember his championship speech for years to come.

Three Tips for Keeping the Audience Emotionally Connected to Your Speech

Tip #1: Give the Audience a Release

In public speaking, it is effective to vary the pace, volume, and vocal variety during a speech to keep the audience's attention. The same process should be followed for emotions.

Don't hold your audience's emotions captive. If you bring the audience to an emotional high or low, don't keep them there for too long. Offer them a release. Invoke humor when necessary or bring forward a positive outcome or solution. The audience will stay engaged as they feel a shift or change in their emotion.

Tip #2: When You Are Overcome with Emotion as a Speaker, Move Forward

The atmosphere can become awkward and uncomfortable when a speaker needs to pause for an extended period of time to regain composure. The audience rapport that was built up earlier in the speech increasingly fades the longer it takes to regain composure.

The best thing to do is to try and get right back into the speech and keep it moving forward, even if it means talking through the tears. You can inoculate the audience if there's a strong possibility that you may lose control of your emotions.

Tip #3: Inoculate the Audience

Inoculation is widely used in public speaking to prepare an audience for an upcoming argument or negative behavior. When the argument is heard later, the audience has already been exposed to it and it doesn't carry as much of an impact. As you can imagine, this technique is often used in a court of law to soften the opposition's arguments. This process can also be used to prepare an audience for a potential emotional situation.

If the speaker feels they might get emotional later on in a speech, they can use the inoculation process. For example, the speaker can say, "I always get emotional every time I talk about my children and how proud I am of them" or "It always gets to me emotionally when I think about all the hungry children in the world." If the speaker does get emotional later in the speech, the audience has already been introduced to the possibility. The emotional moment becomes less of a surprise and therefore less of a distraction.

Four Tools to Control Your Emotions with Preparation and Practice

Tool #1: Understand the Audience's Emotional Level before You Speak

What is happening around them in their environment? What current events are happening that affect the audience? You will know what emotional level you need to start your speech at to make a connection and take the audience to the emotional level you want.

Tool #2: When Audience Members Display Emotion

You may see emotion from members of the audience, which in turn can increase the emotion you feel as a speaker. If this happens and it is affecting you, look elsewhere!

If you are telling a story about losing your pet dog and you see the gruff grizzly bear of a man in the back row bawling his eyes out, focus your eye contact on another member of the audience.

Tool #3: Desensitize Yourself to the Subject Matter

The more you practice the speech, the more desensitized you become to the emotional circumstance. This will help the speech be delivered as planned without awkward surprises. Retaining some emotion is helpful in delivering the speech in the sincere, authentic way in which it was intended.

Tool #4: Add Release Points to Your Speech

A good test to see how you will react while giving your speech is to place a picture of the person, place, or event you are talking about in front of you as you practice. Make eye contact with the picture as you deliver key lines from the speech where you believe emotion will be felt.

Find points in the speech where you experience strong emotion. Surround these sections with humor or material that is easy for you to talk about.

You have a great story to tell so be sure to use these tips and tools to incorporate emotion into your message and delivery. Remember:

- without emotion there can be no effective long-term memory
- you can connect emotionally with your audience using the VIP Method to:
  - enable your audience to *visualize*
  - encourage your audience to *imagine* and *reflect*
  - utilize your *passion* for your subject matter and message
- three tips for keeping the audience emotionally connected to your speech
- four tools to control your emotions with preparation and practice

You will leave knowing you used your emotions and stories to build lasting emotional connections with your audience and that your audience left remembering—*everything!*

Tim Juda is an award-winning speaker and certified World Class Speaking coach who has studied and practiced communication and leadership skills for over fifteen years. Growing up a shy child has led him to become an avid believer in teaching children to have the courage and confidence to speak up and to encourage adults that it's never too late to begin. Find out more about Tim at www.timjuda.com.

27

Bring Your
Characters to Life

Valerie Fuson

Your purpose is to make your audience see what you saw, hear what you heard, feel what you felt. Relevant detail, couched in concrete, colorful language, is the best way to recreate the incident as it happened and to picture it for the audience.

—Dale Carnegie

The biggest mistake most speakers make is giving presentations that are boring. Many presentations are filled with PowerPoint slides, statistics, and facts but little reference to how the information relates to real-life situations and people. Even if the presentation includes stories they are often told in a passive narrative style. If characters are included the presenter describes the characters' reactions and words without emotion. They may even refer to the characters as *they, them, he, she, she said, he felt.* In other words, they narrate the story instead of reliving it.

Stories are meant to impact, influence, and inspire. If you want the audience to think differently, reflect on their own life, and take action, your stories need to include charismatic characters that the audience can relate to, sympathize with, and rejoice with. Characters are the heart of your story. A story well told can deliver your message and sell you or your product or service.

This chapter will focus on:

- why characters are the heart of your story
- three types of dialogue
- reliving your story
- World Class tools to bring your characters to life so they can be *seen*, *known*, *heard*
- coaching in action

Why Characters Are the Heart of Your Story

Do you remember your favorite story from when you were a child? As an adult what is your favorite story, movie, book? Chances are it's not the story or events in the story that you are fond of but the characters. Sure, the events may be exciting, the conflict and resolution could take you on an emotional roller coaster, but the characters make you love or hate them. You may relate personally to the character(s) in your favorite story or to the transformational journey they go through.

As a presenter you want the audience to care about your story but more specifically about the character. When the audience connects emotionally to the character they are reliving the story with you. They have an invested interest in the outcome of the story. You want them to feel the conflict and transformation the character goes through. Why? If you are telling a story of conflict and take them through a journey they may be experiencing, and you show how the character discovered a solution, made a change, and was successful with their aspiration, subconsciously the audience will think, *Maybe I can do the same thing... maybe it will work for me too*. You can give them hope and inspiration through your character.

Next we will discuss the best way to move the story forward through dialogue.

> *The purpose of a storyteller is not to tell you how to think, but to give you questions to think upon.*
> —**Brandon Sanderson**, *The Way of Kings*

Three Types of Dialogue That Move Your Story Forward

There are three key types of dialogue to include in your presentation:

- dialogue between characters
- dialogue between you and the audience
- self-dialogue

Dialogue is the most neglected part of a story. Why is it important? Effective dialogue reveals the emotions, thoughts, aspirations, personality, conflict, and relationship between characters. Dialogue also lets the story unfold in front of the audience and moves your story forward. Your listeners get to relive the story with you. If your story is all narration it becomes a report, easily forgotten, and puts your audience to sleep. If you use all dialogue it becomes a play and not very interesting. When everything is the same nothing stands out. Let your dialogue stand out by putting the right amount of dialogue in your story.

Two key points that dialogue uncovers is your *key message* and *humor*. Let your characters be the heroes or gurus by giving them the best lines. Let your characters convey the key message of your speech. When your message comes from a character other than you, your audience will listen. If you convey the message you could come off as preaching or arrogant. When you tell your audience what you learned from a character in your story, you become similar to the audience, not smarter or better. Your audience will be more likely to experience the learning also.

One of the best ways to uncover humor is through your *self-dialogue*. When you let your audience into your head and allow them to know what you're thinking, they feel like they are invited into your life. Let them know your innermost thoughts, fears, frustrations, surprises, and failures and they will connect with you at a deeper level. Often your audience may be in a similar situation. When this happens they think you got into their minds.

Dialogue between *you and the audience* can also reveal humor. You may want to go into the audience and give them a line of dialogue. For example, you could say, "I know what you're thinking," "I know you were thinking the same thing," or "If you were in my situation you would have done the same thing." Because it is unexpected it creates humor. When you get into the minds of your audience you make them reflect on their own lives. When your audience reflects on their lives they begin to experience the emotions attached to their circumstances.

Relive Your Story and Let Your Characters Experience the Emotion

Get the audience invested in what happens to the characters. Stir their emotions. Why should you stir their emotions? If you don't engage your audiences' emotions they won't connect with you or your message. They may think *that was a nice speech*, but you didn't connect with them at a personal level. You didn't get them to relate to you or your characters, which means they won't connect with your idea, message, service, or product.

Tell your story as if it were happening now. Let the story unfold in front of your audience. Tell the story with the appropriate emotions throughout the story. Take them on a ride with you from frustration, confusion, and unhappiness to hope, inspiration, and finally success. When this happens your audience will get excited and pulled into the story. You could step out of your story and say, "Has that ever happened to you?" or "Have you ever felt like that?" Show them how it's possible to get what they want when they learn new techniques and strategies they can use in their lives. Show them how they can go from frustration in their lives to success.

World Class Tools to Bring Your Characters to Life
So They Can Be Seen, Known, Heard

Bringing your characters to life means making them real and believable. If your audience doesn't believe you or your characters they won't believe in your message. If they don't believe in your message they won't buy into how you can help them.

So how do you bring your characters to life? Let them be *seen*, *known*, and *heard*.

Let Them Be Seen

Let your audience know what your characters look like. Give them enough description of your characters' appearance and mannerisms, but let your audience fill in the rest. Allow them to see the characters the way they want to see them. Make them do a little work with their imagination but not so much that they can't follow the story.

> *Make them do a little work with their imagination but not so much that they can't follow the story.*

Let Them Be Known

Give your characters charisma and personality. Give small details about who your characters are, their experience in work or life, whether they are a parent, child, caretaker, addict, CEO, etc. What are their aspirations, integrity, challenges?

Another tool for letting your characters be known is to give them a name or nickname. It is especially important in the story to let the audience know who is speaking. Instead of saying "she said" or "he said," call your characters by name or nickname. For example, if you are speaking to your spouse or child you can call them by name or sweetie, honey, or a special nickname. If the character is speaking to you they can call you by name. Referring to your characters by name makes it clear to the audience who is speaking.

Let Them Be Heard

How can you let your characters be heard? Give them a voice. Let them take a stand for something. What are they struggling with? What are their values and integrity? Give them dialogue throughout the story, and let them express their emotions—fears, love, happiness, frustration.

How can you let your characters be seen, known, and heard without narrating all the information and boring your audience? You can give information about them through dialogue. In one of my stories about my mother I could say, "Mom, just because you're a Beatles fan doesn't mean you have to buy me all the Beatles albums. I like Ricky Nelson, and I want his album for my sixteenth birthday." This is an easy way to say my mom is a Beatles maniac and is trying to cover it up by buying their albums for me. While my sixteen-year-old self may like the Beatles, it doesn't mean I have to have everything Beatles. I have a teenage crush on my heartthrob, Ricky Nelson. "Beatlemania" just started and hasn't affected me yet.

In dialogue we can give tidbits of information with fewer words and reveal character descriptions and circumstances. Dialogue moves the story forward and unfolds it in the moment before the audience.

Now that you have learned how characters, emotion, and dialogue can take your presentation from dull to engaging and keep your audience on the edge of their seats, how do you implement these World Class Speaking techniques? Find out in the section below.

Coaching in Action

Practice!

I know that's not what you wanted to hear, but practice—when you know what to practice and how it can transform your speaking—can be fun and inspiring.

Practice how to let your characters be *seen*, *known*, and *heard*. *Characters*, *emotion*, and *dialogue* are the three key secrets that will transform your presentation the quickest, yet most speakers don't use them. Here are some other tips for bringing your characters to life:

1. **Make a list of your characters.** Depending on the length of your speech and story, only have key characters that may be yourself and one or two other characters, perhaps even the audience.

2. **Let them be seen.** Write down a couple of important characteristics such as appearance and mannerisms. Do they slouch? Are they shy or charismatic, young or elderly? What kinds of quirks make them stand out?

3. **Let them be known.** What is important in their life? What are their challenges, their values? What do they want? What was the change in their life?

4. **Let them be heard.** What are they thinking? What are they saying? What are their aspirations? Let them share their emotions in dialogue.

5. **Relive your story.** Don't just tell it. Your voice and body language should match your emotions throughout the story. When you are happy show it. When you are frustrated show it. Let the audience feel your emotions. Take them on a ride with the characters' journey.

6. **Step out of the story to have a conversation with the audience.** Take a step forward or move to another place on the stage.

7. **Write down the dialogue for each character.** Just as you don't want to narrate the whole presentation, you also don't want to have only dialogue in your presentation. Give your characters the best lines. The key message is best delivered by the guru in your presentation, not by you. When you deliver the dialogue make sure you use the appropriate emotion, body language, and tone of voice.

8. **Now for the fun part: emotions.** How do you practice emotions? In my seminar called "Improv for Storytelling" we bring the speaker up

onstage and have them tell a one- to two-minute story. Then we give them an emotion and have them repeat the story in the new emotion. This is an improv technique that teaches emotional range. Have you ever seen a musical conductor use his hands to get the musicians to play the music louder or softer? We do this same technique in our "Improv for Storytelling" workshop. The conductor motions the speaker to take their emotional range from a 1-10 scale. We then give the speaker a new emotion and have them take the new emotion through the same scale.

You can do the same by practicing different emotions and varying the range for each emotion. Practice the same one- to two-minute story with new emotions so you can experience the difference on the emotional scale of 1-10.

Most speakers are afraid to increase their emotional state because they think they are overacting or being too dramatic. After this improv game the speakers experience what the difference really is between a 3 and a 10. To their surprise, they realize they aren't demonstrating the right emotional range for their presentation. Make sure you know the range and use the appropriate range for your story.

Have fun practicing your range of emotion with your body movements and also in your dialogue.

Remember, when you are having fun your audience is having fun!

When you use the World Class Speaking storytelling tools (characters and dialogue) and let your characters be seen, known, and heard, you will create magnetic characters your audience will connect with and care about. Use dialogue to create interest, convey humor, and impart your message.

This lively combination of characters that "live and breathe" with interesting dialogue will convey your message and sell your product, service, and expertise. The choice is yours. You can narrate a story that is easily forgotten, or you can create a captivating story with characters that draw your audience in—keeping them on the edge of their seats and remembering the story for months and years later. When your story and characters are remembered, *you* are remembered.

Valerie Fuson is a certified World Class Speaking coach who helps business professionals create their signature story and speech. She coaches speakers to create a dynamic delivery style using influence and improvisational strategies. You can reach her at Valerie@ ValerieFuson.com and www.EmpoweredSpeaking.com

28

Create Compelling Stories
That Sell a Result

Richard Ballard

We've all grown up hearing stories. Most of us have gone to bed at some point in our life listening to a bedtime story. We hear stories when we gather together during holidays, usually told by a very colorful uncle or grandparent about times past or some unforgettable family event that never gets old in the telling. But have you ever stopped to think about how a story is created?

Storytelling is an extremely important part of public speaking. In fact you could say public speaking is all about telling great stories. Not knowing how to develop and tell a story can make you a forgettable public speaker. Knowing how to develop and tell a story can make you a World Class Speaker. In the next few pages you will learn how to:

- discover stories from your own experiences
- use key phrases in your stories to sell a point or product
- create compelling stories that have your audience wanting more
- use the PARTS formula to anchor your stories

Discover Stories from Your Own Experiences

One of the first questions novice storytellers ask is "Where do I get my stories?" Let me start by explaining where you don't get them. The one cardinal sin in any speaker's career is to use another speaker's story. Be original. A speaker's story is their trademark, their sweat and toil, their life. Nothing will kill your career faster than to "borrow" a story and make it your own. Give credit where the credit is due.

So where do you get your stories? You get stories from your own experiences, even if you haven't had that many. Everyone has experienced something in life. You are unique; there is only one of you. So it is with your stories. They are alive within you; you just need to draw them out. It's really quite simple.

Start by creating a matrix or outline with the following information:

- the decades of your life
- specific events that happened in each decade
  - birthdays
  - deaths
  - vacations
  - boyfriends/girlfriends
  - schools
  - breakups
  - victories
  - failures
- your reflections on each of these events

You now have the basis for your stories. You have the raw data that makes compelling stories. They are true, they are yours, and they are unique. A question at this point might be how you know they are relevant. Let me answer that question with a story of my own.

While I was traveling in China in the early eighties I ran across a professor of physics. Now you have to understand what had just taken place in China prior to my visit. China was coming out of a deep trauma called the Cultural Revolution. During this time China purged a whole generation. People were relocated from one part of China to another based on their education. The more educated the person, the more remote the relocation. What was tragic is that the leadership used the younger generation to purge the older generation.

I grew up being reminded of all the starving children in China and how remote the country was. To say the least, I never thought we would have anything in common. But the story the professor told me that day has been in my soul ever since.

To avoid the purge, this professor had locked himself in his lab at the university and relied on the old adage "out of sight, out of mind." For him it worked. He managed to remain in his village until the purging was over.

But during the Cultural Revolution, his oldest son bought into all the government was doing and actively participated in the removal and disappearance of several of the village elders. As he was telling this tale, he began to weep for the loss of his son's respect. At that moment I came to realize we had much more in common than I had ever dreamed.

As humans we all laugh and cry about the same things: family, friends, and life-changing events. Your story is relevant because of this truth. You can move mountains with a well thought out story about the truth in your life.

Use Key Phrases in Your Stories to Sell a Point or Product

Speakers like to say that anytime you try to persuade someone with a speech, the audience is always tuned into one radio station the whole time: WIIFM (What's in it for me?). If you don't keep this radio station in mind, you will lose your audience.

> *The audience is always tuned into one radio station the whole time: WIIFM (What's in it for me?).*

So when opening your speech, you need to lay the foundation early. The best way to do this is to begin selling from your very first words.

Every time you speak you are selling. You are either selling yourself or your ideas. When you create your stories, keep in mind how you intend to sell it. As a rule, never sell a product, idea, service, or yourself. Always sell the results.

The easiest way to accomplish this is with a simple phrase: "with this you can…" The formula goes like this: Your Product + "with this you can" = their result.

In World Class Speaking we have a process for everything we do. It is no different with storytelling. The process used here is called the EDGE sales formula. Here is a golden nugget: with the EDGE formula you decide what results you want to achieve. Everybody wants either more *Esteem*, to *Do* more, to *Gain* more, or to *Enjoy* more. By tapping into one or more of these desires, you will tune into your audience's very own radio station, WIIFM.

I thoroughly believe that no matter who you speak to—whether it is presidents or CEOs, profit or nonprofit companies, or Little League baseball teams and Girl Scout troops, the sooner you learn to write compelling stories the sooner you will achieve huge success.

Create Stories That Have Your Audience Wanting More

Once you lay the foundation and decide what results you are seeking, you insert the four most important areas of your story. They are the *characters, conflict, climax,* and *conclusion.* Another way of describing these areas would be to ask yourself who is in the story (main characters), what happens to them (conflict), what is their turning point (climax), and what is the result (conclusion).

With your *characters*, give them a chance to be real. Give one- or two-line descriptions so your audience will have an image in their mind of that character.

Give them a chance to be known. We need to know your characters. How else will we care about them? Also, speak in dialogue. Narration leads to a dissertation while dialogue leads to a great story.

Give them a chance to be the hero. Give them the best lines. You do not want to be seen as a know-it-all.

With your *conflict*, identify the kind of conflict. Everyone likes a struggle. So give it to them. The classic question in any writing class is: what are the four types of conflict in any story. They are

- person vs. person
- person vs. society
- person vs. nature
- person vs. environment

In World Class Speaking, we add one more: person vs. themselves. This is always the best conflict. Remember, people will always move away from their own pain and toward their own pleasure. Show them how to do this and your story will touch more lives.

Establish the conflict early, the sooner the better. Throw them in the fire, get them into trouble, and set the stage early. Grab the audience's attention right from the beginning.

> *Establish the conflict early, the sooner the better. Throw them in the fire, get them into trouble, and set the stage early. Grab the audience's attention right from the beginning.*

Intensify the conflict. Ramp it up. Make it unbearable. Get your audience to want release. Conflict is the hook, the bait of your story. Get them to bite. Get them on the line so they struggle to get free.

Your *climax* should be a significant emotional event. It should include some wisdom, lesson, or strategy. Make it a new way to act, think, or look at something. This is your chance at being a wise sage. Don't blow it!

Your *conclusion* should conclude your story, not your speech. Each story should have a conclusion. It will sell the people on your message. And ask yourself has your character changed as a result of the story.

Don't just tell the story, relive the story. But relive it through dialogue not narrative.

Use the PARTS Formula to Anchor Your Stories

The final part of your story should be to create anchors so your story is not forgotten but remembered. It does no good to tell a great story that does not stick with your audience. Getting them to reflect on your message is the magic that makes a World Class Speaker. For this use a process called the PARTS formula.

- Point
- Anchor

- Reflection
- Technique
- Sales

Let's start with the main Point. Ask yourself what it is. Each point should have a *foundational phrase*. Make it brief, fewer than ten words. Make it "you focused." Make it repeatable. One of the phrases I use in my speeches is *"If you can dream it, you can be it."* Another is *"With the proper tools, you can build any dream."*

Now that you have your point, Anchor it. You can anchor a point with one of four methods (we call it the 4 A's to Anchoring): use an *anecdote* or story, an *analogy* comparing it with something else, an *acronym* (such as SMART goals—look that one up if you don't know it), and finally an *activity*. Each of these methods has its good and bad points.

Next you will want to get your audience to Reflect on what you are saying. Craig Valentine teaches that "wisdom comes from reflection." You must constantly get your audience to reflect on their own lives. Questions are one of the best ways to achieve this. I will ask, "What tools have you been using to achieve success? Is it time for an upgrade?"

Then you might want to give them a Technique they can use right now. At the beginning of each seminar I ask the attendees to write down what brought them here today. What motivated them to break from their busy schedule and spend time with me? Writing down your goal engages the unconscious mind, and you stand a better chance of achieving that goal.

Finally you will want to Sell the results of the idea, product, service, or yourself. Remember that all speaking is selling. Also remember that everyone is tuned into WIIFM. So to sell, instead of saying "today I am going to share, show, teach…" say "today you are going to learn, discover, receive, walk away with…" Make it about them.

Let me close this chapter with a story.

Most people don't move or take action until they are at the end of their rope. It is your job to make them face that reality.

I tried college five times and quit five times. I gave up on ever having a college degree. I was destined to be a laborer working for small wages. That was my mindset. I was at the end of my rope when it came to trying to get a degree.

One of the jobs I had was working on a construction site where they were building a large power plant to generate electricity. The plant needed to be very sturdy so the task was to blow big holes in the ground to fill back up with reinforced concrete to make a stable base.

My job was to go down into these blasted-out holes and smooth down the sides. The gear I had to use was a 90-pound jackhammer. It wasn't the easiest job around. Daily I was lowered into the hole on a rope and the jackhammer was lowered down beside me on another rope.

Let me describe how the smoothing of walls went in the hole. I would position myself over a jagged outcropping and swing the jackhammer up and onto the outcropping and hammer away until the rock broke loose, and as the jackhammer fell I would swing it up onto another outcropping. I would work my way around the hole—which was about 20 feet wide and 60 feet deep—continuing this routine of swing, hammer, swing, hammer.

After I smoothed out the rocks at the current depth, I would be lowered five feet and start the whole process over again. Each day I came to work I was lowered into this manmade hole that had been blasted deeper the night before.

When the hole got to the required depth, it was filled back in with reinforced concrete. Concrete is reinforced with what is called rebar, or steel bars about a quarter-inch in diameter. In this hole they would be sticking up ready for the next fill of concrete. So my view looking down into the hole was the business end of about ninety pieces of rebar. If I fell I would instantly look like Swiss cheese on a bed of rebar.

One day I was about 40 feet down and at the end of my rope. I looked down at the approaching rebar. I looked up at the ever increasing depth I was going. And like an epiphany it came to me that if I kept digging this hole I was in, and I kept swinging this 90-pound jackhammer, there was a good chance I would reinforce concrete at some point.

I made the decision to quit jacking around, and, starting at the end of my rope, I put one hand over the other and climbed out of the hole I had dug myself into.

Sometimes in life we all have dug ourselves into that hole and are swinging by the end of our rope. Quit jacking around and start climbing.

I did go back and finish what I started and got my degree, but that is another story.

Richard Ballard is a certified World Class Speaking coach, author, and keynote speaker. He currently lives on Amelia Island in Florida. You can reach Richard at info@ rballard.com.

29

Transform Your Speaking with Eye Contact

Willie Joe Robinson Jr.

hink back to the last time you saw a truly captivating speaker in person. Perhaps while seated in the audience you looked around and realized you were nestled between tens or hundreds of other event participants. There might have been the smell of fresh cups of coffee nearby, and you felt a sense of excitement in the air as you eagerly anticipated what was to come.

Suddenly the lights dimmed, and the speaker was introduced and took the stage. From the very start the audience was captivated. Every communication element used by the speaker had purpose. The content began with an attention-grabbing Big Bang, and then flowed into a clear, relatable message. The speech was delivered at a comfortable pace and with vocal variation that perfectly matched the intended emotion. The congruent nonverbal cues used by the speaker, such as gestures, stance, and movement, were executed naturally, with confidence, and complimented the message.

Then something truly amazing happened. The speaker looked directly at you—yes, you—and made eye contact. For that moment, though seated in a large audience, you were engaged in a one-on-one conversation with the speaker.

How did that make you feel? My guess is that it was an uplifting experience that helped to create an amazing connection between you and speaker.

If you want to be an authentic, captivating, and successful speaker, effective eye contact is an important element to incorporate into your speaking arsenal. But it is often one of the most misunderstood or incorrectly used public speaking elements.

The aim of this chapter is to demystify and transform your speaking through the successful use of eye contact. This will enable you quickly develop rapport and build trust with your audience in half the time, while developing deeper and longer lasting connections. The topics in this chapter include:

- benefits of making effective eye contact
- elements to making great eye contact
- techniques and strategies to improve your eye contact

> *The eyes unveil a story that words alone can't.*

The Benefits of Making Effective Eye Contact

From a very early age, we have learned to decipher elements in the communication process. Since we can't read minds, we look into the eyes of a person to get an indication of what is actually going on inside their mind. Often when looking into a person's eyes, we can pick up on a number of nonverbal signals, such as whether they are in agreement, confused, considering, unimpressed, dishonest, honest, open, concealing, and many other things. So, there is a degree of truth in the saying "The eyes are window of the soul." As a public speaker, having rock-solid eye contact that is consistent with your true underlying intent is crucial.

Using eye contact correctly can:

- **Reduce speaking anxiety and help settle nerves**. Have you known people comfortable speaking in one-to-one situations, but panic when forced to stand before an audience? Effective eye contact changes your perspective from trying to speak to an entire audience at once, to the manageable task of speaking to one person at a time.

- **Help create trust and integrity**. Have you ever heard a person say to another "Look me right in the eyes and tell me ..." to help establish if the truth was being told? A speaker who can look a person in the eyes when speaking with them is more believed and trusted.

- **Gaining valuable feedback**. Public speaking is not broadcasting; it is an interactive two-way communication process. When you are speaking with a person and establish eye contact, you can often get a reasonable idea of what's going in their mind. Nonverbal feedback received might include a facial expression, eye moment, head nod, or other body language. This feedback can provide confirmation that you are on the right track or alternatively signal that you will need to make adjustments to keep your audience.

- **Enhance connection with the audience**. There is something wonderful about being in a conversation with a person who appears to be sincerely interested in you. Dale Carnegie, a pioneer in interpersonal skills, stressed the impact that being truly interested in the person you are speaking with has on establishing a connection. When you are speaking to an audience, and hold a conversation with a single person for a complete thought (in the context of eye contact, a thought is from the start of a sentence to a punctuation mark), do you think that for that moment they feel special and connected? In turn, when you see that person responding back to you and your message positively, don't you as the speaker also feel uplifted and connected?

- **Maintain train of thought**. Doing too many things at the same time seldom works out well. When you attempt to make eye contact with multiple people within a single thought, you are doing way too much. Instead when you focus on only one person for an entire thought, you have the freedom to enter into a more flowing conversational mindset. This will enable you to think more clearly, better remember what to say, and eliminate inappropriate interjections or filler words such as *ah*, *um*, and *er*.

- **Slow speaking pace**. Making eye contact with one person for a complete thought allows you to enter into a more conversational mode rather than a broadcast mode of speaking. Your speech rate will naturally slow down and you will take greater care to be understood.

Successfully using great eye contact will provide you with a number of tangible benefits, and quickly elevate your public speaking outcomes to the next level. So now let's discover what you can do to create magnetic eye contact.

> *Your audience takes flight when your eye contact's not right.*

The Keys to Making Great Eye Contact

On the surface, making a powerful audience connection using eye contact sounds dead eye. How hard can it be, right? You just have to look out at your audience. After all, you are clearly visible, standing front and center, possibly even elevated by a stage. The audience can't miss you, right? That's all there is to making eye contact, right? Wrong, wrong, wrong.

Let's face it: as a speaker you have so many things to do. You have to be comfortable with material presented, use your voice and gestures appropriately, and concentrate on your stage movement, all while appearing calm, confident and looking natural on stage. If you look at it that way, it all seems pretty challenging, doesn't it?

But let's look at it another way. When you are in everyday, one-on-one conversations, you do similar things without feeling the same degree of stress. So, one of the most important things to remember before taking the stage is to be the same natural person you are in your everyday conversations.

The following points should be used as a checklist or reference when practicing or evaluating you eye contact.

- **When speaking to an audience, instead of thinking of the group as a whole, imagine that you are having individual conversations with one person at a time.** Your goal should be to speak to each person for a complete thought or hold contact for three to five seconds. Use whatever seems most appropriate.
- **Make eye contact with as many people in the audience as possible.** Just like a good host of a party, it is important to meet all your guests. Be careful not to focus exclusively on certain people or sections of the room. It's a

natural tendency to favor people we know or who send positive feedback. Resist that temptation.

- **Your transition of eye contact from one person to another should be as smooth and controlled as possible.** Imagine it as a dance, where you gracefully release one dance partner and graciously receive another.
- **Be sure to know your speech well.** This will give you the freedom to concentrate on the feedback gained through eye contact, and make any required adjustments to keep your audience connected.
- **When asking a question to a person, maintain your eye contact until you get a response** (nod, smile, eye movement, etc.) or until a reasonable amount of time has passed. Breaking eye contact too soon gives the impression that you don't really care about the person's answer. It is similar to when a person asks you a question, but continues to speak without providing you with an opportunity to respond. If a person is hesitant about responding, you can try things like nodding to get agreement, or adding a comment such as "Do you agree?" These prompts will often help you to get a reaction.
- **If you really must read your speech, select spots where you can look up from the page for longer amounts of time.** Questions or points of reflection are ideal. When you look up from the page, make actual eye contact with someone in the audience. Throughout your speech, make eye contact with as many people as you can.
- **If you use a PowerPoint presentation, make sure that you, rather than the presentation, is the star of the show.** Instead of looking back at the screen, use a computer monitor positioned to enable you to face the audience. You should know your speech well enough so that the monitor is only referenced as guide.
- **Just as pauses can add impact, allow for reflecion and variety.** You can break eye contact to move across the stage or reflect on a point. The majority of your stage time, though, should be spent making direct eye contact with members of your audience.
- **Speak with honesty and believe in your message.** When you attempt to deceive, your eye movement will give you away.
- **Smile when speaking, especially when beginning your speech.** Combined with eye contact, this will help your audience warm to you more quickly, while helping to soften your eye gaze.

- **The larger the audience, the greater your eye contact span.** For example, when you make eye contact with one person in a large audience, multiple people will feel that you are making direct eye contact just with them.
- **If the audience is too large, or lighting too dark, for you to actually see a person's eyes, visualize their eyes,** as if you could actually see the person. Also break the audience in a reasonable number of zones to provide sufficient coverage.
- **Be sure to move your whole head, and not just your eye, when making eye contact.**
- **Don't turn your head more than about 45 degrees to the left or right when making eye contact.** Otherwise you run the risk of some audience members seeing the back of your head. Well-thought-out stage movement will help you to cover the entire audience.
- **While direct eye contact is valued in most Western countries, it can be considered an invasion of privacy or disrespectful in some places.** When speaking to such audiences, don't focus on one individual for too long, as it could embarrass them.
- **Be genuinely interested in getting to know your audience.**

Using effective eye contact will make a real difference to how your audience reacts to you and your message. As a speaker you will also benefit from making deeper connections and gaining quality feedback from your audience. In the next section, we will examine techniques and strategies that will help you to refine your eye contact skills.

Techniques and Strategies to Improve Your Eye Contact

As with all skills, to become proficient in a new area requires practice. The techniques presented in this section will help you to work through the steps required to become both confident and capable of establishing meaningful eye contact.

To become more comfortable making eye contact during one-on-one conversation

Since your objective as a speaker is to connect with one person at a time rather than broadcast to the masses, extending your comfort zone in this area is a crucial starting point. The following suggestions will give you a starting point for achieving this initial goal.

- If you are uncomfortable making basic eye contact, choose a spot directly between or slightly above the listener's eyes. If this doesn't feel comfortable, try letting your eyes go slightly out of focus. This has the added benefit of softening and relaxing your gaze. Your goal is to eventually make direct eye contact.
- Create one-on-one conversation opportunities to practice and develop your skills. Start with people you know and are comfortable with. Afterwards create short impromptu speaking opportunities with random people that you encounter daily. For example, consider asking for the time or directions while practicing your eye contact.
- After you are comfortable making direct eye contact, you will then be ready to move on to the following techniques.

Things You Can Work on without Assistance

- If you prefer an initial pattern to help move eye contact from person to person, the triangle contact method might be helpful. For this you will start with making contact with a person in the front and center of the audience, the next person selected for eye contact will be in the rear left corner of the audience, followed by someone seated in the right rear corner of the audience, and then return to the person seated in the front center of the audience. The pattern followed resembles that of a triangle. After following this rotation for a couple of times, you invert the triangle so that your new starting tip of the triangle directs your attention to a person in the rear center of the audience. Please note: This is only a starting technique until you become more comfortable shifting your eye contact comfortably around an audience.
- When rehearsing your speech, visualise the room layout and audience, and practice your eye contact as though you are speaking to an actual audience.
- Video yourself speaking in front of an audience. During playback, was it obvious that you were looking with a particular pattern of eye movement? If it gave the illusion that you were naturally looking at various members

of your audience, you have accomplished your goal and made effective eye contact with the majority of your audience in a meaningful way.

Things You Can Work on with Assistance

- When speaking to an unfamiliar audience, be sure to arrive early, and take the opportunity to meet and introduce yourself to as many people as possible. This provides you with a comfortable landing spot for your initial eye contact, and the selected people will be thrilled you sought them out.

- As a group training exercise, have the audience members raise their hands at the start of your speech. They must keep their hands raised until you have made eye contact with them for one complete thought, or three seconds have elapsed. Your primary focus should be on establishing and maintaining suitable eye contact, not just getting hands down.

- As a variation to the previous group training exercise, at the end of your speech ask for a show of hands of people who felt that you made meaningful eye contact with them during your speech.

- Get together with trusted friends, join a local speaking group, or join an international organization such as Toastmaster's, which can provide a supportive environment to hone your public speaking skills.

- Until you are comfortable with your ability to make suitable eye contact, it can be helpful to have your live speeches evaluated by a qualified speech coach or a skilled and experienced speech evaluator.

When you prepare for your next speech, I hope that you will review the components that will facilitate great connections with your audience, as well as practice the techniques detailed in this chapter.

Using rock-solid eye contact will enable you to transform your speaking and achieve amazing speech outcomes quickly.

Willie Joe Robinson Jr., MEI, is an engaging motivational speaker, speech coach, and trainer. As a speaker, he entertains and inspires audiences to exceed perceived limitations and unleash the greatness within. As an educator, he unveils proven techniques that will enable you to quickly transform your speaking and achieve more personally and professionally. For more information, visit his website at http://www.transformyourspeaking.com/.

30

Mastering
the Q&A

Dell Self

Conducting a question and answer (Q&A) period is a common aspect of speaking. Unfortunately, too many speakers are unaware that there is a right way and a wrong way to handle it.

In this chapter, you will learn:

- why having a Q&A in the wrong "location" can devalue your entire message
- where to put the Q&A in your message
- how to get your audience ready to ask questions
- how to keep the Q&A from taking over your message
- how to have your audience leave fired up by your message rather than confused by the Q&A

You've spent so much time working on your message making certain everything is just right. Don't let a poorly done Q&A period ruin your message, leaving your audience with nothing but questions.

It's all about location, location, location.

When working with clients, I like to use common illustrations to drive home points. One of my clients, Harry, a well-dressed realtor, was conducting a series of workshops on how to become a successful realtor. While his workshops started well, they seemed to end in utter chaos. This prompted me to ask him three specific questions:

1. How do you end your workshops?
2. When do things start to get out of hand?
3. What do you think might be the problem?

In his slow and methodic way, Harry responded, "I end my workshops with a precise call to action, and then I have the Q&A. Dell, I started to notice things getting out of hand during and after the Q&A. Do you think I should stop having the Q&A?"

"Harry, you're doing workshops," I said. "People expect to be able to ask questions. Keep the Q&A."

Harry's workshops went well until he got to the Q&A. Time and time again Harry would unknowingly defeat his own efforts by having the Q&A at the end of his presentations. As I talked with Harry further I discovered two issues going on. He treated the Q&A as totally separate from the workshop, and he included it during the wrong time of the workshop—or, in realtor language, at the "wrong location." After I made a few comments regarding the Q&A, it became apparent that Harry would need additional input from me at our next session.

That evening I stumbled upon a TV show, *House Hunters*, which explained the importance of location. The light bulb came on. I knew exactly how I could get Harry to grasp why the location of the Q&A mattered.

In our next session, when we got to the Q&A discussion, I looked Harry straight in the eye and said, "Harry, you're a realtor. You're going to love this. It's all about location, location, location."

Having a Q&A in the Wrong Location
Can Devalue Your Entire Message

Just as the wrong location will devalue an otherwise great house, a Q&A in the wrong place will devalue an otherwise great presentation.

As Harry and I talked, he indicated that he understood the structure but still didn't quite see the big deal about not putting the Q&A at the end of the workshop. I offered him the following scenario for why the Q&A never goes at the end of the presentation: "People will remember best the first thing you do and the last thing you do. If the Q&A is the last thing you do, do you want your audience to remember the little woman in the back who asks where you got your shirt because her husband would like a shirt like yours since "he's hard to fit—are you hard to fit too?"

I continued, "Someone else might have a question about the first point you made. Another person might want to talk about a matter that is loosely related to the third point. All of this is fine—you want people to ask questions. However, the question about the shirt is completely off topic and will be the one question everyone remembers! Additionally, as the questions get further away from your message, people start holding their own private meetings; some are gathering their things to leave, checking phone messages, and others are leaving." Harry agreed that questions and comments all over the place was not the way he wanted to close out his workshop.

If the Q&A is handled poorly, the audience leaves and the message is devalued. The audience ends up remembering the Q&A more than the speech. The next section shows how the value of the message can be increased by moving the location of the Q&A.

Where to Put the Q&A in Your Message

You can increase the value of your message by simply putting the Q&A directly before the closing. Harry's issue was that he saw the Q&A as being separate from the actual workshop. If done right, a Q&A can enhance your message. Keep the closing as the last thing. Don't let the conversations about the shirt be the last thing your audience hears. Instead let your carefully crafted closing thoughts be the last thing your audience hears—and remembers.

Now that the Q&A is in the right location, it still won't be of much use if you have no questions to answer. There are methods to get your audience primed to ask questions.

Get Your Audience Ready to Ask Questions

Begin preparing for the Q&A long before you start speaking. Think it through in advance as to how you want to handle questions. Some speakers take questions as they're going along while others prefer to hold all questions until the Q&A period.

Although not always the case, my experience has been that most speakers who encourage the audience to ask questions at any time haven't prepared enough content (or any) and they're trying to use up the allotted time. Here's what I recommended to Harry and why.

Anticipate questions. Tell your audience up front that there will be a Q&A later on. Instruct them to write down their questions, and let them know you will be happy to answer them during the Q&A. Doing it this way addresses a few issues.

- Your audience now knows there will be a Q&A.
- Your audience has ample time to formulate their questions and eliminate the ones answered in your presentation.
- Your audience has a heads-up not to blurt out questions whenever they feel like it.

Often, allowing audience members to stop you and ask questions whenever they wish is beneficial to no one because the more questions you stop to deal with, the less content you can deliver. These audience members are cutting into instruction time. However, there will be times when you need to make exceptions; use your judgment. Most of the time, just ask them to write down their questions for you to address later. Once the audience is prepared to ask questions, make sure the questions don't take over the message.

Keep the Q&A from Taking over Your Message

Quantify. When you get to the Q&A, state how many questions you will entertain. Whether it's four or five questions, or more, this lets the audience know there are a limited number of questions so they can't afford to waste time with irrelevant ones. Be certain to say that you will wrap up your presentation after the Q&A so the audience knows it's not time to start leaving.

Avoid the trap of the Q&A that goes on and on with no clear ending in sight. Consider quantifying it another way in terms of how long you will take questions. You could say something like this: "I would like to take the next seven or eight minutes to address your questions before I close." Again, the audience knows there's a limited amount of time, and they can't wait for someone else to ask a question first.

*Avoid the trap of the Q&A that goes
on and on with no clear ending in sight.*

Don't ask. Inform. In other words, don't ask if there are questions; inform your audience that it is now time for questions by saying something like "What are your questions?" or "I'll take your questions now." Even though you have adjusted your Q&A, there are still a few more things to do to make a greater connection with your audience.

Have Your Audience Leave Fired up by Your Message, Not Confused by the Q&A

Remember, the goal is to keep the audience focused on your message. I asked Harry to put himself in the audience's seat and pretend that I was the speaker.

"Harry, how would you feel if I only answered questions from one section of the room and you happened not to be in the privileged section? What if my body language suggested that neither you nor your question was worth addressing? If I spent more time off topic than on, how would that impact the message?"

After some thought, Harry arrived at the following conclusions:

- The speaker should not favor one side of the room or the other. Encourage questions from all sides of the room so no one feels left out.
- Body language can speak volumes. When you take a question, don't point. Instead, recognize the person by extending your hand, elbow slightly bent, with your palm up, in the direction of the person asking the question. You're serving the audience, not demanding. Acknowledge and validate. Thank the person for the question. Tell them it's a good question. Smile. Raise your eyebrows a little. Look interested. Be interested.
- Repeat the question and rephrase if necessary. Sometimes audience members take a long time to ask a simple question. Repeat it so the other audience members can hear it, or rephrase it so they can understand it. After you have answered, ask the person who asked the question if you have satisfied their question or if your answer made sense or if they understood your answer. Generally this is not necessary, but if your response is in multiple parts, you

should let them know it has more than one part. If you want people to stay fired up about your message, don't douse it with stray responses. Keep your answers short, stay on topic, and provide opportunities for the audience to reflect back on key points in your message.

Recently, Harry shared with me about his revamped realtor workshops. "Dell, things have changed dramatically. Now I use my Q&A to reinforce what I have talked about. Because I have the Q&A right before the closing, and I have quantified it, my audience is eager to stay for the entire Q&A as well as my closing."

By putting the World Class Speaking skills into action, my client removed the frustration of conducting workshops that were doomed to fail. Harry gained the confidence necessary to conduct workshops that were clear, concise, and compelling from start to finish. Without a doubt, Harry was speaking better and closing bigger.

> *Just as the right house in the wrong location can diminish the value of the house, the Q&A in the wrong location can diminish the value of your speech.*

Just as the right house in the wrong location can diminish the value of the house, the Q&A in the wrong location can diminish the value of your speech.

Key Takeaways
- Never close with a Q&A.
- Anticipate and quantify questions.
- Stay on topic and let your responses enhance what you have said in your speech.
- Let your audience leave fired up by your message rather than confused by the Q&A.

Dell Self is a professional communicator, certified speaking coach, book coach, and author of eight books. As the founder of Speak Through Me Communications, Dell is committed to helping ministry leaders deliver messages that are clear, concise, and compelling. Contact Dell at www.SpeakThroughMe.com.

31

Practice: How to Take Your Presentation from Good to Great

Maureen Bell

An Olympic athlete, a fighter pilot, an opera singer, or any professional will practice over and over again before they get to their event. They will also make sure they train repeatedly in conditions similar to where they will perform.

The philosophy used by these professionals applies to public speaking as well. Repetition is the key to success in mastering any skill. What makes a professional go from good to great? The willingness to practice over and over again until they get it right.

As a presentation skills coach I often hear clients say "I'm better when I don't practice" or "I'll wing it" or "I practice so much that I begin to sound scripted and lose the spontaneity" or "I don't need to practice because I have the whole presentation in my head" and lastly "I don't have the time to practice."

The truth is that those people who practice, practice, and keep practicing get better and better. Like the Olympic athlete, they would not be at the top of their game if they did not practice. Practice is the difference between good and great, mediocre and magnificent. The aim of this chapter is to share with you powerful practice techniques that will ensure your practice sessions deliver a confident presentation.

Practice is important to develop the habits you want to use when speaking, particularly to get you through the beginning of your presentation when nerves are heightened.

> *Practice is the difference between good and great, mediocre and magnificent.*

Let's look at some of the practice mistakes people make. Some people:

- do not practice at all
- practice only in their head
- practice the beginning only
- practice once, thinking they have mastered the speech
- practice without using slides, props, or handouts

On the following pages we'll discover techniques to ensure your practice sessions emulate a real environment and are productive so you can take your presentations from good to great. At a glance, the techniques are:

- become comfortable with the spoken word
- make your practice as real as possible
- practice using an imaginary audience
- become comfortable with your stance and delivery
- practice using your voice
- time your presentation
- practice making mistakes
- practice the entire presentation, not just the start
- practice questions and answers
- practice using audiovisuals and props
- practice more advanced techniques (voice, movement)

Become Comfortable with the Spoken Word

Once you have your presentation written it is important to verbalize what you will be saying. How you write is very different from how you speak; therefore you must verbalize the presentation many times over to feel comfortable with the words, sentences, and format you have written.

You may stumble over certain words or phrases, or they don't feel comfortable when you say them. This is okay and the reason you need practice. Sometimes you will discover the arrangement of content is not flowing; you may need to move information around, changing your structure slightly. Once again, better now in practice than on presentation day.

Make Your Practice as Real as Possible

The aim of practice is to emulate your real environment as much as you can. This means practicing as you mean to deliver and even practicing in the environment where you will be speaking. If you have access to the presentation room, practice in it several times before you speak.

If this is not possible emulate that environment as much as possible. For example, you may be speaking in a client's boardroom or a conference facility in another state or part of the world, or perhaps in a room that is not accessible. If you are traveling to a destination to speak, allow time before the event to know your room and environment. Practice the night or morning before.

Set up your practice area as if it were the real thing. If you are standing while speaking, when you practice always stand up so that you are used to standing. If you are using slides, have your laptop in front of you with a remote clicker device. Have your notes near you for easy reference and to use as a guide if you lose your way.

Practice Using an Imaginary Audience

Speaking is all about the audience so when you practice imagine an audience right in front of you and speak to them. I have my clients set up their boardrooms or rooms at home with an imaginary audience. Be sure to use eye contact in conjunction with your presentation as you deliver your speech.

Become Comfortable with Your Stance and Delivery

Practice delivery so that when under pressure you will perform well. I recently had a client at a workshop who spoke beautifully; she engaged the audience with her words and voice. However, she moved forward and backward on one foot, which distracted the audience. Rather than focusing on her they began to focus on the sway. She needed to practice standing still or moving with purpose. The only way to overcome her distracting sway was through first acknowledging the sway and then practicing a better way of moving.

Practice Using Your Voice

If you use "ums" when speaking, you have to develop the habit of stopping at the end of your sentences, pausing, and starting again. This will only develop with practice. I used to say "um" when speaking and set myself a goal to never use the word again. So I focused on pausing at the end of a sentence or phrase where I would normally add an "um," and over a period of time I deleted this word from my vocabulary. They say it takes twenty-one days to form a habit so be patient, but also know that practice is important.

Time Your Presentation

You have been given a certain amount of time to speak. Good presenters use this time well and finish on time—not over time. Practicing your presentation out loud in front of an imaginary audience and timing it will ensure you deliver in the time allocated.

Get used to timing yourself so that you know where you should be at the major stages of your presentation and to eliminate hidden surprises. When you practice allow for:

- laughter from your audience (pause and pretend the audience is laughing)
- giving out handouts
- audience participation (if appropriate) and then asking for their attention once again
- passing around props, which will slow down your delivery

Key point: When you actually deliver the presentation in front of an audience it always goes longer than you timed during practice. The explanation for this is your delivery of "ums," "ahs," and pauses; audience involvement such as laughter and comments; and bringing them back to attention. Allow for the extra time. Build it into your overall presentation time.

Practice Making Mistakes

When you practice, if you make a mistake just keep going, don't start all over again. This will allow you to build your confidence knowing that you can make a mistake and get back on track without it being a big deal. It's likely to happen when you give your live presentation, and sometimes making mistakes allows you to change your delivery for the better.

Practice the Entire Presentation, Not Just the Start

The presentation you have to deliver may be quite lengthy: twenty minutes, thirty minutes, an hour or more. Finding the time to practice this over and over again is a challenge. Many people find they start practicing from the beginning, get interrupted, and then when they go back to the practice they start all over again. This develops a strong, well-rehearsed opening but does not allow enough time to develop the remainder of your presentation. To overcome this challenge, break your presentation into segments such as:

- opening
- first point
- second point
- third point
- question and answers
- close

Practice your presentation in segments or chunks; this is more realistic and manageable. For example, you may take time out to practice your introduction, a couple of hours later practice your first point, later in the day your second point, and so on until you have practiced all segments of your speech. This will ensure you have rehearsed all segments equally and that you are confident with the delivery of all parts of the presentation.

> *We are what we repeatedly do. Excellence,*
> *then, is not an act, but a habit.*
> **—Aristotle**

Practice Questions and Answers

Many people are daunted by the fact that they may be asked a question they will not know the answer to. My advice? Anticipate as many questions as possible and practice answering them. One good way to achieve this is by having colleagues ask you the questions and you providing an answer. If this is not possible, prepare a list of possible questions you may be asked during your presentation, then imagine an audience member asking you a question. Practice answering it out loud as if you were giving the presentation.

When an audience member asks a question, repeat the question back to all audience members. This will show you have understood the question and also ensure all audience members hear the question. Then proceed to answer the question.

Practice Using Audiovisuals and Props

Once you are comfortable with what you are saying, include your slides into your practice. Practice changing slides with a remote or manually on a laptop.

Practice instructing the group if you are using activities, discussions, or brainstorming sessions. For example, how many people do you want in a group? How much time will you allow for discussion?

If using a prop, practice holding the prop and passing it around. Know that the audience will touch and feel the prop; be sure to focus their attention on the prop rather than on you.

If you are using a whiteboard practice writing on the board with the pens and colors you will use in the real presentation.

Once you have the basics right...

Practice More Advanced Techniques (Voice, Movement)

Practice is the part of the process many presenters don't do. In many cases standing up and delivering their presentation in front of a group is the first verbal out-loud run, and it will show. The secret to practicing is that each time you say your presentation out loud you will improve it as you see what works and what does not work.

Knowing and understanding the skills to present effectively is not enough; they have to be practiced over and over again so that they become learned motor skills. Find an environment where you can practice on a regular basis to enhance your skills, which will lead to increased confidence.

Don't let the hard work of preparing your content and structure fail because you have not practiced how you will deliver. The only way to become a polished and confident presenter is to practice how you are going to present. It does take time and effort, but the rewards are huge.

Maureen Bell is the founder and CEO of Speak with Presence, a Sydney-based boutique consultancy that coaches business leaders and executives in the art of delivering phenomenal presentations. With a powerful program drawn from almost two decades of experience, Maureen helps high-performing individuals overcome their fears and stresses in the public arena. Her passion is to enable clients to master their voice, heart, and communication skills so they can influence and inspire others to make a difference.

Part 5

WORLD CLASS SELLING AND MARKETING

32

Two Steps to Earn Commitment to Your Coaching Business

Michael Davis

She called me at 3:15 on a Tuesday afternoon. "Michael, I understand you're a speech coach. My name is Sarah and I really need your help."

I said, "Tell me more, Sarah."

"If I want to get promoted in my job, I have to give presentations to clients. I'm really intimidated. I didn't used to be afraid like this. I won awards for speaking in college, but now that I'm in the business world, I freeze up when I have to talk to higher-ups or clients."

At this point I had a decision to make—either continue the conversation with Sarah and get more information, or tell her about all the services I offer and how I could help her.

Which would you do? Most coaches jump in and "sell" themselves. Unfortunately, they don't understand that at this early stage in the conversation you haven't gained the client's trust and confidence yet. You need to delve further into her world before she'll commit to you. That's what this chapter will teach you to do.

By the end of this chapter, you will know the foundational steps to earning a prospective client's confidence and how to position yourself as a speaking coach people should hire. You will learn:

- a two-step process that creates a need to do business with you
- a tool to create a mutually beneficial experience
- how to move from hourly fees to being properly paid for the value you provide

Why should you learn these concepts? Because they'll help you overcome the frustration many coaches feel from being underpaid and under-hired.

There are many reasons why people may balk at paying for coaching:

- They have preconceived notions about coaching and struggle to understand the value you provide.
- They're in self-preservation mode. They may have been burned by others. Their skepticism is a product of bad experiences—it's nothing personal against you.
- To keep from feeling "taken" they have developed pre-programmed responses. Your job is to get past those responses to uncover their real issues and determine if you are a good match for them.

Here are the keys to developing a deep and trusting relationship with prospective clients:

- **Uncover their pain.** People won't change (i.e., hire a coach) until they're uncomfortable and feel a *need* to change.
- **Talk about money.** Many coaches are uncomfortable talking about money, yet most people understand that you don't work for free. The longer you wait to talk about money, the more suspicious prospects will feel. Discuss money as soon as possible.
- **Learn their decision-making process.** How does the prospect decide whether he needs a coach? How does she decide who to hire?
- **Present a solution that eliminates their pain.**

So how do you do this? Start by using a two-step process that has worked for the most effective leaders, salespeople, and coaches since human beings first learned to speak:

1. Ask questions.
2. Close your mouth and listen.

It's that simple, but it's not that *easy.* If you're reading this, you may be a coach, and chances are good that you're also a *speaker.* You're conditioned to talk. And this means you probably want to tell people how much you can help them because that's what coaches do.

Learning to listen actively—rather than launching into "sales" mode— is a difficult habit to develop. With practice and repetition you can become an empathetic listener.

> *Learning to listen actively—rather than launching into "sales" mode—is a difficult habit to develop. With practice and repetition you can become an empathetic listener.*

World Class Questions

To develop this skill, use the following questioning "funnel." The concept is taken from the book *You Can't Teach a Kid to Ride a Bike at a Seminar* by sales trainer David Sandler. When you ask a series of questions, you gradually guide a prospective client to narrow her response to the core issues that are creating her problems.

These questions are merely a guide and not meant to be a word-for-word memorization. You might not need to ask every one. As you develop this skill, ask as many of the questions as possible, in the order given. With experience you'll use fewer questions and uncover problems quicker.

Question 1: Why is it important that you speak?
Question 2: Why do you feel you need coaching?
Question 3: What is your biggest challenge?

Question 4: How long has this been a problem?

Question 5: What actions have you taken to solve it?

Question 6: What were the results of those actions?

Question 7: If you continue to get these results, how will you feel?

Question 8: What is this costing you?

Question 9: What do you want to do about this?

Keys to Making These Questions Work Effectively

Don't ask them in rapid-fire succession; that will make your prospect feel as if he's being interrogated ["Where were you on the night in question? Can anyone vouch for you? Did you know the victim? Where did you hide the murder weapon?"]

In the conversation that started this chapter, Sarah told me that not speaking well was "hurting my career." I asked, "How long has this been a problem?" "Michael, I've been with this company two years. The problem seems to be getting worse. If I don't get over this, I will have *no chance* to advance in this company."

At this point, many coaches stop asking questions. They assume they know what a client means because they put their own interpretation on phrases like *advance in this company.* However, that term can have different meanings. Until a client clearly defines the problem *in her world,* and why she needs to solve it, it will be difficult to get her to commit time and money to coaching. This leads to the second key…

When you don't understand what you're hearing, make this statement: "Please tell me more." This encourages the client to elaborate and, in turn, can compel that person to divulge the deeper emotional issues underlying the problem. When they share these emotions, they are building trust in you.

In my conversation with Sarah, my follow-up statement was "Sounds as if advancing in the company is important to you. Tell me more about that." She replied, "Well, advancing means I get to work one-on-one with clients, and that's what I really love to do. Working with them directly means I get to use my creativity and build good relationships with them. It's also the best way to earn bonuses."

Now I understood why this was important to Sarah. This led to the most important question…

"What is this costing you?" Of all the questions in the series, this is the one that uncovers the pain that will compel them to take action—in this case, hire you as a coach. It is important to note that this question will *not* work if you ask it too soon in the conversation.

Imagine that you just met someone and he says, "So, you're having a tough time at work. What's that costing you?" Chances are you'd be a little put off and wouldn't trust him.

"What is this costing you?" should be asked once you've developed rapport with someone. With practice, you'll sense when the client is comfortable with you. The question will often elicit a response related to money. What you want to elicit here is the *emotional* cost to the client. In Sarah's case, I asked, "Other than money, what is this costing you?" After a thoughtful pause, she said, "It's costing me in my career… it's hurting my confidence…it's hurting my self-esteem."

Bingo! Now I understood the root of her pain. This was developed through empathy and patience in listening to her responses.

At first glance this process is a pre-scripted conversation. However, with repetition the questions will feel less scripted. They will become a guidepost to encourage your clients to open up and lead to your goal of understanding the underlying reasons for his problem.

The last question is **"What do you want to do about this?"** Traditional salespeople usually cringe at this one. You can't ask that question, Michael! You'll be giving up control of the conversation, and you can't close the sale.

Consider this: if you've gone through this series of questions and have uncovered the source of the client's problem, there is no need for a hard "close" or drawn-out process of overcoming objections. If the client gets to this point, he wants to solve the problem. The only question left to answer is "How much is your fee?"

> *If the client gets to this point, he wants to solve the problem.*
> *The only question left to answer is "How much is your fee?"*

How to Structure Your Fees

There are a number of ways to structure fees, with no right or wrong method. However, the vast majority of coaches are *grossly* underpaid because they fail to use the questioning process above; thus they don't create the need for their services.

The challenge with pricing speech coaching is that you're providing an intangible service. For instance, it's impossible to quantify the value of a better speech, improved storytelling skills, or increased confidence.

To be fairly compensated for your coaching you must have the right mindset. There is no better authority on this than consultant Alan Weiss, who works with several world champion and highly successful professional speakers. If his ideas are good enough for them, they're good enough for you and me.

In his book *Value-Based Fees* (which I *highly* recommend), Alan offers a plethora of great ideas. Some of the most important:

Never Charge by the Hour

Hourly fees turn you into a commodity. If you price yourself in this manner, people are more likely to negotiate your time and your fee. For example, a prospective client might say, "I don't think I need to learn how to structure a speech. I just need some delivery tips, so I'd like to buy forty minutes of your time." This is not cost-effective for you, and it cheats your client out of getting the full scope of your knowledge.

Focus on Results

Results are more easily determined when you clearly understand the client's problem. For example, I asked Sarah, "How much would a promotion be worth to you in the next twelve months?" After careful thought, she said, "Probably eight to ten thousand dollars."

Now we had a reference point for her to compare her problem and my fees. Best of all, *she* provided the number. To borrow an old sales adage, if *you* say it, the client can doubt you; if *she* says it, it's fact. Compared to what her speaking problems were costing her, my coaching fee was comparably small.

Never Offer the Option of Whether to Hire You as a Coach

Instead, offer different packages of service. This gives the prospective client choices on *how* to hire you under criteria that best meet his situation.

Structuring your offer in this manner increases the likelihood that you'll be hired. You haven't given a yes-or-no option; you're letting the client choose the best option for him, but each one means you'll be hired. These are the packages I offer:

- **Package 1**—*Essentials of Creating and Delivering a World Class Story.* This includes the fundamentals of structuring a story (the World Class Speaking 9-C formula), opening with a bang, concluding with a call to action, plus an extra session in which the client delivers the story, followed by a debriefing and recommendations for improving the delivery. This typically consists of four sessions.

- **Package 2**—*Essentials of Creating and Delivering a World Class Speech.* This includes the elements of *discovering* your speech topic; creating a logical, easy-to-follow *structure*; uncovering the essential *material* to support your main points; and how to deliver in a dynamic style. This typically consists of six sessions.
- **Package 3**– *Six- and twelve-month retainers for coaching.* These include all elements of Package 3. This choice makes coaching available on an as-needed basis for clients. There are stipulations for issues such as maximum number of sessions, minimum amount of time notice before each session, locations for sessions, etc. These are worked out between the clients and me before we enter into the agreement.

The fees I charge have increased since my first year. Before being introduced to the wisdom of Alan Weiss, I charged hourly fees of $100. After Alan, I adjusted to these packages:

- 2 sessions for $250
- 3 sessions for $350
- 5 sessions for $500

I also offered a 10 percent discount if clients prepaid for all sessions. Each year I have increased my fees. As of January 2014, packages are priced as follows:

- Package 1 = $ 997
- Package 2 = $1,597
- Package 3 = negotiated with each client

A common question I'm asked is "When do you know it's time to raise your fees?" Again, there is no right or wrong answer. I believe that clients *always* receive many times the value from my coaching than what they pay. I typically raise my fees when I am comfortable with the current fee structure. I want to feel slightly uncomfortable when quoting fees. Why? Because I'm moving into a higher level of client. Not everyone can pay that higher fee. But the ones who can tend to build long-term relationships and can introduce you to other people like them.

A concept to keep in mind: you are *always* delivering more value than the client is paying for. When you internalize this belief, you will have the courage to ask for higher fees. These fees mean both the client and you benefit from your coaching.

I leave you with this final thought. There are many people like Sarah in the world. They need the coaching you provide. They know they are being held back by their own fears, lack of knowledge, or lack of skills. When they come to you, avoid the temptation to sell yourself right away. Begin with a question-based conversation that will help you understand the root of the client's problem. Build rapport and trust, and you'll develop a solid foundation for a coaching experience that is mutually beneficial—and most likely will open the door to many more opportunities.

Michael Davis, the Speaking MD, is a passionate student of the art of public speaking and training. His company, Speaking CPR, was founded on the principle that the most important marketing tool you have is you, and that becoming an effective communicator is a key to long-term personal and career success. He provides individual and group training for speaking and storytelling. For more information, visit SpeakingCPR.com.

33

How to Make an Offer When You Speak without Sounding Scared, Slimy, or Slick

Deirdre Van Nest

Imagine for a moment that you could forever answer the question "Where is my next client going to come from?" How does that make you feel? Excited? Relieved? Well, if you use speaking as a marketing strategy to generate leads for your business, you can answer that question once and for all. How do I know? I've done it and my clients have too. Here are a few examples:

- I sold more than $11,000 worth of my home-study course Speak and Get Patients™ with one seventy-five-minute talk.
- At a sixty-minute talk my client Amy, a Financial Advisor, had eighty-five out of one hundred attendees signed up for her College Planning Strategy Session. Her session led to thousands of dollars in immediate revenue and even more through the client relationships she forged thereafter.
- My clients Dr. Becky Perry and her partner Dr. Matt Hanson brought in 103 new patients from one 60-minute talk. This talk doubled their practice almost overnight.

The examples above may sound dramatic, and I don't want to oversell what speaking can do. Your results will depend on your talk, your skill level, your audience, and your offer. So let's be ultra conservative. If you could bring in one or two clients every time you spoke, would that excite you? If so, I encourage you to use speaking as a marketing strategy.

There is a catch however. To reap the rewards speaking can bring, you need to structure your talk so that it fosters leads and grows your business. It's not enough to know how to write a keynote. It's also not enough to be an engaging speaker. A lead-generating speech is a different animal. To rely on speaking as a marketing strategy that consistently brings you business you must know how to write a talk that *educates*, *engages*, and *sells*.

> *To reap the rewards speaking can bring, you need to structure your talk so that it fosters leads and grows your business.*

This type of talk has seven key elements. In this chapter we will discuss key pieces of the fourth element: How to make an offer without sounding scared, slimy, or slick. (For a description of the other six elements, download my free report "How to Get More Warm Leads in One Hour Than Most Business Owners Get in One Month" at www.speakandgetresults.com/gift.)

In this chapter you will learn:

- why making an offer is critical if you want to grow your business through speaking
- how to master your mindset to avoid feeling uncomfortable or apologetic when making your offer
- how to get people to accept your offer on the spot
- what to say when transitioning into and making your offer

Making Offers Is Critical to Growing Your Business through Speaking

To use speaking as an effective marketing tool, you need to make an offer. I've spoken with many presenters who think if they hear me speak and want my services, they'll reach out to me. Those presenters are relying on the audience to figure it out. But the reality is that your audience won't figure it out. Take my client Mike for example. He spoke for years and rarely made offers; occasionally someone might contact him about his services after a talk. Sure, he increased his visibility, but Mike was tired of the low return on his talks.

A few months after he enrolled in my Speak and Get Results™ program, he gave a talk where he used my B.I.G.™ formula for making his offer. Twelve out of forty-eight people took him up on his offer! That's a 25 percent conversion rate compared to his previous nonexistent conversion rate. He was thrilled!

So you know you need to make an offer, but you might be asking "What is an offer?" An offer is inviting your audience to take a next step with you. Some examples include offering tips, e-zines, strategy sessions, products, books, or programs. What you offer will depend on your current business goals.

Master Your Mindset to Avoid Feeling Uncomfortable or Apologetic

I was sitting at a coffee shop with my client Lee, an international speaker and business consultant, when he said, "I don't want to be out there hawking my books! Can't I just have the event organizer sell them for me?" Maybe you can relate to Lee. Nobody wants to "hawk" their products or services, and because of that many professionals are scared to make offers. They don't want to feel like the dreaded used-car salesman and so they make excuses such as "I ran out of time" or "it just didn't feel right" or "this audience wasn't right for that."

This fear is so common I named it Offer Aversion Syndrome (OAS), and I'll tell you a secret: I too used to suffer from OAS. I avoided making offers for years because I was afraid of rejection. I finally got sick of losing opportunities so I determined to get past OAS. I want to help you do that too.

Three things will help you move past OAS. The first is to just get out there and do it. It's like exercise. You've got to build muscle and tolerance. The second is shifting your mindset when making offers, and last is learning how to structure your talk so that it's natural to make an offer that converts the audience into leads. Let's start with your mindset:

Imagine this scenario: You're at your favorite restaurant for a cooking demonstration. As you watch the chef and smell the ingredients, your mouth starts to water. You're excited to taste the food. You even start thinking about having a dinner party next weekend so you can try your hand at making the chef's special dish.

But you get to the end of the demonstration and something's not right. You realize, Oh no, the chef has not told me what the "special" ingredient is that he's mentioned all evening long. I can't make this at home without it! Not only that, but after the food is prepared, you're not allowed to sample it.

How would you feel if this happened? Ripped off? I would! Now imagine yourself as the chef and your offer as the special ingredient. If you give a powerful talk that entices your audience without telling them how to get more, you're shortchanging them. You are doing to your audience what the chef did to you.

So the key is to stop telling yourself I don't want to be sales-y and instead start thinking, I'm offering something powerful, an opportunity to transform. It's their choice if they want to take me up on that or not. This simple shift will be critical to your success in making offers from the stage. The more you practice believing that your audience wants what you have to offer and rejecting your old OAS beliefs, the easier it will be to make your offer.

How to Get People to Accept Your Offer on the Spot

How you structure your talk is critical for your comfort and your conversion rate when making offers. We won't cover every detail of the structure, but I have included three overarching principles to get you started. To convert audience members into leads or paying clients on the spot, you have to be B.I.G.™

1. Begin with the End in Mind

Have you ever heard or given a talk that sounded like one-part instruction and one-part sales pitch? Most people don't like to hear that kind of talk. It's also the kind of talk most presenters try to avoid. For example, my client Dr. Becky and her partner Dr. Matt used to give a talk where they provided helpful information about nutrition. At the end they made an offer for a chiropractic exam. Rarely did people sign up for that exam because they didn't understand why they needed the exam in the first place. You see, Dr. Becky and Dr. Matt offered numerous insights on how to improve nutritional habits, but chiropractic care wasn't included as a method for achieving overall wellness. You can avoid their mistake by beginning with the end in mind.

Instead of writing your talk and then tacking on an offer at the end, write your talk knowing the exact next step you want your audience to take. Then write content that leads your audience to the conclusion, "I want his offer so I can apply this information to a deeper level in my life!" In Drs. Becky and Matt's case, once they rebuilt their talk—connecting how chiropractic care helps absorb nutrients in the body—their conversion rate skyrocketed to 70 percent!

2. Invite Buy-In

If you want people to say yes to your offer you have to lead your audience to "buy-in." You do this by evoking an emotional response in them. One of the most effective ways to do this is by using the World Class Speaking "Then, Now, and How Storytelling" formula. You may have heard the adage "facts tell but stories sell." It's true. Stories tap into people's emotions and people buy first based on emotions and then validate their decision with logic. It's not enough to supply information. You have to make your audience feel something.

A Then/Now/How story will do just that. I recommend you add this story to your opening or first point so you can establish credibility for your product or service early on. Later in your presentation you can callback to the results the characters in your story received. For a detailed description of how to create your Then/Now/How story, go to chapter 36 of this book.

3. Give a Precise Next Step

If you want people to say yes on the spot versus do nothing (or just ask for your card) do the following when making your offer:

1. Provide an easy-to-read order form for each person.
2. Do not offer more than two items or people may get overwhelmed and confused. For example, I often offer my free report that comes with twenty-six tips to Speak and Get Results™ (you can see this by going to www.speakandgetresults.com/gift) and a complimentary Speak and Get Results™ strategy session.
3. Create urgency and give them a reason to buy today. Offer a special-event-only price, put a limit on how many you have available, or offer a bonus to buy or sign up today.
4. Give specific sign-up instructions. If you want your audience to check the boxes on a form and provide contact info to indicate they're interested in your offer, tell them that. If you want them to meet you at the back table after your talk, tell them that. Don't leave anything to chance. Spell everything

out step-by-step. This sounds simple but I've seen many presenters leave out this critical step and when they do they are leaving money on the table.

What to Say When Transitioning into and Making Your Offer

One area most presenters struggle with is how to transition from their content to the offer without sounding like they're going into sales mode. In fact, knowing how to do this one thing can go a long way toward helping you recover from OAS. So I want to give you an idea of what an offer may sound like, including how to transition into it.

Let's pretend I've just finished making my last point and my offer is my free tips and a strategy session. I would say:

Everything you learned here today will help you become a more effective speaker and help you bring in more business when you speak. But we have only scratched the surface. If you want results like Dr. Becky (she is the subject of my Then, Now, and How story) has had then you'll really want to dig into the entire Speak and Get Results™ system and learn it step-by-step. To do that I have two free resources to get you started. [Someone now hands out my order form.]

The first is my 26 Tips to Speak and Get Results™. If you check box number one and fill in your name and email address, every month you'll get two short tips from me helping you grow your business through speaking. The second resource is a complimentary Speak and Get Results™ strategy session. Now this is not for everyone; this is for you if you are serious about using speaking as a marketing strategy. In your session you will learn the specific speaking skills you need to work on to grow your business through speaking. And if it seems like we're a fit, you'll discover how our program works and if it can help you get from where you are now to where you want to be in your business.

I have cleared six priority spots on my calendar for this group. The way to get one of those sessions is to check box two and then fill in your contact info at the bottom of the form. So to get your tips and strategy session come see me at that table [point to it] at the end of my talk. I've got my schedule here so you can sign up today for your session.

[Now you would move into your close. Note: your offer is not your close.]

> *Imagine giving a talk where your audience rushes to your table to sign up for your offer. Imagine walking out of a talk with new leads and/or new business.*

And that's it! By using the B.I.G.™ formula throughout your talk you make it easy to move into and present the offer in a way that is helpful and authentic.

Imagine giving a talk where your audience rushes to your table to sign up for your offer. Imagine walking out of a talk with new leads and/or new business. And imagine how great it will feel to see clients consistently on your schedule and no longer worry about where your next client will come from. It has happened for me and my clients over and over again, and when you use these formulas it will happen for you!

Deirdre Van Nest, owner of Accelerated Performance, LLC and creator of the Speak and Get Results™ Business Building Blueprint, is a certified World Class Speaking™ coach and a professional speaker for a variety of Fortune 500 companies. Her specialty is helping business owners get more warm leads in one hour than most get in one month. To learn more go to www.acceleratemyperformance.com or www.speakandgetresults.com

34

Becoming a
TEDx Speaker

William Reed

TED Has Changed the World of Presentations

Over the last thirty years a quiet revolution has changed the face of professional speaking, led by the nonprofit organization TED—a grassroots initiative launched in 1984 as a conference to unite people and ideas in technology, entertainment, and design. Today its scope has grown far beyond that, and the TED stage is a coveted "feather in the cap" for leaders and thinkers and artists at the top of their game. TED is a celebration of diversity and excellence and an agent of social change.

TED has raised the standard for public speaking through its signature style of

- speakers on stage without podium or notes
- simple slides that tell a story
- personal and intimate communication
- no selling from the stage
- emotional takeaway
- ideas worth sharing, recorded and archived for the world to see

TED Curator Chris Anderson says in his article "How to Give a Killer Presentation" (*Harvard Business Review*, June 2013) that "a successful talk is a little miracle—people see the world different afterward." The eighteen-minute or shorter format challenges speakers to deliver an appealing mix of persuasion and narrative brought to life with multimedia or live demonstrations. Although TED topics often touch on technical issues or specialized knowledge, the message must be brought home to the live audience as well as the global audience who may watch the video. Authenticity and originality are paramount.

> *A TEDx Talk is an excellent opportunity to share your ideas on the world stage, to position yourself in your field, and to clarify your message.*

A TEDx Talk is an excellent opportunity to share your ideas on the world stage, to position yourself in your field, and to clarify your message. It is an important opportunity for personal branding, which is why so many people now seek to become a TED speaker. However, this undertaking is not to be taken lightly. To do a TEDx Talk justice takes a lot more time and energy than you might imagine. If you don't prepare adequately, your lack of preparation will be evident on video for the world to see. TEDx organizers make efforts to help you put your best foot forward. They select and audition speakers as well as provide coaching and guidelines for a TED-style talk. But ultimately it is up to each speaker to prepare and rehearse for their eighteen minutes of fame.

How to Get Selected as a TEDx Speaker

A TEDx event is an independently organized TED event. You can find information on TEDx events around the world at www.ted.com/tedx, including videos of previous speakers. If you want to become a TEDx speaker, understand that it is a highly competitive and selective process. You have a greater chance of being selected if you understand what event style the TEDx organizers are expected to maintain under their license, the theme of the scheduled event, and who will make the final decision on speaker selection. This information is partly posted on the organizer's website or made available to candidates.

During Anderson's presentation on "What Makes a Great TED Talk," given to more than one hundred TEDx organizers from forty-three countries at TEDGlobal 2013, he made it clear that TED is not interested in *motivational* speakers, telling the organizers, "Just say no. We're not interested in inspiring talks. We're interested in minds being shifted. What is the core idea that you have that is fresh?" This reflects not just TED policy but a shift in what audiences are looking for from speakers. There is more room for new voices and fresh ideas and less tolerance for sales and self-promotion.

If you know someone connected to the event, it helps to have a personal introduction. If you do not live close to the event, or if the event is being hosted in a foreign country, your interview will likely be conducted on Skype. Most TEDx events have limited budgets, so you may only be reimbursed for local travel and lodging. Nevertheless, if you prepare well it is worth the investment for what you will learn and what you will have to show others for your effort.

The best way to gain the confidence of the interviewer is to ask good questions, demonstrate that you understand, and show them why you are a good fit for their theme. Videos of your previous speaking engagements can help if relevant to the theme, and if the quality works in your favor. Endorsements and experience are helpful, but ultimately TEDx organizers want to know if you will live up to their expectations. They are taking a chance on you. Show them that you understand this, and be respectful of their deadlines and requests. They will want to see your slides and your script well enough in advance of the talk that they can advise or coach you as needed.

The TEDx organizer's website will feature your photo and profile, so study how other speakers have been introduced and provide something that fits the style. There will likely be a Facebook page for the event as well, which offers information on incremental updates. This can be a way to build anticipation among your own friends and associates. Some TEDx events are streamed live, but it can take up to a month after the event to get the videos edited and posted to the site. The purpose of editing is to create a blend of the best camera angles, close-ups, and slide shots and sometimes to add subtitles. Once posted, you have a permanent link to your talk that you can use for promotional efforts and refer to people.

How to Prepare and Rehearse Your TEDx Talk

Once you have been selected as a TEDx speaker, the clock starts ticking. Your success depends to a large extent on how well you use the time to prepare and polish your message, rehearsing and refining your presentation until everything flows and looks natural. Do not underestimate the importance of preparation and rehearsal. Most less successful TEDx presentations result from underestimating the importance of what happens before you step onstage.

> *Do not underestimate the importance of preparation and rehearsal. Most less successful presentations result from underestimating the importance of what happens before you step onstage.*

The biggest evidence of insufficient preparation is running out of time or going over the allotted time, something painfully obvious to the audience. Another sign of non-readiness is the speaker calling attention to mistakes, such as reading or being on the wrong slide. If you do make a mistake, take it in stride and maintain your poise. You will get *one* rehearsal onsite, but all the speakers need to rehearse, so there is not much time to make changes at that late hour.

How much time should you use to prepare and rehearse? For a basic business presentation I recommend a ratio of ten hours of preparation for a presentation of one hour or less. For a TEDx Talk I recommend closer to fifty hours of preparation. If you are acting in a play, it might be closer to one hundred hours of rehearsal. Here are eight ways to spend that time wisely.

- **Clarify your message.** If you cannot clearly state your message in thirty seconds, you will not be able to explain it clearly in eighteen minutes. However, this may not be easy when you first start preparing. Like a work of sculpture, it takes time to remove the excess material that obscures your message.
- **Find your passion.** If you do not feel passionate about sharing your message, you should not take it to the stage. Passion not only gives you the energy you need to prepare intensively, it also helps the audience to share your energy and emotions.
- **Polish your presentation.** To ensure that your message makes sense to your audience, be very clear about the *purpose* of your talk, help them *remember*

it with anchors such as illustrations and metaphors, make it *relevant* to the listeners' lives, and give it *impact* with a powerful opening and closing.

- **Prepare yourself as a presenter.** Rehearse and record yourself. Get feedback on your *posture* for poise and professionalism, your *body language* and gestures for depth and expression, your *eye contact* for audience engagement, and your *voice* for emotional engagement. Ultimately, *you* are the presentation.

- **Master your stories.** The most effective way to get your message across is through stories. There are many ways to improve your storytelling style: develop different *types* of stories, use *metaphors*, write and practice your *script*, audio or video *record* your stories, make *illustrations* of the poster scenes in your story, use *humor* where appropriate, incorporate Craig Valentine's *9 C's of Storytelling* (curiosity, circumstances, characters, conflict, cure, change, carryout message, call backs, and conversations), and study the *resources* that can make you a better speaker (recommended resources listed below).

- **Make a TEDx Talk file.** Keep all of your notes, apps, recordings, scripts, and reference resources in one place, ideally on an iPad or tablet that you can carry with you. Be creative in finding new places to rehearse your material— mentally or physically—such as coffee shops, parks, long walks, or before going to sleep. If you live and breathe your message for several months before your TEDx Talk, it will flow naturally. As with Craig Valentine when he delivered the talk that made him the 1999 World Champion of Public Speaking, it should feel like *deja vu*, as though you had already been on that stage a thousand times.

- **Practice the parts.** Break your talk down into manageable sections, and give loving attention to each of the parts. They will gradually come together as a whole. The most important reason to practice your talk as a whole is to get a sense for how long eighteen minutes is and to make sure you can comfortably deliver your message in or just under that time. A digital clock shows the speaker the time elapsed.

- **Enjoy the process.** Enjoy every aspect of the process, from preparation to rehearsal to performance. Your enjoyment will naturally engage your audience, and your performance will be preserved for posterity in the TEDx video archives online.

As Craig Valentine says, make your TEDx Talk part of your Hall of Fame, not Hall of Shame. The best way to do this is to follow the eight points listed above and leave yourself ample time to prepare and rehearse.

Finally, imagine and strive for three things:

1. **Give a TEDx Talk that you can be proud of.** This will clarify your sense of mission, give you greater confidence, and share your ideas with the world.

2. **Continue to evolve and share your message.** Your TEDx Talk is the beginning not the end of the process. Find ways to reach more people with your message. Use it to launch a new career, write a book, or initiate a project.

3. **Show your gratitude.** Although your efforts are important, nothing can be achieved without the support and understanding of your family, friends, coach, event organizers, and most of all your audience. Show them your love and respect.

View My TEDx Talks

- "Physical Finesse through Nanba" (http://youtu.be/Imyj85h8m2Y). My first TEDx Talk was on Nanba to connect mind and body (delivered in Japanese with English subtitles) at TEDxKG, on June 30, 2013, at Kwansei Gakuin University, Japan.
- "Restoring Natural Movement through Nanba" (http://www.youtube.com/watch?v=-BLhcIRxhck). My second TEDx Talk was on Nanba as the solution to the sedentary syndrome (delivered in English) at TEDxTrondheim, on September 28, 2013, held in Trondheim, Norway.

Recommended Resources

1. www.ted.com. This website is the source for hundreds of videos of TED speakers around the world, organized by events and searchable by themes such as persuasive, ingenious, and fascinating and categories such as technology, global issues, and business. Most of the talks come with full transcripts and are available with subtitles in dozens of languages.

2. www.ted.com/tedxTEDx. TEDx events are independently organized licensed events around the world that follow the TED format. Usually organized around a theme, TEDx events provide an opportunity for people

in many fields to share the TED platform. Events are archived and posted on YouTube.

3. TED Talks are viewable on smart phones and tablets. TEDict is an excellent app for downloading and studying your favorite TED Talks.

4. *Talk Like TED: The 9 Public-Speaking Secrets of the World's Top Minds* by Carmine Gallo.

5. *How to Deliver a TED Talk: Secrets of the World's Most Inspiring Presentations,* revised and expanded new edition, with a foreword by Richard St. John and an afterword by Simon Sinek, by Jeremey Donovan.

6. *How to Deliver a Great TED Talk: Presentation Secrets of the World's Best Speakers* (Kindle edition) by Akash Karia.

7. *Speeches That Will Leave Them Speechless: An ABC Guide to Magnifying Your Speaking Success* by Kathryn MacKenzie.

8. An iPad or tablet. It is important to have a portable digital means to record your talk, write scripts, create slides, draw illustrations, make notes, and store reference books. Rehearsal is the key to success in any presentation, and it will help to have all your notes and practice materials in one place.

One Final Thought

You may not have many opportunities to speak in public. Perhaps you feel it may not be worth the extra effort to speak on a TEDx stage. However, consider the words of author/speaker Patricia Fripp: "Outside of the privacy of your own home, all speaking is 'public speaking.' There is no such thing as 'private speaking.'" You never know when you will be asked to present on a stage beyond your previous experience or comfort zone. Presentations can help or hinder your career opportunities, so it is best to be prepared. If you aim higher and put yourself through the extra trouble, your communication will improve at every level. You will be a better speaker in the boardroom and a better conversation partner at the dinner table. Stretch yourself, prepare properly, and do your best to share your message with the world.

William Reed is a two-time TEDx speaker and corporate speaking coach who has lived for many decades in Japan. Completely bilingual and a bestselling author, he has experience in many areas of communication including a long-running newspaper column, translation, and television. He also has a seventh-degree black belt in Aikido. Reach him at info@williamreed.jp or on the Web at www.williamreed.jp.

35

Copyright, Trademark—
What Should You Do?

Jocelyne Vézina

I n the course of your speaking career, you'll no doubt face the questions "Should I copyright this material...or trademark it? And what's the difference between the two?" This chapter is designed to help you decide whether you should pursue trademarking or copyrighting; it is not intended to give you legal advice. I am not a trademark lawyer. I am using my personal experience from the corporate world to show you where it's appropriate to protect your work.

This chapter answers the following questions:

- What is intellectual property?
- What should you copyright or trademark?
- Should you do it yourself or hire a lawyer?
- What are the steps to filing for a trademark or copyright?
- Who polices the misuse of your trademark?

Do the same rules apply to the Internet?

There are international agreements such as the Berne Convention for copyright that protects each member state's intellectual property (with 165 country members as of March 2012) and establishes minimum standards for copyright laws.

What Is Intellectual Property?

According to entrepreneur.com intellectual property is: "The ownership of ideas. Unlike tangible assets to your business such as computers or your office, intellectual property is a collection of ideas and concepts."

In North America, you can protect your ideas through patents (e.g. a product design), trademarks (e.g. the name of your company or its logo), or a copyright (e.g. a course you have created, a CD you have recorded, or your website).

Trademarks and copyrights are the best tools for you to protect your ideas. Keep in mind, however, that because you are dealing with ideas and not something tangible, even these tools have limitations.

> *Trademarks and copyrights are the best tools for you to protect your ideas. Keep in mind, however, that even these tools have limitations.*

A copyright will protect your document and give you the exclusive right to copy it, modify it (such as creating a CD or DVD from it), publicize it as a book or e-book, distribute it through a distributor or your website, and perform it.

Think about the last book you read. On the copyright page you always see a small paragraph that reads: "No part of this book..." You know the paragraph I'm talking about!

According to entrepreneur.com, "A trademark is like a brand name. It is any word(s) or symbol(s) that represent a product to identify and distinguish it from other products in the marketplace. A trademark word example would be 'Rollerblades.' A trademark symbol would be the peacock used by NBC."

You could trademark the name of your book in a manner similar to what has been done with the For Dummies® series. If you look closely you can see the ® after the For Dummies®. The For Dummies® is even in a different font and color to emphasize the trademark. However, the content of those books cannot be trademarked, only copyrighted. The icons used in the books could also be trademarked as long as they are unique and distinct from any other icon used. For example, the little target icon with the arrow in the middle that is used throughout the books to indicate a "tip" could be trademarked if it was designed specifically for this series of books and was never used anywhere else before in other context.

The content can only be copyrighted because there is nothing unique or distinct in the way the books are written. They use the same sentence structure as any other books; there is nothing unique in the vocabulary used—only the ideas presented and the interpretations given are unique.

The distinction between a patent, a trademark, and a copyright is clear. If you invented a new widget you could patent its design, trademark its name, and copyright the instructions on what components were used and how to build it.

In our world of ideas and concepts the line might not be so clear. The question becomes:

What Should You Copyright or Trademark?

A document, CD, or DVD you have created—that represents your ideas and interpretations of a concept—can be copyrighted. A song, a movie, and its music that you have created can be copyrighted as well. Keynotes, speeches, and PowerPoint presentations that you have created can also be copyrighted.

A copyrighted document should have the following symbol attached to it: ©. This is a universally recognized symbol that will help you defend your rights should you find somebody copying your creation.

A trademark is the way to go if you wish to protect a logo, a name for your business, or a slogan that you have created and want to use in all your marketing material. The trademark goes beyond just protecting your rights; it speaks to the integrity of the brand you are creating. Anything that represents your brand should be protected. If you ever want to sell your business, think about the added value it would have if its name is a recognized trademark.

There are two symbols used in a trademark. The TM indicates that you have started the process of registering the mark in your country and are serious about defending it against infringers. However, you are not protected yet. The ® does protect you from infringers. You cannot use the ® if your mark is not registered; in the UK it is an offense under the UK Trade Marks Act 1994. In the United States, you can lose your trademark if you don't use the ® after you have received your registration. Sometimes you may want to register in the United States in the anticipation that you might use it. Be aware that the United States will ask you, at the five-year anniversary of the registration, to prove that you are using the trademark.

When registering a mark you should look at the Nice Classification (classifies goods and services) to determine under which class or classes you should apply. The World Intellectual Property Organization (WIPO) administers the Nice Agreement. As of January 2012, 83 states were members of the Nice Agreement. However, more than 150 trademark offices around the world apply the Nice Classification. The classification has 34 classes of goods and 11 classes of services (source of statistics: www.wipo.int/classifications). Of course the big advantage is that it simplifies the process when you want to register your mark outside of your country.

The symbol should be placed after the name or at the upper right corner of your logo. If you are going to trademark your work, make sure every piece of marketing material or correspondence (even an email to a friend) where your logo or name appears has the symbol attached. By doing that you are telling the world you are serious about your trademarks.

The fees associated with a registration are at least twofold: the fee to the governing entity and the fee to your lawyer. Those fees vary widely from country to country. Check with the trademark office in your country. You also have a renewable fee. In India it is every ten years, in Canada, every fifteen years. Check your trademark office to know when the renewal fee is due. Do not be late in renewing; you could lose your registration, and somebody who has been watching can register your mark for themselves.

Should You Do It Yourself or Hire a Lawyer?

It is getting easier to copyright or trademark your work, especially online. Yet it is getting more complicated than ever to protect your intellectual property. The Internet has made finding your work easy but also easy to copy.

Although it is expensive to hire a lawyer, in the long run it might be a better approach than to do it yourself. In the European Union you will need to hire a local lawyer if you are a foreigner. You will not be allowed to register a trademark by yourself via the Internet.

Before you go to a lawyer you can do some research to make sure your idea or name or logo is not in use by someone already. Here are some of the resources you can use:

- a phone book
- Google (search online for the name)
- a trademark office database
- a trademark publication
- an independent database such as LexisNexis, Dialog, or Compu-Mark (found on Wikipedia.com)

Research as many variations as possible of the spelling of the name or logo you are trying to trademark. As you read above there are classes in which you can trademark a name or logo. Be sure to research every class that applies to you.

Once you have done your research and feel confident that nobody is using your name, consider hiring a lawyer.

A lawyer will also be helpful if you want to register outside of your country. He or she can find a competent lawyer in the other country. Between the two of them, they will take care of the registration—for a fee of course. Don't be alarmed if it takes much longer than you anticipated. In some countries such as Brazil it can take up to five years if you are a foreigner.

Too expensive to hire a lawyer? Decide to do it yourself!

What Are the Steps to Filing for a Trademark or Copyright?

According to the USPTO (the United States Patent and Trademark Office www. uspto.gov) here are the steps to register in the United States of America.

1. Determine whether you need trademark, patent, or copyright protection.
2. Determine whether you should hire a trademark attorney.
3. Identify your mark format: a standard character mark, a stylized/design mark, or a sound mark.
4. Identify clearly the precise goods and/or services to which the mark will apply.
5. Search the USPTO database to determine whether anyone is already claiming trademark rights in a particular mark through a federal registration.
6. Identify the proper basis for filing a trademark application.
7. File the application online through the Trademark Electronic Application system.

After following the above steps the office reviews your application. You might be asked for more information or clarification.

After the trademark office has determined that your request is legitimate and meets all requirements, the office will publicize your request for registration in their trademark publication. If someone wants to oppose your registration they have three months to do it. Of course there are fees attached to that process. The opponent has to explain why he or she is opposing the registration. It is now up to you to decide if you want to continue the registration or abandon it.

Here are a few examples of what an opposition could look like.

- The Intellectual Property Office rejects the application because a similar name was already registered by another company.
- You try to register a name that is already owned in another country. Let's say a company from Finland opposes your application. After exchanging correspondence with the other company, you agree not to register under one classification and the Finland company lets you register in your country.
- Over the years you trademarked a name around the world. In Australia, however, you could not register the name as it was trademarked by somebody already. In 2013, to your surprise, the renewal was not paid. You quickly filed an application. The other company did not oppose and your application was accepted. However, the Australian Intellectual Property Office (www. ipaustralia.gov.au) needed more clarification before allowing the publication in their trademark journal. It can take you up to two years before you get your registration.

These examples illustrate how important it is to protect your intellectual property in the proper categories. You have to be prepared for oppositions and the cost associated with fighting those oppositions.

You may choose to register your mark in several countries. Take a look at the Madrid system (the International Trademark System). According to the WIPO, the Madrid system states the following:

...geographically, an applicant using the Madrid system can apply for protection of a mark in over 80 territories ("Contracting Parties") by filing a single application in one language and by paying a single set of fees, instead of filing separate applications in the different IP Offices of the various territories....

Once your name, logo, or slogan has been registered your involvement does not stop there.

Who Polices the Misuse of Your Trademark?

The burden is on you to police your trademarks and copyrighted material. This is not easy to do if you are a small business. On the Internet you can set Google alerts that will let you know every time somebody uses your trademark name. How you set your alerts will determine what kind of response you get.

Pay attention to the marketing material others in the same industry as yours have published. The marketing material for trade shows where exhibitors are advertising can be very revealing.

You can also read the trademark publications to see if somebody is trying to register a name that is so close to yours it could be confusing to the general public. You might decide to oppose that registration. Sometimes a simple letter to the registration office will do the trick, but be prepared to defend your opposition.

What happens if you find somebody copying your material on the Internet?

Do the Same Rules Apply to the Internet?

The biggest challenge an author faces today is the protection of his or her ideas on the Internet. The World Intellectual Property Organization Copyright Treaty adopted in 1996 addresses issues raised by the Internet. One of the biggest issues is the domain name. Can it be trademarked? According to ARVIC (www. arvic.com/library/domanuse.asp) the answer is yes.

An Internet domain name that is used to identify and distinguish the goods and/or services of one person, from the goods and/or services of all others, and is also used to indicate the source of the goods and/or services may be registered as a trademark providing it satisfies all the other rules for registration.

To find out if your domain name qualifies for registration, ask yourself the following question: Is my website going to offer a service to others and/or helpful information or merely be a point to sell my products and talk about my own business? If your site is strictly to promote your own business, it does not qualify for registration.

All other rules established under the copyright laws apply to the Internet.

> *The biggest challenge an author faces today is the protection of his or her ideas on the Internet.*

I encourage you to search the Internet for domain name registration and copyright/trademark laws. You can start with the WCT (WIPO Copyright Treaty) and the WPPT (Performances and Phonograms Treaty).

Whether you decide to do it yourself or hire a lawyer, you are now armed with some insight when considering the protection of your intellectual property, some of the rules to follow, and a few pitfalls you may come across throughout the process.

You worked hard to get where you are as a speaker or presenter. Now take the necessary steps to protect your valuable intellectual property!

Jocelyne Vézina, DTM, is a certified trainer of the Simply Strengths™ and Strong Manager™ programs offered by The Marcus Buckingham Company (TMBC) of California. She also has created her own workshops and seminars based on her more than twenty-five years of experience in the human resources field.

36

Then/Now/How Is Your
Cash Cow to Keep Sales Moo-ving

Diana J. Canaday

Remember the first time you tried to catch a butterfly? When I was in first grade, I got a butterfly net for my birthday. The next weekend we went to visit my grandmother in the country. I felt confident that I would catch at least a dozen butterflies, perhaps even the granddaddy butterfly of them all—a Monarch.

When we got to my grandmother's house, I jumped from the car and ran to the flower garden and set about hunting the butterflies. I went to the first bush and beat the bush with the butterfly net. Then when the butterflies took flight, I dropped the net and tried to catch the butterflies with my hands. Do you know how many I caught? NONE!

There were so many I thought I could surely catch one. But all the butterflies would gently flit away beyond my fingertips. Even the large Monarchs hovered just out of reach, seemingly taunting me, singing in rhythm with the beat of their majestic wings *"Neener, neener you're a wiener!"*

No matter how high I jumped, my little fingers grasped air. I tried to jump higher, which only made me tire faster. At the time it was frustrating to be outsmarted by a butterfly. However, looking back it is embarrassing to have been beaten by a critter that is dumber than a chicken.

Do you feel this way after giving your sales presentation? After beating the bushes with your speech your prospects flit away like the bright orange butterflies in a hot afternoon breeze?

By learning how to craft a Then/Now/How story you will have the tools to keep your listeners hooked and emotionally engaged—often just what is needed to close the sale after your presentation.

Using the information in this chapter you will

- build rapport with your audience
- learn how to craft a Then/Now/How story
- discover the power of Then/Now/How in action

Your Pain Can Be Your Gain to Build Rapport

It was the worst five minutes of my life! I was on the phone with LaQuetta, a sister "queen" from the World Elite Pageant. She had made me an offer I simply couldn't refuse. I wanted to learn more about makeup and had always wanted a business of my own. It was horrible.

I couldn't say no so the answer was yes. I signed on the dotted line and became an independent beauty consultant. Yes, a saleswoman, but I despised sales. I was no good at sales. I couldn't sell water to a man dying of thirst. It was incredibly stressful learning a skill that was the polar-opposite of what I do as a state investigator. But this setup appealed to me; I could work for the state in the daytime and do my beauty consultant work in the evening.

The regulatory field is very police oriented. My job dealt with facts not feelings. Now I would have to go outside that box and learn a different way to motivate. I was more than just a little afraid. But LaQuetta assured me that she and her director were going to be there to help.

Training day came and I received a fat notebook filled with information and scripts. The instructions directed the consultant to have a skincare class, which in turn would sell the product. To build rapport the materials directed you to give an "I Story" during the skincare class. The guidance in developing an "I Story" consisted of sharing why you signed on the dotted line.

Based on this guidance, I prepared my "I Story" and confidently presented it at my first skincare class. However, like the butterflies of my youth, my potential customers flitted out of reach. My two-hour investment resulted in no sale! In short, I worked for free. That happened time after time after time. My lack of sales hurt my ego, my pocketbook, and my health.

After talking to three people I would have a mild asthma attack and need to take a breathing treatment. Nothing shuts down communication like an asthma attack. In *Book Yourself Solid* author Michael Port gives the guidance that you need to talk to one hundred people a week to get ten customers, which for me would equal thirty-three asthma attacks and subsequent nebulizer treatments. I needed a shortcut to weed out the ninety to get to the ten!

Today my "I Story" helps me to quickly identify prospects who want to buy and can save my breath. During the close at least three out of four people end up buying.

I feel good knowing that my customer has the products that fit her needs, and each time she uses the products she will remember my speech and smile. Not only will she use the products, but she will share the experience with her family and friends—which results in more parties and more sales.

What made the difference?

I discovered the power of the Then/Now/How story formula.

How to Craft a Then/Now/How Story

For sales professionals, a Then/Now/How story is the story of how your product chavged your life for the better. It is the result. Since your product makes your customer's life better, the money they spend will be an investment rather than an expense.

The first component of this story is "Then," which is the problem you faced, or it could be a situation you want to avoid. This is when you reveal the pain of failure (verbal knife) and a prime opportunity to insert the seed of price comparison. With this verbal knife you reveal pain, both emotional and financial.

The "Then" portion of the story should be a failure, flaw, or "first"—like the first time you learned to tie your shoes.

Let's take a brief journey back to your kindergarten class when you learned this important skill. Do you see your construction paper shoe outline with yarn shoestrings? Think about the first time you tried to tie the yarn shoestring into a neat bow. Did you tie a perfect bow the first time? Probably not. I know I didn't. In fact, I remember tying the yarn so tight I ripped the construction paper shoe. It took a lot of practice but eventually I got the job done and am a productive shoe-tying adult today.

> *The pain of your failure will connect you to your audience faster because failure is a human commonality.*

The pain of your failure will connect you to your audience faster because failure is a human commonality. In short, everyone has failed and can identify with your failure. Since you have shared a failure you will not appear special and have removed yourself from the pedestal so that you can put your product on the pedestal. The "Then" portion of your story gives flavor to the result, which is the "Now" portion.

The "Now" portion of your story is about you in the present after using your product. You are contrasting the past with the present. Your "Now" story should enumerate at least three or four positive results. For instance, with skincare, my customers get smoother, younger looking skin at a recession-conscience price.

The "How" should be your product or service. Earlier I shared a story about becoming an independent beauty consultant and trying to write an "I Story" that would persuade a prospect to buy. I wasted a lot of time, energy, and breath following the path of the conventional "I Story" wisdom. Next was the "Now" part of the story, in which I enumerated the results. Finally I shared the secret to my success: the power of the Then/Now/How story.

How will a Then/Now/How story increase your sales?

You have identified the problem (Then) and enumerated the result that can be achieved (Now). The final step is the "How." Your "How" should be your product. The "How" should be an exact next step—that is, to purchase and use your product or service. A Then/Now/How story is the path to the one next step. The next step is the process or product that makes the difference for you and your prospect. The "How" part of your story is the time to look into your audience and observe who is smiling and nodding in agreement. Those are your potential buyers.

> *The "How" part of your story is the time to look into your audience and observe who is smiling and nodding in agreement. Those are your potential buyers.*

The Power of Then/Now/How in Action

This is my "I Story" which I can modify to fit the situation. The parts of the story are identified in boldface italics enclosed in parentheses.

(THEN—verbal knife)

Have you ever shared your dream with someone and that person mocked you? How did that make you feel? I felt this way in 2009 when I shared one of my big dreams with my best friend. If you were sitting next to us on the beach, you would have heard me say…

"Mary, I'd like to do some modeling."

"Ha! I wouldn't get my hopes up," Mary said with disdain.

*Did you feel a knife stabbing you in the chest? I did. I was going to prove her wrong—even if it killed me. It didn't matter that I was over the hill, overweight, and had never worn makeup (**flaw**). I am Scotch Irish and have stubbornness issues.*

Upset and depressed, I ate a brownie. Well, to be honest, a whole pan of brownies, then called my mom to get advice.

"Diana, find a beauty pageant because that is how many models started."

Mother knows best, so I found a local pageant, then Mom and I went shopping. We started with makeup at a large retail department store. Ms. Laura, the counter sales clerk, started bringing out bottle after bottle of skincare products and applying it in meticulous order to my face while proclaiming the benefits of each product.

*In thirty minutes she had applied eight bottles of beauty potion to my face before any foundation was applied. Since I was older…uh, more mature…my mom insisted that I do some sort of skincare to fight the signs of aging. For me aging consisted of wrinkles, age spots, and sagging skin (**verbal knife to self-esteem**). So I agreed to purchase the set. The register totaled a little over $1000* *(verbal knife to pocketbook)! Did you feel a stabbing pain in your pocketbook? I did.*

I recovered from sticker shock when my mom bought the eight-bottle set for me. Since it was so expensive, I used it only on Sundays for a pampering session. Sadly, I didn't get the guaranteed result because I was unwilling to invest an hour each day and $1000 every three months (price comparison seed).

(NOW—result)

Thanks to my mom and her credit card, I was ready for my first pageant. But I didn't win. However, three years later I received a big pay-off with four national titles: 2012 Global America US Woman, 2012 Global America Woman, 2012 Global Woman, and the 2012 World Elite Director's Service Award. As of this writing I am currently the 2013 Ms. Woman South Carolina World Elite.

During my journey to prove Mary wrong, I discovered the best skincare system that has only three steps. Now I get a five-minute pampering session in the morning and evening. I saved that $120 makeup artist fee by doing my own makeup at beauty pageants. Even with the recession, I don't feel guilty treating my skin to the very best in skincare at only $200. I love the results of reduced wrinkles, fading age spots, and firmer skin (desired result).

Strange that my determination made me a role model, a beauty queen, and a business owner. Can you keep a secret? It also made me a superhero.

A superhero wears a costume—I wear a beautiful evening gown. A superhero has a logo—I have the Ms. Woman World Elite name on my sash. A superhero has a special power—my special power is wearing my crown. Because when I wear my crown people notice me. Now when I put on my crown at an appearance I sing "Here I am to save the day, and I look glamorous thanks to MK!"

What would you do to be a superhero?

(HOW—desired outcome)

I won the titles because of my commitment to skincare and makeup application. After my first pageant, I looked at the photos and was shocked to see how much I had aged. I had wrinkles everywhere—or so it seemed. I used the MK repair set to ease the signs of aging and reduced my wrinkles. Indeed, when I am in the field my skincare helps to fight the damaging effects of the sun with a sunscreen built into the morning moisturizer and foundation primer. My improved facial tone gave me an edge on the runway, and the camera proved it.

I realized that while I am at work (my 9-to-5 job that I love too) I am still onstage because I am a state employee. I discovered that wearing makeup increased my credibility. Studies show that when a woman wears cosmetics, even a little makeup, it increases her credibility 30 percent. Thus wearing cosmetics is a career investment.

You may not want to be a beauty queen, but you can be a role model for girls. You can do that by looking your best and feeling your best. I would like to meet with each one of you after your pampering session to discuss your skincare needs and tell you how you can be a superhero.

Conclusion

Over time I have become wiser and altered my method of catching butterflies. I now use a camera with a telephoto lens. Works every time! I don't get hot or tired or frustrated. With my camera I can even catch the granddaddy butterfly—the Monarch.

This is how I felt when I discovered and applied the power of the Then/Now/How story. Do I get a sale at each presentation? Yes. Not all the prospects buy, but enough buy so that I don't feel like I am grabbing at the wind.

Diana J. Canaday is a pesticide investigator with Clemson University Department of Pesticide Regulation. In 2014 she won her fifth national title as 2014 World Elite Ambassador for World Elite Pageant system. She endeavors to harness the power of the Then/Now/How story for her work, her title, and her community.

37

Increase Your Income with Back-of-Room Sales

Mark A. Vickers

Depending on the type of presentation you're making, you may be able to offer your audience an opportunity to purchase products or services directly from you. Back-of-room sales of your products and services provide you a huge opportunity to increase your income.

You may offer a variety of products including:

- books
- CDs and DVDs
- coaching services
- training services
- Mastermind Group memberships

While the sale of your products and services can drastically increase your income, turning your presentation into a "sales presentation" will annoy your audience and hurt your income.

In my book *Speaking Is Selling—51 Tips Your Mother Taught You* I share that "Good Things Come to Those Who Wait." Rushing your audience to your offer is a sure way to alienate them and reduce the likelihood that they will purchase.

By implementing a cohesive strategy throughout your presentation you will provide value to the audience and make your back-of-room offer irresistible.

In this chapter we will cover the four key elements to generating back-of-room sales:

- have a defined strategy
- sell the process and result *first*
- call back to emotional hot buttons
- have appropriate price points and bundles

1. Have a Defined Strategy

You are in front of your audience for a short period of time during which you need to entertain, educate, motivate, and drive the desire to make a purchase. People buy based on emotion and justify the purchase with logic.

> *"People buy based on emotion and justify the purchase with logic."*

By understanding that the purchase of your resources is driven primarily by emotion you begin to grasp the importance of the many techniques discussed throughout this book. It is critical that you create an emotional connection to your audience and that they connect to your presentation and stories.

When you are presenting and making back-of-room offers, let your audience know you truly care about them. Based on your focus and mindset, your audience will know if you are being genuine, looking out for their best interest, or are just trying to sell them something.

Back-of-room sales require an additional level of strategy that wraps around your speaking skills. Before developing your presentation ask:

- What do I want them to purchase that will support *their* achieving more in their lives?

- What process do I recommend *they* follow using what they purchase so they can most effectively achieve results?

With the answers to these two questions you can start developing the elements of your presentation that will support your sales.

2. Sell a Process and Result *First*

Your presentation needs to help your audience see the value and benefit of change and understand that they too can achieve the desired results using your processes and resources.

There are a number of questions to answer for your audience:

- Why should I make a change?
- What is the benefit to me of making a change?
- Who else has been able to make the change I need or want to make?
- Were they like me and in a similar situation to me?
- How did they go about making the change?
- What did they do?
- What tools, supports, or help did they use?
- Can I actually make the change?
- Do I have the time, money, and skills to make the change?
- What do I do next?

Your Then/Now/How Story

Your Then/Now/How story, discussed earlier in this book, is one of the key elements supporting your back-of-room sales. Remember that your story should connect to your audience emotionally and answer many of the questions listed above.

Through your story you should help your audience understand that:

- You were in a position similar to theirs.
- You are basically like them.
- You found a *process* that helped you change.
- Where you are now is better than where you were then.

Since people buy based on emotion, helping them connect emotionally to your story will position them for the process and eventually the purchase.

As you share your story, maintain a clear focus on a process that will help your audience members believe they can also make the desired changes. If your presentation focuses on you and your abilities instead of the process, your audience may doubt their own ability to achieve.

The Process Focus

The focus of your presentation should be on a simple step-by-step process that anyone can follow. During your Then/Now/How and other stories you will highlight the steps and ease of the process—"selling" the process. Always remember: people will buy a process faster than a product.

> ### People will buy a process faster than a product.

Here are some simple tips to help you establish your process:

- Use an acronym to make it easy to remember (KISS, Keep it Simple Silly).
- Use rhyming words that lay out progressions (Efficiency, Proficiency, Self-Sufficiency).
- Outline a process with an odd number of steps (three-step process, five-step process) but never more than five steps.
- Keep each step extremely simple.
- When possible provide a time commitment (fifteen minutes per day, and it will take three months).

The Result Focus

Through your stories you will also highlight the successes and results that you and others have achieved by following the process you recommend.

To be relatable to your audience and help them believe that they can also achieve the desired successes, it may be beneficial to limit the size of your success. While this may seem counterintuitive (not to mention hard on the ego) the focus is on the audience and not on you as the presenter.

As an example, assume you are presenting a program aimed at helping your audience improve their income and standard of living. Your story highlights a real situation where you or someone else:

- went from broke to millionaire
- moved from a shack on the outskirts of town to a 5,000-square-foot home in a gated community
- dropped 200 pounds to arrive at your ideal weight

If you are telling the story for your own enjoyment, realize that you are losing sight of your audience. Many speakers create huge differentials that make it difficult for the audience to believe in the change and unable to comprehend the new situation.

Result Differential

The result differential is the gap between where you were then compared to where you are now having followed the prescribed process.

If the result differential in your story is too small it can leave your audience thinking, *Well, it's hardly worth the effort if that is all I get.* On the other hand, if the result differential is too great (even though 100 percent true), your audience may begin to think:

- Is that gain really true?
- Is it really possible to improve that much?
- There must be something else they did to achieve that much.
- I could never make that big of a change.
- I don't want to make that big of a change.

Audience Differential

Similar to the result differential, the audience differential can cause your audience to disengage from your presentation and ultimately your offer. The audience differential can be measured from two different perspectives:

1. where are they now compared to where you were then
2. where are they now compared to what you describe in your story

If your audience perceives that you were considerably further ahead at the start of your story than they are today, they may believe the gap is simply too great. For example, if you were previously successful and then became more successful, those in your audience who do not believe they have ever achieved any success are likely to disengage. This is a form of being dissimilar to your audience.

If the differential from where your audience is now to what you are speaking about is too great, they may not believe they can do it even if you did, and they may not be able to relate to the end result you presented. For example, an audience member who has never earned more than $20,000/year can have difficulty imagining a scenario where they could earn $200,000/year.

The Solution to Differential Gaps

To ensure the gaps are not too large, ask the following:

- Would my average audience member believe this is true and achievable?
- Do I really believe that my average audience member could make the same achievement?
- Will my audience be able to relate to the improvements and believe they can too?
- Can I effectively show the steps required to move them from where they are now to the level I am describing?

The simplest way to eliminate gaps is to use percentage- or ratio-based changes in your stories. For example:

- increase income by 50 percent
- double your income
- create a threefold increase in production
- convert twice as many prospects to customers

The person currently making $20,000 can probably imagine making $40,000, and the person making $200,000 can probably imagine earning $400,000 per year.

Dream Building

Having shared the process you recommend and the results you achieved, you have successfully "sold" your audience on making a change and doing a process to achieve results. As a final step in preparing your audience to purchase your back-of-room offer, move them to a dream-building mindset.

Many speakers spend considerable time explaining all the wonderful things they have done and the incredible benefits they have gained through improvement. The issue is that what you did with the rewards of your improvement may be very different from what each member of your audience wants.

You may have undertaken a change and achieved results so that you could purchase a larger house and a nice car, but some members of your audience want nothing more than to get out of debt and stop working weekends. By allowing your audience to build their own dream they will develop their own emotional attachment to the results you are promoting.

The Product or Service

Having developed the need for change you will now want to discuss specific products or services that support the process you have shared. Depending on the nature of your presentation, you may have mentioned the names of specific tools or even used them to teach a particular point.

Ideally you will share with your audience information about other people's products that will support them in achieving their goals. This shows that you are confident enough in your offering to provide them with other possibilities.

When it is time to share the details of your products and services your audience should already have "bought" into the process you are recommending, and your products are nothing more than a toolkit for achievement.

If you find that you are selling your offer instead of presenting a call to action, you have not effectively implemented a strategy that triggers the need for your offer.

3. Call Back to Emotional Hot Buttons

As you are making your call to action it is beneficial to call back to emotional hot buttons that were set earlier in your presentation. Referring back to the situation your audience is currently experiencing—and the benefits they can achieve—will retrigger the emotional responses created earlier and the need and desire for your resources

As you deliver your call to action include phrases that will help your audience remember:

- what they want more of
- what they want less of
- how they will feel when it happens

4. Appropriate Price Points and Bundles

Even if everything else in your presentation has been masterfully developed and delivered, your back-of-room sales can be supported or hurt by the price points you choose.

If you have a single product or service, the back-of-room offer is typically the retail price (or the price offered on your website) less some special discount for purchasing at the event. While the discount may be small it should be enough to motivate your audience to act now instead of waiting until later.

When you have a variety of products and services, bundling provides your greatest opportunity for high back-of-room sales. Determining your bundles and their price points is as much of an art as it is a science.

The most important considerations in bundling are:

- Which product combinations best support the process described?
- Do you want a single offer?
- Do you want a two- or three-tier offer (e.g., Bronze, Silver, Gold)?
- What price points can be realistically supported by your audience?
- Do you want to use scarcity to drive immediate action (e.g., today only, limited quantities, or bonus items available only at the event)?

The key to delivering your offer lies in its simplicity. The easier you can present your offer the easier it will be for your motivated audience to say yes and move to the back of the room to make their purchase.

To increase your back-of-room sales and your income always remember:

- Have a *defined strategy* that will create a compelling offer.
- Sell the results and the process *first*.

- Prepare your presentation from the perspective of the audience to avoid *differential gaps* that are too large to imagine.
- Offer a limited number of tools and resources.
- Price and bundle your offers realistically based on your audience.

Mark A. Vickers is a certified professional coach, a certified World Class Speaking coach, professional speaker, and author of Speaking Is Selling—51 Tips Your Mother Taught You.

38

From Conversation to Contract: Objectives to Meet Before You Finalize the Deal

Jeanne R. Lee

T hat first contact with a prospective client is like a first date—you want to get to know one another.

From the moment you pick up the voicemail or open an email or, by gosh, the potential client actually is able to connect with you on their first try with a phone call, you have the opportunity to build a professional relationship for life—and sometimes a personal relationship as well. It's all about that initial contact, and the conversation that follows is equally important.

In this chapter we will cover the process from "conversation to contract." The goals of the conversation, before terms and compensation are determined, are to:

- get to know who the potential client is and where they are in the present moment
- really listen to what they want (you will be able to better serve them)
- develop a rapport as the conversation unfolds so that you each get to know one another and thus build trust
- determine from the conversation if other items should be addressed

- before determining compensation, find out what other items can be negotiated that would add value to your fee
- know what they want to accomplish with your speech; in other words, where they want to be after your presentation.

If their first words to you are either "what do you charge?" or "we can only afford this amount," guide the conversation to learn more about them after they have disclosed the topic they want you to speak on. Through your *curiosity* of thoroughly understanding why they have come to you, you will know if you are a good match or if you need to refer them on to a colleague. Empathetic listening to their needs and wants, learning the history of how they decided on the range of topics that will address their "objective," and fully engaging to help them get the results they want allow you to begin building a professional relationship for life. It is an old marketing adage that people like to do business with people they "know, like, and trust." The conversation you have before you get to the terms of contract allows the client to get to know, like, and trust you. The better you understand them, the more likely they will like you and hire you and refer you over and over. So be yourself!

The Conversation Begins

Start the conversation by talking about the organization the client represents. (If you are lucky enough to have some time to do background research on them do so, but don't assume that what you find on the Internet is all you need to know.) Be open and listen to what your client wants you to know. Ask follow-up questions to clarify any statements that are unclear to you or questions that can assist you in distilling better their wants, needs, and objectives. Who were their past speakers and topics, and what did they want to achieve with each of them? Were they able to achieve their desired goals? If the organization is choosing you on a similar topic, why have they done so? Is their objective the same, or how is it now different? Will there be other speakers and if so who are they, what will their topics be, and where do you fall in the lineup? Can you have a proposed agenda as well as a final one? What are the demographics of the audience? Age range? Male/female ratio? Political leanings? Diversity? Topics they would suggest you avoid? Will there be any cheerleaders in the audience for the objectives you want to achieve even before you give your speech? And will there be any naysayers that are difficult to win over and why? (With this information you may decide to meet or speak with any of these identified people beforehand to tweak your stories or speech.)

I have personally met with people before an event to connect with cheerleaders and naysayers so that I better understand their perspectives. If they give me their permission I weave their stories into my speech, and I may even ask if they would like to participate. I have found that audiences enjoy being interactive and are more engaged when their fellow members are called upon to participate.

Finally, listen to what is not being said. Sometimes I can draw the answer to that last question by asking "What is the one question you are so glad I did not ask?" And then I ask that question. Usually, asking that question will generate laughter and relief. This is another sure sign that you are connecting with your client.

> *By looking at the incidentals, you may actually receive a value that exceeds your speaking fees.*

Explore the Incidentals before Determining Price

At some point in the conversation, you may already know what they are willing to compensate you for. You may be satisfied with that number or you may want to explore other incidentals that will give you a "value" commensurate with your speaking fees. By looking at the incidentals, you may actually receive a value that exceeds your speaking fees. Here are some ideas of items to consider:

- What type of reimbursements are they considering and the amounts— ground transportation, amount allowed for meals, any and all tips, plane costs, and how many nights of hotel expenses they will cover. (Remember to consider additional nights due to time zone changes.)
- What type of advertising will they have to promote the event? In what ways can you ask them to leverage this for you? For example, are they willing to keep the ad(s) posted after the event (get a time commitment so that you can put it in the final contract) and post testimonials? Would they be willing to post a video on their website with your website address to create a buzz before the event?
- If the event is being video recorded, have the parties agreed to whom the recording belongs and each party's rights to use the same? If it belongs to

the client, have you negotiated how you might be able to use it and for what price? If it belongs to you, what steps have you taken to ensure that all recordings of the presentation will be returned to you?

- Regardless of who owns the rights to the video recording, will the client agree to get live testimonials after the presentation to give to you?
- Will the client allow you to audio record the presentation? You could use these recordings in the future as audio CDs to be sold to future audiences. You can even transcribe the speech and turn it into an e-book or supplement to a home-study course or training program.
- Will you be able to have back-of-room sales? Some clients do not like to have a sales pitch in their presentation. However, if you can walk them through how your sales pitch is really a soft sale, you may be able to get around the "NO sales pitch" position. You can even ask how you might be able to work around the "NO sales," so don't take no as a final answer.
- Will they allow you to have a prize drawing whose relevancy has been worked into the talk? This would be a way to add to your mailing list. Or perhaps you could have a sign-up sheet in the back of the room for a specific purpose such as sending a "tip sheet" related to the presentation for those who sign up.
- Ask if they plan to do other workshops that year. Are you qualified to lead them? If so, they have already paid your transportation there. What details are required to add a workshop to your engagement? The topic could be related to the presentation or it could just be within your realm of expertise.
- Will they allow you to sign books at the end of the speech?

These are just a few ideas that I have used. What other ideas do you have or have you employed?

When Life Interferes with the Speaking Engagement

Sometimes a speaking engagement will need to be canceled either through events out of our control—such as unforeseen strikes that affect transportation, acts of God, or an incapacity that precludes you from performing. Providing for future contingencies will help nurture the relationship ahead of the cancellation of your presentation. Keep in mind that the best way to avoid too much disappointment for your failure to appear—other than to show up as planned—would be to place disclaimers on promotional materials that state: "Speakers may be substituted at the last minute." Because life does happen, I strongly suggest that you provide the language or similar language as stated above. Below are some items you might want to consider for managing the unforeseen now (by no means exclusive).

- If there is a speaker deposit to hold the date open, is that subject to refund if either party cancels?
- Up to how many days before the event may either party cancel with no penalty? Likewise, if either party cancels thirty days before the event what is the cancellation fee? What is the cancellation fee one to three weeks before the event? What happens if the cancellation is one week or less before the event? Can the parties negotiate that you as the speaker can find a substitute with no penalty, and how many days will they give you to find a substitute? Can the parties agree to a list of substitute speakers now?
- Under what circumstances can a party be excused from performing under the contract?
- Do you want to state the actual dollar amount that each party is entitled to if there is a breach of contract? Be aware that some states may not honor the amounts that the parties have agreed to.

Now to the Contract

Once you have followed the steps above, you have a fairly good idea as to the compensation that both parties can agree to and other terms that should be reflected in the agreement. So the final step is to get a contract in place. While I am not advising you as to all aspects that need to be considered to make a contract enforceable, or all items to be included (you should retain an attorney to review the enforceability of your agreements), you will want to consider at a minimum the following. Again, this is not an exclusive list, nor is this content to be considered legal advice. This list is from my own collective experience as well as the experiences of other colleagues.

1. First and foremost, you need the names of the entities who are parties to the agreement, with a statement that they have the power to bind whatever entity they represent. Be sure to have the agreement dated and state that any changes will need to be agreed to by both parties in writing.

2. Next be sure to detail all the items you have agreed to. Consider the date, time, venue, the format (lecture, case study, etc.), how the room is to be arranged, number of sessions and contact hours, if your presence is required before and/or after the presentation, who is to pay for any copies to be required and if so when do you have to have them sent, who will be distributing the materials and in what manner, what type of audiovisual equipment will be required and who is to provide the same, an agreement as to how the class day will proceed (registration times, scheduled break times, lunch, etc.).

> *With respect to incidentals, you need to be clear if your speaker's fee is for the total costs or only for the presentation itself.*

3. Third, you will want to set forth the compensation structure and cancellation timetable and whether your speaker deposit is required to be returned. In addition, with respect to incidentals, you need to be clear if your speaker's fee is for the total costs or only for the presentation itself. Specify who will make the travel arrangements, who should be billed for airfare and transportation, what mileage rate you are allowed, how many days of per diem, and the dollar amounts. (There are generally three ways to handle travel. Option A: Client will prepay all travel expenses. Option B: All travel expenses are to be arranged by the client and billed directly to them. Option C: All travel expenses are to be arranged by the speaker and billed directly to the hiring organization for payment from their funds. Option D: Speaker bills the client for expenses. If you choose this latter route, be sure to include some statement that they have to make payment within ten days of your expense submission or there will be a late fee charged of $100 per day to encourage prompt payment.) With respect to hotel, speaker can ask for reimbursement or have the client be responsible for providing the hotel room and that the speaker will not be required to use her own credit card to secure lodging. Be sure to specify the dates of your lodging and other room details that will keep you fresh for your presentation.

4. Agreements as to who owns any recordings or if the client is barred from recording the event in any manner.

5. Set forth the remedies and damages if either party fails to perform.

6. In the event of a dispute, set forth what state will have jurisdiction over the matter. Consider a mediation clause as well should a dispute arise.

7. Also consider a copyright clause. This clause would represent that your materials are to be used for the sole purposes of the attendees. They may not be copied, sold, or given away for any other purpose without your expressed written permission.

8. Finally, consider a Force Majeure Clause. This clause generally states that in the event either party is unable to perform under the terms set forth in the agreement due to events or causes outside the control of the parties (think war, acts of God), each party shall not be deemed to be in breach of the agreement.

You have built the trust through your conversation, understood where they are now and why and where they want to go and how they will know what they want has been achieved; you now have the knowledge of how to make your presentation meet their needs. If you reduce into the agreement all that you have agreed upon in writing, you are set to GO!

Jeanne R. Lee is an executive coach for executives, lawyers, and high-performing individuals who are committed to the next levels of success in their professional and personal lives—a service that often includes presentation and communications CPR. A certified World Class Speaking coach, she is called to speak on leadership, courage, time management, negotiations, and networking with grace, agility, and fun. Jeanne can be reached at Jeanne@lawyermentorcoach.com.

39

Tapping into Asia:
Don't Let It Faze You!

Carl Dusthimer

Are you ready to meet the widening circle of challenges in the twenty-first century? Since 1910 the Boy Scouts motto has been "Be prepared." Recently, my student's speech theme was "We must be ready to take advantage of all opportunities." Well, the opportunities are here, and they will only increase as the world continues its march toward globalization. Asia is diverse. Asia is dynamic. Asia is a driving force. Perhaps it's time to get prepared and make Asia part of your portfolio.

Night and Day. Yin and Yang. East and West. Do you see these pairs as polar opposites, as extremes of a continuum? Or do you see them as complementary, as balancing components of a continuum? The latter is how they are viewed in Asia, and recognizing and embracing this is a step toward speaking and making well-received presentations to Asian audiences.

In a Marketing 101 class I remember reading Philip Kotler's *Principles of Marketing* textbook. He mentions the classic mistake General Motors made when introducing one of its cars, the Chevy Nova, in Mexico. In short, GM tried to sell that model under its English name "Nova," not realizing that in Spanish "Nova" means "doesn't go." That simple example in language differences, which resulted in a complete failure to sell the Nova in Mexico, points to the main theme of this chapter on tapping into Asia: know your audience.

To connect with an Asian audience in Beijing, Brussels, or Buenos Aires and get across those important ideas you have to share, you need to take the time to get to know the people you're talking to. The world is full of intelligent people who want to listen, laugh, and learn. To share our ideas and ourselves, we as speakers have to put on their shoes for a moment and walk the path into their hearts and minds. To get started, this chapter will cover:

- similarities (not everything is different)
- cultural considerations
- language considerations
- presentation pointers
- dos & don'ts

Similarities: Not Everything Is Different

Many of the World Class Speaking principles are just as valid in the East as in the West. Whether in Asia or on another continent, we want to share our ideas, persuade others to think in a certain way, or get our audience to take some action. To do any or all of those things we first have to connect with our listeners. Here are three characteristics of exceptional talks that cross all borders:

Stories pack 'em in. Throughout human history people have communicated through stories, and that hasn't changed. Triumph or tragedy, serious or sad, hilarious or happy, everyone loves a story about other members of the human race. To make whatever you are talking about seem relevant to another person or to a group, there is no better and more universal way to make the connection than with a story.

Pixels pack a punch. A picture is worth a thousand words. It's an old saying, but it's as true now as when it was first penned. Whether it's Asia, Africa, Europe, or the Americas, everywhere there are people there are pictures and graphic art. The mind loves visuals more than it loves words! The mind can process images much faster than words, so it seems natural that pictures or graphics can bring into sharper focus the words we use. We will look at visuals more in the *presentation* section below.

Structure packs it right. Though there are differences in Eastern (spiral) and Western (linear) logic, the norm for structuring speeches and presentations reflects the Western approach, as it is more straightforward and less nuanced than the Eastern approach. It is also quite similar to the World Class Speaking approach, which can be used as a model:

1. Open with a bang. Start off with a statement that will get the audience's attention and make them want to listen to you.
2. Convey your main message or point(s) in a short foundational phrase or sentence that they will remember.
3. Anchor your talk with a compelling story.
4. Bridge your points with smooth transitions.
5. Summarize by recalling your foundational phrase and a call to action or reflection.

With the comfort and confidence gained by being aware of these broad similarities, we can move on to the subtleties that can easily be overlooked, many times with dire consequences.

Cultural Considerations:
They Sure Look Different from My Usual Audiences!

Imagine speaking to a group of people. They smile at you warmly, they nod in agreement at your points, and thvy clap when you finish. Then you find out later from a trusted acquaintance that your talk was a dismal failure. Most Westerners in Asia have experienced this at least once. Luckily, you can avoid this "presentation culture shock" by being aware of and keeping in mind a few cultural differences. Here are three from the audience's point of view.

> *In Asia, maintaining harmony and balance are more important than wearing your thoughts or feelings on your sleeve.*

It's not what I say, it's what I mean. For the most part, Asians will not directly express their feelings or thoughts, particularly in business situations. Maintaining harmony and balance are more important than wearing your thoughts or feelings on your sleeve. Thus Asians will normally not say they don't like something or disagree with a statement or point of view. Instead they will be non-committal or may even "say" they like something or "verbally agree" with a statement. Their actual stance will eventually become clear through later actions or inaction. So for speakers, the immediate reaction from the audience may be a bit misleading. A frequent complaint from Westerners is "but they said yes! It was clear…" Again, politeness and maintaining social harmony tend to guide most interactions.

It's not what I do, it's how I feel. As you might experience a smiling audience nodding at you, you might also experience people laughing at your jokes or stories, only to find out that it wasn't the joke or story they were laughing at. Certainly Asians love a good joke and a funny story as much as anyone. But Asians will commonly laugh when they feel uncomfortable, embarrassed, or simply at a loss for a proper response. Considering this, it is usually best to simply accept answers, reactions, and responses as they come and not press for more clarity. The clarity will come at the appropriate time for your host.

It's not what you know, it's who you are. Westerners, especially Americans, often come across as cocky and arrogant. Perhaps it is a "Wild West" kind of swagger or simply the result of an enthusiasm to show people how it's done. Whatever may be the source, it is very often perceived in Asia as rude, kind of like a bull in a china shop, if you'll pardon the pun. Patrick Hwang, a Korean publisher with over 20 years experience presenting in Asia, emphasizes that in line with the importance of harmony and balance, western speakers should try to practice humility and be genuine. Focus on the "you" or the "us" not the "I". Actually this is quite similar to the World Class speaking way, where the speaker never builds him or herself up. It's all about the audience and the idea.

Language Considerations:
I Know What I Want to Say, but How Do I Say It?

Asia is diverse in both cultures and languages, so naturally presenting in English could be a barrier to connecting with an Asian audience and delivering a memorable message. Fortunately, English is accepted as the international language throughout Asia. It is good, however, to make some slight adjustments since the mother tongue of most audiences will not be English.

It's not a race. It may take a little practice, but setting a more deliberate pace when speaking is a good first step. A native speaker usually talks at about 130-150 words per minute. For a non-native speaking audience, 80-100 words per minute would be about right. It is also good to give audience members enough "think time" to process what you are saying. Marc Helgesen, a textbook author who has spoken to audiences in almost every country in Asia, finds "think time" a better tactic since slowing down one's speech can sometimes make you sound artificial. It is interesting to note that Asians find Steve Jobs, who spoke at about 10 words per minute, much easier to understand than Bill Gates, who speaks at about 22 words per minute.

It's not an IQ test. Some speakers, especially at conferences, like to cram as much information into their sentences as possible. That's very efficient, but it makes the language more complex or dense than it needs to be. It is better instead to use the KISS principle and keep sentences short and simple. After all, the goal is to communicate, not to impress.

It's not free association. It is common but not good practice for speakers to expect the audience to follow the bread crumbs and keep track of everything they say. A better approach, particularly in an EFL (English as a foreign language) environment like Asia, is to follow World Class Speaking practices. This means always showing how the major points fit together and calling back to the foundational phrase so the audience can follow and remember.

Presentation Pointers

Having looked at culture and language differences, let's move on to some presentation tips to consider when putting your talk together. When you are up there in the spotlight talking to your audience, listen to them. Here is what they are telling you:

Show it to me. As pointed out earlier, visuals are indispensable in getting points across effectively and efficiently for any audience. Add the possible culture and language barriers and visuals take on even greater importance. The writing systems in Asia are not the same as English, so it naturally takes slightly longer to process English text. This means we should keep text on slides to a bare minimum.

Do it for me. Another way to overcome communication barriers, especially when introducing new ideas, is to demonstrate what you are talking about rather than explain it. It is really just an extension of how a picture or graphic will help the audience understand a concept or point, and it applies to products, processes, or some action you want your audience to take after your talk. It further helps if the steps in the process or procedure can be remembered using an acronym.

Know about me. It is critical that you use local examples in your talks. Showing how well something works in Europe or North America does little to convince someone in China or Indonesia how it will benefit them. Taken even further, referring to how well something—an education program for example— works in Korea if you are talking to a group of people in Malaysia does little to help sell your program in Malaysia. Another example might be mobile devices. If you happen to refer to cell phones in Korea, you should be aware that they are referred to as "handphones" in Korea and that 95 percent of people use Android devices rather than Apple devices. Andrew Todd, a Scottish executive working in China, makes it a point to download and include local pictures whenever presenting in Asia. He says it shows a respect for your audience and sensitivity toward the local culture.

> *Showing how well something works in Europe or North America does little to convince someone in China or Indonesia how it will benefit them.*

Do This, Don't Do That

Finally, here are some "Dos & Don'ts" that may not fall neatly into one of the above sections. Because harmony and balance are so highly valued in Asia, taking these tips to heart can save you from some awkward or embarrassing situations.

Dos

- Bow to your audience at the beginning and end of your talk. This isn't expected, but doing so shows respect.
- Get out from behind the podium. Though traditionally Asians speak from the podium, a relaxed, informal style is appreciated these days.
- Use a simple phrase or two like "hello" or "thank you" in the local language. This simple act, as much as any other attempt you make to know your audience, can have a huge impact on how you are received.

Don'ts

- Don't use local symbols like flags or other national symbols unless they are a real part of your presentation.

- Don't tell jokes. In general, jokes translate very poorly across cultures.
- Don't point at (or to) other people using your index finger. Instead, point using an open palm gesture.
- Don't show strong emotions. Asians are typically reserved, unless around very close friends or associates.
- Don't beckon someone using an upturned palm and curling your index finger. This is how Asians usually call dogs. Rather, extend your arm with your palm facedown and curl your fingers toward your body.
- Don't use English idioms. Like jokes, they are very culturally based and rarely translate well. Stick with clear, standard English.
- Don't be overly enthusiastic or use large, sweeping gestures. This is seen as over-the-top and disingenuous.

The opportunity to speak in Asia, or to a group of Asians in the West, can open up new worlds for you as a speaker. And there are enough similarities to speaking to Western audiences that the transition is not too drastic. Just remember, people everywhere want to listen, laugh, and learn. If you get the chance, take it; share a little of yourself and make some new friends. They could be right around the corner in your neighborhood or maybe just across the Pacific. And that's really not far anymore!

Carl Dusthimer has been an educator in Korea since 1988. He speaks at conferences across Asia and develops curricula and other materials for young learners. He teaches at the Korea National University of Education.

40

Guidelines for Speaking to a Diverse Audience

Danish Qasim

Our beliefs and experiences set the frames through which we understand the world. These frames establish moral code, etiquette, and common sense. When speaking to people of different backgrounds it is imperative to understand their worldview. Otherwise you risk offending, insulting, or in a best-case scenario not being understood.

The diversity you may encounter as a speaker is endless so I will give you a few scenarios and anecdotes to serve as a guide to establish maxims that will apply to every particular situation.

In this chapter we will cover the following:

- Choose your words thoughtfully.
- Be universal in examples.
- Learn to empathize.
- When you show appreciation, you will be appreciated.
- Learn the norms.
- Don't be ethnocentric.

- Master the art of code switching.
- Know your audience's value system.

Choose Your Words Thoughtfully

Speaking intelligently and speaking intelligibly are not mutually exclusive. Your insight should reflect your skills, not your ability to speak above your audience's comprehension. A golden rule of writing, and it applies to speaking, is the famous Orwellian mandate "never use a long word where a short one will do."

> *A golden rule of writing, and it applies to speaking, is the famous Orwellian mandate "never use a long word where a short one will do."*

Speaking to a high school audience would require a different vernacular than speaking to college students. Again, the essence of your message needs to be tailored to the specifics of the audience.

Research shows that a reader ceases to pay attention upon encountering an unfamiliar word. The unknown word demarks the beginning of unfamiliar territory. With reading, a dictionary will swiftly get the reader back on course. A speech, however, is constantly moving, and a tirade of unknown words will mercilessly set the listener off course for good.

When speaking to an audience of foreign English speakers, it is important to assess their fluency. Simple research beforehand by conversing with a few members should be sufficient. Remember not to use idioms and colloquialisms.

Be Universal in Examples

America is a pluralistic society. Try to make your allusions mainstream or draw from the interests of the subculture you are engaging. For example, if you are engaging high school students learn what high school students are into. Sports is always a safe way to go. Never try to fake expertise or even interest. However, use familiar points of reference in examples and analogies.

On this topic, public speaking professor Matt McGarrity told me:

Audience adaptation is key. Most chapters on speaking to a diverse audience in public speaking textbooks tend to simply default to "avoid all stereotypes," which is sound advice. But this diverse audience is showing up at the speech for a specific reason. There are norms and expectations embedded in that situation. When I find myself speaking to a widely diverse audience, I try to be as universal in my examples as possible, avoid colloquialisms, and try to be very transparent about the cultural assumptions I perform. So, I want to be accessible, but I can't not speak like an American; it's who I am. So, I try to indicate that I'm aware of my positionality and make it open for people to talk about the different performed cultural assumptions. It would be the same when you have inter-faith discussions across cultures, but there the differences are more readily apparent.

Learn to Empathize

The transcendent quality every World Class speaker must possess is empathy. You will not share the same experiences, hardships, privileges, advantages, or disadvantages as every audience, but with empathy you will be able to bond and connect with your audience whether they are from Beverly Hills or South Central.

I remember asking Dr. Michelle Mazur about speaking to a diverse audience. Her advice was straightforward:

You must develop a deep empathy for your audience. Understand how they feel. Do research on their background and their experience. Interview potential members of the audience to understand them. When you don't take the time to understand your audience, your presentation could be a huge miss. An interior decorator client of mine was asked to present to new moms about how they should redecorate their home with a baby in mind. She gave tons of information about toy-free zones, a sweep every night, and a baby-free space for Mom. The information was good, but she wasn't a mom. She didn't understand at all how new moms felt: tired, overwhelmed, delirious with joy, and terrified they were going to break their newborn. Developing an empathy for how new moms felt, she was able to revamp her message so that it was helpful and didn't overwhelm.

When You Show Appreciation You Will Be Appreciated

I remember my first phone call with Craig Valentine. I asked him how to balance "opening with a bang" with following tradition, such as opening with a prayer or greeting. He told me, "You never want to break from tradition. For example, whenever I speak in Saudi Arabia or Kuwait, I begin with 'Asalam Alaykum.' The audience responds very positively to that." The reason is obvious—when you appreciate your audience, they will appreciate you.

I have witnessed time and time again that when a speaker greets the audience in their native language the audience responds very positively and an immediate bond is established.

I remember giving a talk at a Mexican wedding. I do not know Spanish and was not expected to know Spanish. But to show appreciation for the audience, in my speech I used just a few Spanish words, *la comida es muy deliciosa* (the food is very delicious) and *gracias* (thank you) at the end of my speech. Just these few words did wonders for connecting with the audience. I had multiple audience members come up to me saying how they loved my Spanish and thought that was really nice of me.

Learn the Norms

When you speak in another country, you will not be expected to follow their norms. They know you are coming as a visitor; they have invited you and are honored by your acceptance. They will be accommodating to you and expect you to be yourself. Although this takes the pressure off, you would do well to conduct some basic research such as learning what obscene or insulting hand gestures are in the local culture. Even though you may not be taken as offensive and your "breach" will be excused, you sure will create an unforgettable distraction for your audience.

> *World leaders, dignitaries, and celebrities speaking abroad have gestured with their fingers the equivalent of the "middle finger" in our culture. You can imagine the distraction that causes....*

World leaders, dignitaries, and celebrities speaking abroad have gestured with their fingers the equivalent of the "middle finger" in our culture. You can imagine the distraction that causes and how suddenly every member in that audience loses focus on the words and can't stop thinking about the speaker's obscene gesture. Imagine how you would feel as an audience member in that setting. Immediately the focus shifts from content to gesture. The blooper becomes more memorable than the content.

Don't Be Ethnocentric

Respect is a universal principle, but how respect is shown varies from culture to culture. Some of these norms are based in religion and principles of modesty, such as in Islam and Judaism where a man is not to put out his hand to a woman lest he offend her. Rather he should maintain his boundary of respect and wave or nod as a greeting. The opposite is also true. This is because touch is sacred and reserved only for family members.

It is important not to be ethnocentric when encountering new practices or norms. Celebrate the diversity and welcome new experiences. Do not be offended. Embrace the honor and diversify your palate.

Master the Art of Code Switching

Another way to connect with your audience is through successful code switching, or changing your speaking style based on the background of your interlocutors. The keyword here is *successful*. This is not being inauthentic, it's being empathetic. Code switching is increasingly important as our melting pot grows richer in diversity. Misery and embarrassment are the likely results of a failure to code switch effectively.

A good example is Malcolm X, who intoned his words in a manner very close to African American vernacular, but if you read a transcript, you'll see that his speeches read like Standard English. The syntax and diction are congruous with the rules of the language, but sometimes for rhetorical effect he broke the rules in a manner native to his audience.

A good time to add colloquial English or slang is during dialogue. Everyone knows people do not converse in fully Standard English, so dialogue is more authentic when spoken in colloquial English. Another effective use of colloquial speech is when a speaker expresses the thoughts of the audience, such as saying "I know ya'll thinkin' *he don't know what he talkin' about*." Although this isn't dialogue, it serves the same function where the speaker is speaking as the audience—in their conversational manner.

You must strike a balance between sounding out of touch and too informal to the point where you are not revered. Just as a speaker is expected to dress a level above his audience, so too is the expectation for speaking a level above.

I taught a lesson on this to high school students. I told them to pretend they had just witnessed a fight or car accident and then to take five minutes writing about it as if they were describing it to a friend. Five minutes later I told them to write about the same event, but as if they were presenting it to a judge.

Here are some examples:

To a friend: Was up Fred, this one guy got whooped on today. He got knocked out.

To a judge: Today as I was walking to school I witnessed a fight. A pedestrian was walking and another fellow came from the back and assaulted him. I felt sorry for the fellow. But I finally stopped all the commotion by calling the Hayward Police Department. They took care of everything.

This exercise shows we all know that each scenario has a specific rhetorical situation. Part of being a World Class speaker is identifying what the rhetorical situation is at every engagement.

Adjusting to your audience will go a long way in establishing your ability to relate. It's very common to speak slang with your friends but Standard English in a professional setting. Public speaking is a cross between formal and informal, standard and colloquial, so learning this delicate balance is essential.

Know Your Audience's Value System

When you speak to an audience you are conveying a message. To effectively convey your message you must understand the value system of your audience. Persuasive speech does not exist *in vacuo*. Understanding your audience's values will help you understand what they deem important.

Marketers know this very well. How much do car commercials have to do with the specifics of the car? How much do perfume ads have to do with the specifics of the perfume? Do they ever mention the ingredients, how the perfume is made, or even describe the smell? No. They advertise the lifestyle associated with the car and the glamour associated with the right perfume. When a television is being sold do you notice how comfortable the couches look in the commercial? Is there only one person viewing or is there a family or group of friends? Why is this important? What separates a commercial from an infomercial?

With just thirty seconds to impact and persuade, commercials are loaded with the images and myths of a glamorized lifestyle. Incidentally, the first thirty seconds of a speech are the most important to make an impact.

Americans value the "camaraderie system" where everyone is "in it together" as buddy-buddy. A boss and employee or professor and student are on a first-name basis to give the illusion of equality while the power difference remains clearly slanted. The speaker is to come off as personable and just one of the guys or girls telling stories to be relatable.

This would be looked down upon or seen as weakness in more formal cultures where there is a distance of respect between a speaker and audience, or teacher and student, or boss and employee. Getting too personal would lead to a lack of reverence, mentioning one's spouse would be seen as too personal, and sharing a religious view would be intrusive and imposing.

In Germany, identifying with the speaker is not important. Germans are more interested in the information than the personality conveying that information.

In African American culture the speaker and audience have a unique dynamic. They cooperate in a speech in what's called "call and response." This style reflects the egalitarianism in the speaker-audience relationship. Although there is one speaker, statements are punctuated by the audience making encouraging remarks such as "that's right!" to show pleasure and encouragement, or "yes" to show agreement. This style resembles a conversation more than a one-way address in which the speaker is the group representative best suited to articulate their challenges, ethics, and emotions. Because these speeches are not about the individual, the speaker does not need to tell personal stories. Rather, pathos and ability to relate is judged by effective "calls," which will be evaluated immediately by the enthusiasm in the responses.

A human is the same in essence, no matter race, culture, or religion. If this were not so, one culture would not be able to appreciate another, nor would you find religious conversion. A World Class speaker is able to speak to this unvarying element in the human soul while tailoring the message to the specifics of the audience.

Danish Qasim is a speech coach specializing in cross-cultural communication. He is a graduate of U.C. Berkeley where he studied linguistics and religious studies. Upon graduation Danish continued his studies by traveling abroad studying religion, spirituality, different languages, and cultures.

41

Keep 'em Hooked So
You Get Rebooked

Malachi Talabi

I magine this: you are the keynote speaker at an event. All the flyers have your face on it, and people are sending you messages on social media about how excited they are to hear you speak. You spend twenty hours practicing a twenty-five-minute keynote; you get onstage, deliver your speech, and when you finish you realize you flopped so badly the host has to ask the audience to clap. Ouch!

I will never forget the embarrassment of being the keynote speaker at the Toastmasters International Division H conference in 2010. I was still finding my feet as a speaker, one hundred people had come to see me—the 2011 UK and Ireland speech champion—and I bombed! My speech was awful. I went to my sales table and had to *beg* people to buy my book; I stocked fifty and sold ten! I was too embarrassed to ask the organizer for a testimonial.

Six months later I gave the keynote speech at another event, but after this speech my sales table was *bombarded*. The audience was in a frenzy. I sold out of products. I left the event with five invitations to be the keynote speaker at upcoming events, the host was over the moon, and I walked away with a huge profit.

What made the difference? *My story.*

In this chapter you will learn:

- how to make your story irresistible
- how to keep your audience hooked from beginning to end
- how to overcome the number one problem speakers face when telling stories
- the number one sales tool for a speaker
- a step-by-step process for making your audience curious and creating conflict

You will also get two tools that will help you engage your audience and impress those that book you.

If you can implement the tools in this chapter, not only will you find yourself getting rebooked more frequently, you'll also have the undivided attention of your audience when you speak—they'll be glued to your every word!

Are You a Marketing Maniac?

I was! Like most speakers I thought *If I'm going to get booked or rebooked I have to market like crazy! It's* all *about marketing.* I bought tons of marketing books, subscribed to mailing lists, and read blog after blog. I got one or two engagements now and again, but I never got rebooked. I struggled to turn one engagement into a repeat engagement or a new opportunity.

When it came down to it, after a lot of printed business cards, unanswered emails, and other time-consuming marketing gimmicks, I discovered that *the best sales pitch is a story well told!*

Is there a way to have the event organizers and audience members buying your products begging for your card and booking you again? Yes, there is. It is your story!

Marketing is extremely important because it can open doors, but once you are onstage your best sales tools are your speaking skills. The truth is that most event organizers go with what they know.

Think about it—if you are *not* good onstage, why would they want you back? Why would the audience want to hear you again? Why would they recommend you to anybody else? The organizers won't think *His speech is extremely boring; in fact, I saw half the audience sleeping—let's book him again!*

On other hand, if you have your audience on the edge their seats, leaning forward itching to hear your very next word, you'll be the speaker that they'll want to hear time and time again and I can guarantee you that one engagement will open up hundreds of opportunities.

How to Make Your Story Irresistible

What makes a story irresistible? Why is it easy to listen to some stories but a struggle to stay awake during others?

After that nightmare engagement back in 2010, I was brave enough to listen to the recording of my speech. I pressed play on my little dictaphone and discovered that my story was missing two things that every story needs to be irresistible—I call them "attention magnets."

Do you ever find yourself fighting for your audience's attention? You're not alone!

The number one challenge that speakers face when telling stories is gaining the audience's attention. Audiences have heard story after story, so they won't just listen—attention magnets help speakers overcome this challenge.

Most speakers fight for attention; World Class speakers attract it! If you want two tools that will make your story irresistible, hook your audience from beginning to end, and increase your chances of getting rebooked, here they are: curiosity and conflict.

Two Key Attention Magnets: Curiosity and Conflict

Have you ever seen a magnet in action? Put it near a pin and it will attract that pin and have the pin clinging to it. Curiosity and conflict are like magnets—they attract a wandering mind.

You don't need to shout, you don't need gimmicks, all you need to do is create legitimate conflict and make your audience curious, and you'll have an irresistible story. If you can use these two tools in your story you will literally see your audience members look up and lean forward. You'll have them in the palm of your hand.

These two tools are part of the "9 Cs of Storytelling" that Craig Valentine teaches in his home-study course, and for so many years they were absent from my speeches. The only reason my audiences listened to me was because they had to! I was fighting for their attention instead of attracting it.

It wasn't until I went through the 9 Cs of Storytelling that I realized my stories lacked conflict. I failed to make my audience curious—I gave them no reason to listen! Thankfully you never have to be in that position because the next time you speak you'll have two surefire attention magnets at your disposal.

Curiosity and Conflict in Action

One month after I bombed onstage I gave a speech that went very well. Here's an example from that speech of how curiosity and conflict helped me attract my audience's attention. You should have seen the look on their faces when I took to the stage and said:

> *Have you ever heard the phrase what happens in Vegas stays in Vegas? [audience responds with nods] That's not true because something happened that I can't let stay there!*

My audience leaned forward, put down their phones, and a hush fell over the room. I had their attention. Why? Because they were curious! They wanted to know what happened and how it would benefit them. I quickly gained their attention at the beginning of my speech; they couldn't resist. I created a question and my audience wanted answers!

> ### Hook tip: If you hook them at the beginning they'll stay till the end.

Here's how I used conflict in the very same speech later on in the story. I said:

> *I dreamed of winning this contest but I had just lost. All that training, all those hours wasted. I wanted to be alone. I picked up my third-place trophy and made my way to my hotel room. My plan was to lie on my bed and cry, and out of all the Toastmasters I could bump into in the corridor, who do I bump into? [curiosity] Garret Garrels, the second-place winner in my contest!*

At this point my audience started laughing because they could see the conflict of wanting to be a champion and losing—a situation made even worse by my wanting to be alone but bumping into a contestant that had just beaten me!

Although my audience laughed at the conflict they were engaged and wanted to know how I would handle seeing Garret. I had them hooked.

> *Hook tip: When you have your audience hooked they are not hearing your speech they are experiencing it.*

Using these two storytelling tools made the difference in my speech. My audience was engaged, and at the end of the speech I got rebooked. You will be amazed how engaged your audience members are when you use these tools and how many invitations you get after you've given a great speech.

A Step-by-Step Process for Curiosity/Conflict

Now that you know the importance of curiosity and conflict in a speech, here is a step-by-step process for creating it.

Conflict Steps

Step 1: Uncover Your Conflict

First you must analyze your story and decide what conflict you have. Here are some common conflicts:

- man vs. man
- man vs. nature
- man vs. self
- man vs. society

Check your content—do you have a legitimate conflict?

Here is a conflict I use in one of my stories. I turn to the audience and say:

My wife walked up to me and said, "Baby, I love you; baby, I want to start a family…" But I felt too young. I thought, You want to start a family with me? I am not daddy material!

The conflict in this story is man vs. man.

Step 2: Escalate Conflict

World Class Speaking coaching taught me this valuable lesson in conflict. In one of my speeches I had a legitimate conflict but it was static. It didn't go anywhere. Here is an example of the static conflict in my speech:

> *I couldn't find the remote control to my television, and the match started at eight o'clock. I checked everywhere—under the pillow, under the sofa, under the bed...*

For about three minutes I described how I couldn't find the remote control. My audience was bored! I could sense it and I could see it.

> **Conflict tip: The conflict you start with shouldn't be the conflict you stick with; escalate it!**

Here is an example of how I escalated the conflict in a speech I gave when I won the UK and Ireland Toastmasters competition:

> *My mum couldn't afford a washing machine so I had to go to school with a dirty shirt every day, which meant I didn't smell too good.* [conflict] *On Thursday it was time for gym class and the gym instructor said, "Talabi, it's time for gym; go and get changed." I had no choice. I had to take my shirt off.* [escalation]

In storytelling, the conflict should increase or be intensified. It's one thing to have a smelly shirt; it's another thing to have a smelly shirt and body odor and have to get changed in front of your peers! Would I listen to my teacher and risk the embarrassment and potential bullying, or would I get detention for my disobedience? My audience was hooked at this point, waiting to hear what would happen next. Escalation made the difference!

> **Conflict tip: When the consequence is magnified the conflict is intensified.**

Step 3: Early Conflict

I was in a speech contest and had seven minutes to speak. I knew that every minute would count, so within the first two minutes I dived straight into my conflict:

> *I was ten years old, and I had to walk home on my own and past a dark tunnel. Terry was inside. Terry was freckle-faced and filled with fury, and he hated ten-year-olds—especially black Africans...*

My audience was hooked within the first two minutes! I have had times when I took too long to get into my conflict, only to discover this principle: the longer it takes you to get into your conflict, the longer it takes your audience to get into your speech.

The Power of Curiosity

The absence of curiosity is the presence of boredom. If your audience is not curious then they are likely to be bored. Their attention is somewhere else. From now on as a speaker, it's your job to make curiosity a priority.

Curiosity has led to some of the greatest discoveries in the world, and it will lead to some of the greatest speeches you'll ever give. Imagine stepping out to your audience and saying:

> *The number one tool to creating a great speech isn't storytelling, emotion, or even humor; it's something so simple you probably wouldn't guess it. It's something that I failed to see until I gave a free speech and walked away with over $500 of product sales and more Twitter followers and subscribers to my list...*

This is the type of opening that attracts attention, and if it's backed up by a solid point, you've hit a home run with your audience! I have a very similar opening and it works every time I speak.

How to Create Curiosity In Your Speeches

The number one way is to create questions.

> **Hook tip: Curiosity isn't about asking questions it's about creating them.**

You must deliberately and strategically create questions in the minds of your listeners. The answer to these questions should contain the solution to a problem they face, or you can simply use curiosity to get them into your story. For example:

I discovered the number one secret to becoming a millionaire while I was on holiday two years ago…

Anyone who wants to be a millionaire would want to listen to the rest of your speech!

Curiosity Check

Craig taught me this one. After you have written your speech, get your dictaphone and listen to the recording of your speech. Ask yourself, "What questions would my audience be asking?" If there are no questions then your audience members aren't curious! It's your job to make them curious in the beginning of your speech.

Key Takeaways

In this chapter you've received two tools that will help you engage your audience and impress those that book you. You've also learned how to make your story irresistible and keep your audience hooked from beginning to end.

Once you use these principles you'll have your audience hooked, and before you leave the room you'll get rebooked. It has happened for me several times, and I'm so grateful that I discovered these two attention magnets. Without them I would be a very frustrated speaker!

Now that you've got these tools I'm curious to see how you use them!

Malachi Talabi is the 2011 UK and Ireland Toastmasters International speech champion and a third-place international speech contest world semi-finalist. He is a certified World Class Speaking coach, the author of several books, and a lay minister at his local church. His main passion is to help people master and enjoy the art of public speaking. For more information, please visit www.malachitalabi.com.

42

World Class Fundraising
through Speaking

Lisa Vanderkwaak

A
s a speaker you have the tools necessary to mobilize people to give financially to meet a need within their own community or across the globe.

The need for humanitarian aid is growing globally and seems like an overwhelming task to most people. In recent years, it has become normal for businesses, governments, and community groups to raise money to help others affected by natural disaster, disease, or tragedy.

Through this chapter you will:

- learn the power of using speaking to help those who can't speak for themselves
- discover three essential skills you need to successfully raise funds for a charity or cause
- understand why you need to focus less on giving information and more on evoking transformation every time you speak
- have the opportunity to inspire others, shift mindsets, and invite people to step forward and play a role in transforming our world

Three Essential Skills to Help You Fundraise the World Class Way

1. Engage Your Audience

Most people are inundated with solicitors coming to their front door or telemarketers calling them at dinnertime. When speaking to raise money for a charity it is essential that you engage your audience rather than simply give them facts and figures. In other words, you will need to learn the skills to go beyond simply communicating to that of *connecting* with your audience in deeper, more meaningful ways. Emotional connection is vital to establish trust and credibility between you and your audience. Here are two simple yet powerful ways you can engage any audience and connect on personal levels:

Eye contact. Eyes are the gateway to the heart. Engaging your audience means connecting with them emotionally, spiritually, or intellectually—and perhaps all three. The rule that World Class speakers follow is "Look to all, speak to one."

> *Engaging your audience means connecting with them emotionally, spiritually, or intellectually—and perhaps all three.*

"Look to all" means that when you speak your eyes play a key role in making your audience members feel valued and included in your message. Throughout over 90 percent of your message, your eyes need to be scanning your audience *naturally* from one section of the room to the next while connecting by gazing briefly into the eyes of individuals as you ask a question or emphasize a point. This will require that you practice your message to the place where you only have to look occasionally at your notes, if at all. Your goal should be to go beyond simply conveying information to that of evoking transformation in the hearts and minds of all who are listening. Intentional use of eye contact is one way to accomplish this.

Use of stories. Another powerful yet simple way to engage your audience is through storytelling. This is especially important when speaking to raise money for a nonprofit organization. Stories or one main story can be thoughtfully used to connect with audience members in deeper, more personal ways and to inspire them to take action. Through strategic use of stories you invite your audience to walk in the shoes of others and believe in the possibility of their playing a significant role in solving the problem you are presenting.

For example, suppose you are speaking for an organization like Home of Hope, which helps millions of widows and orphans affected by war and gender-targeted crimes. Perhaps you are asked to speak to raise money to help the survivors of the mass genocide that took place in Rwanda in 1994. You may do what most speakers do and provide facts and statistics about what happened in that nation. You may say something like "observers have suggested the number of women raped during the genocide is believed to be between 200,000 and 500,000."

While it is important to paint a picture of what was, it is equally if not more important to paint a picture of what can be by sharing a story of a real person who survived the genocide and is now being helped by Home of Hope.

To fund-raise the World Class way it is important to use the Then/Now/How formula about a person that has been helped. Suppose a widow named Cecilia was left to raise her two children on her own because her husband, father, and brothers were all killed during the genocide. Before coming in contact with Home of Hope, Cecilia walked to the market every day, taking her two hours to get there and two hours to walk back. Often she would return home with just three pieces of fruit that had dropped off the carts of others or food that was left to rot on the side of the road. It was hardly enough to feed even one child let alone a family.

Today Cecilia still goes to the market—not to find food but to run her own business. One year ago she had the opportunity to take a basic course and receive a loan to start her own business. She bought two chickens and started selling their eggs at the market. As the months went on she not only earned enough money to feed her family, she was able to buy two more chickens and with the increased number of eggs doubled her profits. As a result Cecilia has hired two other women to help her in her business and has paid back the initial loan of $150 she received. She now has the means to support her family and is inspiring and equipping other women to do the same.

What made the difference? Two years ago at a meeting just like this a young man named Stephen who was just starting out in business decided to give Home of Hope $150 for their micro-loan project. That $150 was then loaned to Cecilia, who enrolled in the free course Home of Hope offered. During the course Cecilia learned how to write a business plan, develop a business strategy, and found renewed hope for a better future. After a process of interviews Cecilia was selected to be one of the first women to receive a micro-loan. During her first year of business, she had access to a volunteer mentor who helped support and guide her through this initial phase of business development. At the end of the first year, when Cecilia paid back the loan, Home of Hope then gave the $150 to another widow as a micro-loan to start her own business.

By using the Then/Now/How formula in this way you not only share a story of transformation in the life of Cecilia but you also help expand the mindset of your audience members as to how they too can play a part in ending world poverty, for example. The hero in the story was the young man who gave a small donation, to which everyone can relate.

You have probably heard the proverb that says "Give a man a fish and you feed him for a day; teach him how to fish and you feed him for a lifetime." Raising funds to help people who belong to other parts of society or distant countries is often hindered because the audience feels removed from the reality of others. They look to you, the speaker, to help fill in that gap and expand their thinking about what their involvement makes possible. Well-structured stories are one of the most powerful ways to accomplish both.

2. Embrace a Growth Mindset

No matter what the cause or topic you are speaking about, it inevitably targets some need for people to change. When speaking to raise funds your message needs to invite your audience members to embrace a growth mindset. What that means is that to donate money, time, or resources, especially smaller amounts, people first need to believe that what they are giving will help solve the problem you are presenting. As the speaker, you can help them create shifts in their thinking and believe beyond what they thought possible about the difference they can make by their giving.

Dr. Carol Dweck, professor of psychology at Stanford University, has spent most of her career studying the mental attitudes of the most successful people—young and old—as they faced both challenges and opportunities. What her findings revealed was a fundamental difference in the mindset of the most successful people. She called the simple yet fundamental difference a *fixed mindset* or a *growth mindset*.

Many people are stuck in life because they believe that what they currently possess will determine their success in life, and therefore their impact. Often they will resist or shy away from challenges or opportunities because they are unsure they have what it takes to succeed in that area. These people are operating out of a fixed mindset.

People who approach life with a growth mindset believe they can grow through experience and change substantially through taking action. They believe this about themselves and about how their actions can potentially impact others.

Therefore, when speaking to raise funds, give special attention not only to engaging your audience and helping them embrace a growth mindset, but also to inspiring them to take action. Finally, before you close you need to extend a clear call to action.

3. Extend a Clear Call to Action

I have been in the speaking industry for several years, and one thing I have noticed is that most speakers leave their audience hanging without a clear next step to take. If you have successfully engaged your audience and helped them shift their mindset to believe they can make a difference, they are actually waiting for you to show them *how* they can get involved right away.

> *If you have successfully engaged your audience…they are actually waiting for you to show them how they can get involved right away.*

World Class speakers know that "a confused mind says no and a clear mind says go." So even before you write your speech you need to be clear about what next step you will invite your audience to take. If it is clear to you it will be clear to your audience.

A very powerful technique to use at this point is to callback to a previous story that highlighted the impact of one person's donation. For example, in the story about the widow from Rwanda you heard of Stephen, the young businessman who gave $150 toward a micro-loan project that helped Cecilia start her own business. Stephen was the hero in the story. What he did helped transform one woman's life, and ultimately his gift is still helping to transform a whole community. Your job as the speaker is to present the hero as someone similar, not special. By doing so you help the audience relate to Stephen and see him as someone just like them. This leads them to embrace the belief that "if he can do it, so can I."

When extending a clear call to action, have concrete steps your audience can take immediately. For example, you may have volunteers distribute pre-made cards where audience members can fill out their contact information and indicate the donation amount they have chosen to give. Or, if your goal is to generate funds for a certain dollar amount, such as enough to provide five micro-loans, you could show a picture of certain widows who are waiting to receive micro-loans and ask audience members who wants to invest $150, for example, to help each widow start a business.

No matter what the audience, the number one thing people want to take away from hearing someone speak is something they can apply to their life or something they can do to make a difference in the world. That is why having a clear call to action is so critical. It gives the audience a definite "next step" to take.

Whether you are just starting out or are more experienced as a speaker, you have the power to effect change and transformation in the lives of others by the words you speak and the stories you share.

To recap, when using speaking to raise funds for charities or special projects, it is not enough to simply give information; aim to evoke change and transformation in the hearts and minds of the audience members. To successfully raise funds, first master the skills of engaging your audience, helping them embrace a growth mindset, and extending a clear call to action. Developing these skills will set you apart as a speaker and distinguish you as a World Class fundraiser.

Lisa Vanderkwaak, MSc, is the founder and CEO of REAL U Institute™ and is a speaker, author, and certified World Class Speaking coach. To find out more about Lisa or to receive her free Speak To Transform™ toolkit visit www.RealUSpeaking.com.

43

The Secret Recipe for World Class Entertainment

Manoj Vasudevan

World Class speakers aim to *entertain* as they *educate*. Stand-up comedians and late-night show hosts pull in large audiences because they are able to entertain. When you become an entertaining speaker you command more respect, more reward, and higher rehire rates.

After reading this chapter, you will have an edge over other speakers because you will pick up the *definitive process* to make your speeches entertaining. Following that process will put you well on your way to becoming a World Class entertainer.

This chapter will cover:

- the modes of entertainment
- the secret recipe for World Class entertainment
- how to think out of the script

The Modes of Entertainment

Have you noticed how some speakers, performers, stand-up comedians, radio and television hosts, and masters of ceremony keep their audiences entertained? Here are the common modes of entertainment they deploy:

- jokes, comical gestures, clownish acts
- funny visuals or props
- improvisation techniques or crowd work techniques
- stories and anecdotes told in an engaging manner

The primary focus of World Class speakers is on developing compelling stories and anecdotes. The secret of an entertaining speech is that the speaker converts ordinary experiences into fascinating narratives and packages them for a seemingly spontaneous but usually pre-planned dynamic delivery.

In the next section you will pick up the secret recipe for World Class entertainment that will help you to make entertaining anecdotes from ordinary incidents. You will also notice the role that World Class competencies of *storytelling* and *dynamic delivery* play in entertainment.

The Secret Recipe for World Class Entertainment

Wouldn't it be fabulous if there were a process you could follow to make your speeches more entertaining? I have scrutinized several hundred videos of keynote speakers, stand-up comedians, late-night hosts, and other entertaining speakers to uncover the underlying theme and technique of entertainment. What I found is that the speakers who entertain the most are those who follow what I call the ORANGE process. ORANGE stands for Observe, Relate, Analyze, Narrate, Gesticulate, and Exaggerate.

To illustrate the ORANGE process for you, I will use a personal anecdote that I call the MRI anecdote.

The MRI Anecdote

A few years ago a sudden bout of back pain led me to visit a hospital and consult a back pain specialist. The doctor quizzed me for a while, prescribed some medicines, and said:

"Manoj, you need to get an MRI scan as soon as possible."

"What? I feel fine. I don't think I need an MRI scan. Can you just give me some balm and painkillers instead?"

"Manoj, you need to get this done right now. I am the expert on this. I suggest that you trust the expert and follow the process."

I reluctantly accepted the proposal, signed the forms, and went to the MRI room.

Soon, an attendant briefed me on the procedures.

"Mr Vasudevan, remove all metallic objects on your body, change into these hospital robes, and lie down on the MRI machine," she said. "And remember, don't move! If you move, we will have to restart the scanning process."

I removed all metallic objects, changed into the hospital robes, and lay down on the tray of the MRI machine. That was the first time I had ever seen an MRI machine. The attendant slid the tray containing me into the interior chamber of the machine. If you have never seen an MRI machine before, picture yourself being stuffed into a large doughnut. The size and shape of the machine, the rapid thumping sound it produces, and the confined space around the tray on which I lay prompted me to wriggle and say "Oh my God! I feel like I'm inside a coffin!"

The attendant peeped into my coffin and said, "Sir, don't move. If you follow the instructions, we can complete the scan sooner and get you the results. If you do not, you will disrupt the process and delay your results." She quickly disappeared from my view, and I could hear the door closing. The sound of the MRI machine was rising in intensity as if preparing for takeoff. I was feeling increasingly lonely, trapped, and uncomfortable in my coffin. I tried not to move. Then I noticed a tiny red light on the roof of the machine above my head. There was something written around that tiny red light that I could not read from where I lay.

Curiosity got the better of me. I lifted my head and strained my eyes to read the print around that tiny red light. It took me awhile, but I could finally read it: "CAUTION: Do not stare! Laser beam can cause blindness!"

The attendant barged into the room yelling "Sir, you moved! We have to restart the process now. Please allow us to complete the process." I looked at her and said, "Wow! I can still see!"

Eventually the scanning process was completed. The scan report helped me in the early identification and timely rectification of a prolapsed disc.

I use the MRI anecdote for my keynote on World Class speech coaching. You might be wondering what World Class speech coaching has to do with the MRI anecdote. In the upcoming sections you will find out and also learn how I used the ORANGE process to develop and deliver the MRI anecdote.

> *The single most important skill that sets World Class entertainers apart from wannabe entertainers is their keen sense of observation.*

Observe

The single most important skill that sets World Class entertainers apart from wannabe entertainers is their keen sense of observation. *Observation* is the foundation of *entertainment*. The key to observation is to be aware of what is happening around you. The following quote commonly attributed to Leonardo da Vinci says it best.

> *The average human looks without seeing, listens without hearing, touches without feeling, eats without tasting, moves without physical awareness, inhales without awareness of odour or fragrance, and talks without thinking.*

Your observations are the best source for a fabulous speech. You are about to learn how you should incorporate your observations into your speech so that your audience will relate to your experience and be entertained.

Relate

An observation by itself is not usually enough. If all you do is talk about apples, your speech starts to get boring. It becomes more interesting when you find ways to compare and *relate* apples to oranges.

For instance, following are some of my observations:

- The MRI scan
    - The doctor asking me to *"trust the expert and follow the process."*
    - My attitude toward my first MRI scan and how I disrupted the scan procedure.
- World Class speech coaching
    - During my coaching sessions on World Class Speaking, I have observed that certain clients resist trying out new ideas or following the recommended processes. They *disrupt* the coaching process and *delay* seeing their positive *results*.

At first sight, the observations on the MRI scan incident and World Class speech coaching are entirely different things just like apples and oranges. In the next section you will learn how to uncover similarities between different observations.

Analyze

When you *analyze* the observations and delve into the details, you start to see that different observations can be *related* using common characteristics, behaviors, and features. For instance, I had gone to the hospital to consult a *back pain specialist* for *expert* opinion. The expert, the doctor, had my best interests in his mind. However, I doubted the doctor's opinion and disrupted the process of the MRI scan by not following the instructions given to me. That wasted everyone's time and almost damaged my eyes! It caused needless delays in getting my scan results.

Likewise, during speech coaching, the coach is the person with the expertise. Clients engage a coach to seek guidance and to learn new ideas, techniques, and processes. When clients do not follow the processes recommended by their coach, they defeat the purpose of coaching. It disrupts the coaching process and delays the positive results the client could have received. In short, they behave like me during my first MRI scan!

Did you notice how by analyzing two different observations we start to see similarities between them?

Here are some other examples of comparing and relating observations used in the MRI anecdote; I compare the MRI machine to a *large doughnut*. Later I compare it to a *coffin*.

World Class entertainers strive to *relate* observations to acquire such unique perspectives and insights.

From your analysis you will uncover material that is potentially entertaining. What should you do now?

Narrate

The next step is to *narrate* (verbalize) your story.

Key to narration is the choice of words and dialogue used to describe your observations. The secret for superb narration is to be as vivid as possible, invoking all possible senses and building up suspense before the eventual revelation.

In the next sections you will learn the last two components of the ORANGE process to greatly enhance the entertainment value of your narrative.

Gesticulate

The entertainment value of your story hinges on the art of emphasis, hints, and misdirection. World Class entertainers pay particular attention to *gestures* and even plan some deliberate gestures

- to emphasize the emotion they portray.
- to give nonverbal hints about the characters and the scene.
- to intentionally misdirect the attention of the audience before a twist in the tale.

Here are some examples from the MRI anecdote:

- the attendant barging into the room
- hints on the confined space inside the machine
- lifting my head and straining my eyes to read the print

Now let's take a look at an effective technique you can use to make your speech memorable.

Exaggerate

Exaggeration is an effective technique used by World Class entertainers to stretch the audience's imagination. Though the audience might notice the exaggeration, they will love the experience. Exaggeration makes the content memorable, and it can be used in both content and delivery.

> *Exaggeration makes the content memorable.*

Exaggerations used in content

Exaggerations help to paint the scene in your listener's mind. In the MRI anecdote, I used the following expressions to paint the scene: the scare and the struggle.

- If you have never seen an MRI machine before, picture yourself being *stuffed into a large doughnut.*
- The size and shape of the machine, the rapid thumping sound it produced, and the confined space around the tray on which I lay prompted me to wriggle and say *"Oh my God! I feel like I am inside a coffin!"*
- The sound of the MRI machine was rising in intensity *as if preparing for takeoff.*

Exaggerations used in delivery

There are five delivery-related exaggeration techniques. The following illustrates how I used these techniques in the MRI anecdote:

- larger gestures (e.g. large doughnut, confined space of the coffin)
- facial expressions (e.g. emotion of fear, curiosity, straining to read the print around the tiny red light)
- vocal emphasis on key words (e.g. *Don't* move, *caution*, laser beam can cause *blindness*)
- dynamic movements during delivery
- pause (e.g. use of strategic pauses throughout the anecdote)

Here is the little-known secret. While you aim to entertain your audience, watch the movement of your eyebrows and be sure they reflect the emotions you are trying to project. Your eyebrows are the key visual indicator of the emotions you portray.

What you read so far covers

- how to use the ORANGE process to develop an entertaining and memorable anecdote
- how to deliver it with impact

In the next section you will learn how to use the ORANGE process to incorporate the incidents you observe right when you speak!

How to Think Out of the Script

Entertaining speakers are not glued to their script, they *think out of the script.* As you speak there could be interesting observations that you can incorporate into your speech. During one of my speeches I was telling a story in which I mentioned that I was afraid of *my wife*. As I spoke, someone's phone went off. I rushed to that person with earnestness and pleaded "Don't pick up that phone! That must be *my wife*!" The audience broke into laughter. I added, "She is always checking on me!" As you can see, this was a quick deployment of the ORANGE process by relating the phone ringing to the character of the story I was telling.

When you are onstage:

- Always observe. Be aware of what is going on around you.
- When you discover a gem of information, try to incorporate that in your speech. Your audience will love your creativity and presence of mind.

The next time you work on your speech or presentation, ask yourself the following question: *will your speech entertain before it educates?*

When you entertain, your audiences will have less mental strain to learn what you teach and they will better remember your message. Entertainment is a skill you can develop from common observations and consistent use of the ORANGE process. It will help you to transform your ordinary experiences and observations into an exceptionally entertaining speech.

Speakers who use the ORANGE process are well on their way to becoming World Class entertainers. Remember, all around the world entertaining speakers command more respect, more reward, and higher rehire rates!

Manoj Vasudevan, MBA, is a management consultant, international keynote speaker, author, coach, and humor expert. He is the chief expressions officer (CEO) of Thought Expressions. Find out more about him at www.ThoughtExpressions.com or www.TheHumorGuru.com. You can reach him at manoj@thoughtexpressions.com.

Part 6

WORLD CLASS
VIRTUAL SPEAKING

44

Energy and Intentions: How to Connect to a Virtual Audience

Shari Strong

Have you ever attended a teleseminar where the speaker was so monotonous, or the energy on the phone was so low, that you just decided to hang up? Teleseminars, webinars, and virtual meetings are powerful tools for small business owners, speakers, teachers, or anyone who has a message they would like to get out to the world. But as the use of these and other online tools increases, those who are successful at using them will be the ones who learn how to stand out and engage the audience.

One of the very first teleseminars I attended was conducted by an entrepreneur who was offering his services and products, and the purpose was to give you a taste of what he offered. His services and expertise were an excellent offering, but when he started the seminar the energy that came across was so low and so boring it actually discouraged me from purchasing and I ultimately left the call early—and have never joined one of his calls again. I don't say this to scare you, but one of the things that many speakers and small business owners do is underestimate the opposite effect they may have on their business if they don't learn the secrets of connecting with a virtual audience.

In this chapter you will learn how *energy*, *intentions*, and *mindset* affect the engagement of your virtual audience.

Have you ever listened to a speaker in person and thought to yourself *Wow, they are good!* Why? Did they master the use of the stage? Did they master the ability to read the audience? Did they master the art of storytelling?

Key Point: What makes a speaker good onstage is what will make him or her great at virtual presentation as well.

> *What makes a speaker good onstage is what will make him or her great at virtual presentation as well.*

First, energy. The best speakers have a good "vibe" or "energy." If they walked out onto the stage with their shoulders slumped over and started speaking in a tone that had no passion behind it, no emotion, no purpose, you might start to get distracted, maybe look at your phone, and think about everything you need to do for the rest of the day. Your virtual audience will react the same way.

Key Point: The best speakers are aware of their energy.
It takes a lot of energy to perform and deliver a speech in front of a live audience. It takes that same energy plus an ability to be comfortable in a room by yourself to deliver the same speech or content to a virtual audience. The reason I feel many speakers don't do well with a virtual audience is that they underestimate the amount of energy it takes. They go in with the belief that it will take less. It actually takes more! When you are in a room by yourself and cannot draw upon the energy you normally receive from a live audience, you are responsible for generating energy at the beginning, middle, and end all by yourself. A technique to use is to "get into character."

Malcolm Gladwell, a well-known journalist, author, and sociology researcher, has written about how "character acting" is something we all do. Basically his research shows that each "you" you bring forward in any situation is based on your situation.

For example:

1. An audience doesn't respond to you; a different you shows up for the rest of the speech.
2. You present a proposal to a company and they refuse; a different you shows up every time you think of them or speak to them.
3. A homeless person asks for money; a different you shows up.

From his book *The Tipping Point*:

Character, then, isn't what we think it is or, rather, what we want it to be. It isn't a stable, easily identifiable set of closely related traits, and it only seems that way because of a glitch in the way our brains are organized. Character is more like a bundle of habits and tendencies and interests, loosely bound together and dependent, at certain times, on circumstance and context. The reason that most of us seem to have a consistent character is that most of us are really good at controlling our environment.

So when conducting a teleseminar or webinar, the character that shows up has to be the one you would expect if someone else were delivering the information. Beyoncé uses this technique when she performs. She calls it her alter ego, and she even gave the alter ego a name: Sasha Fierce.

It's amazing how many times I have been emailed right after a teleseminar with positive comments about my passion. It's always when I use the same gestures I would use if they were sitting in a live audience. I walk, use my hands, raise my voice, lower my voice—whatever my style is live is the same style I use with a virtual audience.

Key Point: Once in character, it's time to deliver.

Craig Valentine, a world champion speaker, says "Don't speak to many, speak to one." It's the same with a teleseminar/webinar. To connect with the virtual audience, they need to feel like you are speaking directly to them.

It amazes me how some speakers will show up for a speaking engagement and really not know anything about the audience they are speaking to; they talk in generalizations. The rules are the same for the virtual audience. Many speakers just get lazy, become arrogant, and feel that their message is so important—or that they have "arrived"—and that is why people have signed up for the teleseminar. They couldn't be more wrong. The core message or expertise may be something the audience wants to hear about, but you alone are not the full reason they are there.

Take the extra effort to get to know them, their challenges, and their goals. This is one thing that will set you apart. They will relate much better to the information and will connect much more easily to you because you developed something specifically for them.

The best way to become a pro is to practice. The best speakers onstage practice. The best teleseminar/webinar presenters practice. It has to be intentional. If this is going to be a way for you to expand your business, then this is no less important than practicing for a keynote in front of a thousand people. Teleseminars can take your business to another level quicker because you are able to deliver content to many people but with a much more personal touch. Remember, the audience is usually listening from a room where they are by themselves, or a car where they are alone. They too are not in a room of one thousand to draw energy from; they are depending on you to do that. So to them it's just *you* and *them*.

There are many techniques to use that don't take much time and make you look extremely polished. Practice your seminar in pieces; divide it into ten-minute segments and practice each. Be sure to practice without reading a script because you want it to sound like you are speaking from the heart. If you read from a script, your heart will not come through, which in turn will dial down the energy and ultimately your ability to connect with the audience. Record the ten-minute segments and listen to them; pay attention to the words you used, the tone, the pace, and how you would feel if you were a participant.

Statistics are a great way to bring people in and build credibility in any presentation. However, using the same boring old facts that you have heard before will not encourage your virtual audience to stay engaged. If you are going to use statistics, take the time to find statistics that are rare or new. Again, engaging people virtually takes more intention, not less, than a live audience. The real reason to use statistics is to bring emotions to the surface and create a sense of urgency for them to take action.

Key Point: Use words that bring emotions to the surface.

There are many emotions you may want to bring to the surface with your virtual audience. Your choice of words and tone can make that happen sooner, which means you will connect faster. Fear, anger, confidence, or happiness are just a few, and picking the words that mean something to the audience is key. Knowing your purpose and what you want the outcome to be will help you pick which emotions you want to tap and ultimately which words to use.

As you prepare your content, keep in mind this important question: what outcome do you want from the teleseminar/webinar? Most likely you are not choosing to do a teleseminar/webinar just to listen to yourself speak; there is a larger purpose. But to get people to stay on the phone or Internet to hear the message and actually take action, the larger purpose cannot be just to "buy" your products or services. You have to truly believe that the people who do want more or buy more are the ones you will be working with after the seminar. You have no control over who buys and who does not. They may *want* to but can't for whatever reason. The point here is the following:

Key Point: Let go of the results! Commit to the process.

So the question is: *what is the larger purpose to why I am doing this?* If you want to present your speaking system and your goal is to enroll participants, that is what will drive the outline of the teleseminar/webinar, but you really don't know what the results will be. If that is all you are concerned about, that is what will be communicated.

> *So the question is: what is the larger purpose to why I am doing this?*

The question I like to ask my clients is, "What do *you* want to learn?" So if you have done a thousand teleseminars/webinars and the feedback is that they are becoming boring, my question is the same: "What do *you* want to learn from your next teleseminar?" It's simple but profound. The answer should provide a purpose larger than just selling, larger than the audience, larger than just adding fans to your fan base. Do you want to learn how to say more with fewer words? Maybe how you can try new catchphrases?

When we shift our focus to something we want to learn or something that stretches us, usually our energy shifts. When our energy shifts to something that increases our excitement, our intentions become focused on something that is positive and constructive, which ultimately will affect the energy of the presentation delivery.

If you are planning your first teleseminar/webinar, the question is the same: "What do *you* want to learn when you deliver it?" Managing the energy in a room or over the phone is simply bringing awareness to our intentions and how we present those intentions with our actions and words. If we focus on how nervous we are, or wonder if we will sell anything, our energy will focus on the questions we ask. If it is a "worry" or "doubt," the energy will build toward those. If it is a "learning" or "personal challenge," our energy will focus on those intentions. In each case, the audience will feel the energy behind the words.

It's been said that "neglecting passion blocks creative flow. When you're passionate, you're energized. Likewise, when you lack passion, your energy is low and unproductive. Energy is everything when it comes to being successful" (source unknown).

Transparency is a bonus. People often have trouble being transparent because their idea of what professional is prevents them from revealing that they are not perfect. Professional does not mean perfect. When we are not willing to be transparent, we hurt our chances of making a connection with people in the audience. Being transparent doesn't mean telling your deepest fears or revealing your biggest flaws, but it does suggest you tell stories that show you are not always the hero, stories that reveal when you didn't have the right answer, or it could be something that makes you unique. It can be anything that will give them a glimpse into the real you.

Gurus who provide teleseminars/webinars are often great at telling what they do, but the ones who really engage their audiences also share the *why* of what they do. Sharing your *why* will help the audience's perception of your ability to be transparent and authentic.

Key Point: One of the best ways to make sure the audience loves you is to provide solutions to their problems.

If you have done a thorough job of researching your audience, and if your services and products are a match, you already know what their problems are. Most experts offer a couple of solutions that will help the audience, in hopes of "hooking" them to buy their products in order to get the whole solution to their problem. This is where I differ. I believe in giving and teaching your best solutions. Why? Most of the participants will not go implement the solution on their own. It's human nature. We hear it, we get excited, but doing it and putting it into action is difficult. That is why they will ultimately purchase your services or products—not to get more solutions but to help them with the implementation of the solutions you presented. This is where you can separate yourself from other experts in your industry.

Key Point: Come from a place of abundance, not scarcity.

The more you share, the more you will connect with your virtual audience. Many gurus come from a place of scarcity, and it takes them years to build. If they are scared to share or refer and always have an attitude of "what's in it for me," ultimately they will get nothing or it will take years to build their tribe. Think about the people who "give" more in life. Nelson Mandela gave years; Beth Moore gives away her books at the beginning of every year on Kindle; John Maxwell does not allow his certified trainers to charge for teaching "The 21 Irrefutable Laws of Leadership." These are examples of leaders who come from a place of giving.

Nelson Mandela ended up being rich in wisdom and followers, and Beth and John are rich both in followers and finances. I am not saying to give away your products and services; this is about mindset. If you are teaching just "enough" in hopes that they buy more, then you will get just enough to get by. But if you come from a place of abundance and teach your best content and give them your full energy and passion while teaching it, abundance will more likely come your way, and people will want to work with you.

No longer is it good enough to get people all fired up without a clue as to what they will do with their new excitement, knowledge, motivation, or wonder if they are missing a piece of the puzzle. Modern professional speakers bring solutions, a plan of action, and come from a place of abundance. The audience will want more based on the fact that they need you and your guidance to help them implement the solutions.

Final Thought

A teleseminar/webinar can be a highly productive way to market your business and yourself. In the next decade, commit to mastering and achieving virtual success. It will come from your awareness of your *energy*, setting the right *intentions*, and your *mindset*. Your mindset will derive from being focused on your larger purpose—what *you* want to learn from the process—and adopting an attitude of abundance.

Shari Strong is the founder of Success In 4D—Simple Strategies for Success and is a top management development consultant. She helps companies and small business owners take action that allows them to achieve results and experience everlasting success. Reach her at shari@strongorganization.com or on the Web at www.strongorganization.com

45

Making YouTube
Your Stage

Michael Neuendorff

That morning in San Francisco I was meeting with two young energetic women employed by a well-known global nonprofit. They needed a coach to conduct a public speaking training course for a group of thirty of their employees. We'd already talked on the phone, and now it was time to meet face-to-face to decide if this project was a go.

Early in the meeting one of them looked me straight in the eye and said, "Do you know why we chose to bring you in versus others we spoke to on the phone?"

"No, but I would like to know," I said.

"It's because we liked your YouTube channel," she replied. "We like you and your videos."

It felt very good to hear this because I've worked hard for years assembling my YouTube channel, and here was the latest tangible proof that it was paying off.

Fast forward a few weeks after this meeting. I received an unsolicited email that read:

Hi Michael,

I really enjoyed your public speaking lessons and want to discuss bringing you on board as a teacher at Curious.com.

Curious.com is making serious strides in the online presentation of educational videos, and *Time* magazine voted them one of the fifty best websites in 2013. Once again I was flattered by the praise and encouraged to keep at my effort to make YouTube my stage.

In short, online video is exploding, and as a speaker you simply *must* be a part of it.

> ***Online video is exploding, and as a speaker you simply must be a part of it.***

YouTube: The Juggernaut

Did you know that in March 2013 YouTube reached a staggering milestone? For the first time they reached 1 billion unique visitors in a single month. The operative word here is *unique*. Just how fantastic is this number? According to the website Internet World Stats, as of June 2012 there were just over 2.4 billion people on the Internet globally. This means that roughly 4 out of 10 Internet users visited YouTube to watch a video in a single month. The allure of YouTube is so great that, according to Nielson, the platform reaches more US adults ages 18-34 than any cable network.

To meet the insatiable demand for video on YouTube, more than one hundred hours of video are uploaded every minute. Some of it goes viral. As of this writing, the blockbuster video "Gangnam Style" by the Korean pop artist Psy was on its way to 2 billion views.

Here's the last thing to consider as you scratch your head and consider the heft of YouTube anew: Google owns YouTube, and they also dominate the search engine market. Put two and two together here. Video is making it into search engine results pages. Therefore, when someone searches for anything, it's quite possible that video(s) on YouTube will be presented as part of the results on page one. There's no guarantee of such a result, of course, but video on YouTube that's done right has a fighting chance of being found regularly by searchers around the world.

What All This Means for You

I hope you now realize why you might like to invest some time and energy toward creating video footage for YouTube. If you do take the leap you just might find yourself in the same position as I do—having my channel bring me business and recognition in a pretty crowded field.

If you're excited to learn more, let's start with the basics and move toward more advanced concepts to give you a competitive edge over other speakers 24/7 while they work their day jobs, answer email, and catch up on sleep.

The Basics of YouTube

It all starts with a channel. This is what YouTube calls your place on their platform. It's where you upload your videos and people can browse through them. You can title your channel with your name as I have done or go with your business name as companies often do, such as IBM.

The point of having a channel is to develop a following. YouTube calls followers "subscribers." These are people who essentially opt in to receive a notification when you've uploaded a new video. Subscribers are saying they like what they see and they want to see more.

Of course, as with all social media some people only subscribe to your channel hoping you will reciprocate by subscribing to theirs. Don't worry too much about this as most subscribers don't create their own videos. They just watch them.

It's not enough to create a channel and upload a few videos. You'll need to dress up your channel and make it compelling. There are two things people will see first when they come to your channel: your channel art and your trailer.

Your channel art is the large graphic at the top of your channel. At full size it's 2560 x 423 pixels. Depending on the browser and device being used by the viewer, YouTube may show just a slice of the image. They say the safe area of your image is 1546 x 423 pixels. Thus you would want the key imagery to fall within the safe area to show up properly on the variety of devices people use to visit your channel.

This isn't a trivial point as YouTube states that mobile makes up 40 percent of watch time. If you aren't sure what these sizes mean, work with a graphic designer. They will know and can guide you to design and develop your images appropriately.

Now, your trailer. You could call this the commercial for your channel. It is smack-dab under your channel art and only visible to those who have not yet subscribed to your channel. One of YouTube's more recent enhancements, channel trailers do make plenty of sense. Why not welcome someone to your channel and explain what you're about? I believe the trailer is essential, and you should create one from the outset.

You're probably wondering how long such a video should be. The hardest working commercial on television is thirty seconds, right? Don't go too far beyond that as this is what people are accustomed to.

The next step is to organize the videos you have into meaningful sections called playlists. This might not be that important in the beginning if you've only uploaded a few videos, but it will soon become valuable for you and your viewers. On my channel I have three playlists:

- Social Media
- Guerilla Marketing Coaching
- Public Speaking

It's not a coincidence that my public speaking playlist has received the most views. As popular as the other subject areas are, they are not as universal as the interest in improving one's public speaking skills.

Playlists will also help you avoid rambling creations that don't really highlight your strengths. I've seen channels with completely random videos that don't promote the expertise of the creator at all. For situations like that I recommend creating a miscellaneous playlist and parking the odd ones there.

Guidelines for Creating Video

I've tried just about everything when it comes to creating videos. My first few videos are now so embarrassing that I've hidden them from public view. I shot them either with the camera embedded in my laptop or a Flip camera connected to a tripod— with me standing in front of a vinyl backdrop created to echo my brand. Instead it just looked cheesy.

I have also taken plenty of videos using webcams. Other videos were recorded demonstrations of social media activities conducted on my computer screen while I recorded my voice using a USB mic.

When I started working with a professional video producer I got fancy and shot videos against a green screen to simulate a studio effect with floating graphics and the like.

The bulk of my videos are either from live speaking engagements or in a conference room at my office against a plain wall and sometimes with a plant to one side. They range from one minute long to full-length seminars exceeding one hour. The point of all this is that I'm constantly experimenting with different types of videos.

Here's what I recommend to make it easy and to get going:

- Record every live performance you give that you can record.
- Shoot some videos in a controlled space like a studio or conference room.
- Stick to videos that are one to three minutes in length instructing on one point.

What to Do with Live Performance Videos

My favorite tactic with live speech recordings is to have my video producer look for chunks of content that can be pulled out as compact mini-lessons. From a forty-five-minute presentation we can often pull six to ten shorts for posting. I'll then post them one at a time—usually at least one week apart—on my channel. If the speech was good in its entirety, I'll post the full-length video too.

After doing this a few times I discovered that it matters less how many people you're speaking to or even if you're getting paid. Either way you're going to have some video that you can put to work for you. Indeed you'll actually accept invitations you might otherwise have turned down because you're eager for new footage.

> *It matters less how many people you're speaking to or even if you're getting paid. Either way you're going to have some video that you can put to work for you.*

My Process for Controlled Shoots

Editing live footage is good, but it doesn't beat controlling the situation from beginning to end. There will be times when you're speaking in a room where the lighting stinks and the acoustics are poor. Nothing can kill viewership of a video faster than bad sound or an obscure image.

This is why I like to set aside days for just shooting videos to keep the content creation machine going. One of my strengths after training for fifteen years as a speaker is the ability to communicate strongly off the top of my head. I typically just draft some ideas, run through them in my head, and write down key points if necessary before the shooting begins. You may want to be more structured. In fact, many experts claim that scripting can make your videos tighter and more compelling. Do what works best for you.

Recommendations for Gear

Because I like to tape live presentations, I invested $400 in a Canon Vixia HD camcorder a few years ago. It records onto SDHC cards (I use 16-gb class 10 cards made by Transcend), which can be popped out of the camera and copied right into a Dropbox folder for sharing with my video producer very easily.

My webcam is a premium Logitech HD model that runs no more than $100. I also purchased a Logitech USB mic that was very inexpensive and for some reason works better for me than a much more expensive Blue microphone with multiple settings.

For screen recordings I use Camtasia, which isn't cheap but is worth it; for simple voiceovers I use Audacity, a free app.

Getting Your Videos Viewed

Now we're at the part you've really been waiting for and that is what to do with all this glorious video you've created. It must have some use beyond YouTube, right? Indeed it does, and truthfully you'd better do more with it than just post it to YouTube or you might get lost in that hundred hours per minute that's getting posted online.

Here's a list of my favorite uses for my YouTube videos.

1. **Embedding into newsletter articles.** I use Constant Contact for my monthly newsletter, and they make it very easy to feature a video in an article. It's actually a thumbnail of your video with the classic right-facing triangle over the center that links to the real video on your channel.

2. **Posting to a LinkedIn profile, LinkedIn company page, or as an update.** Yes, you can feature your video on LinkedIn numerous ways.

3. **Sharing on Facebook.** You can upload video directly to Facebook, and there are some advantages to doing this such as permanent placement on your business page on a dedicated tab and larger sizing in the newsfeed, but I still prefer linking to YouTube. I want subscribers.

4. **Posting to a SlideShare profile.** This network is primarily known for PowerPoint presentations, but they do allow videos and I've garnered some views there.

5. **Sharing on Twitter.** YouTube videos can be watched directly in the tweet stream, which is really handy and stands out among a sea of links and quotes.

6. **Posting to your website and blog.** People don't want to read just text on your website. They also want video.

7. **Embedded into web pages promoting events.** This is an absolute must in my opinion.

Ensuring Your Videos Are Searchable

It's very important that your videos be found online. To enable this make sure you use keywords in the titles of your videos and write out a full description of the content (don't worry if it's long) as well as add meaningful tags. If you want to go a next step, invest in having your videos transcribed professionally. Google reads through the transcriptions to figure out what's in there.

If you diligently follow the guidelines in this chapter and create videos that serve others, I believe you too will someday hear those delightful words, "I'm hiring you because I really liked your videos!"

Michael Neuendorff is a certified corporate speaker and World Class Speaking coach who has been on YouTube since 2009. He is also a sales coach and online marketing consultant. Michael resides in Northern California with his wife and two children. More information can be found at www.SpeakWellandSell.com.

46

Engage and Grow Your Audience in the Digital World

Anastasia Pryanikova

S tanding on the twenty-second floor of the Marriott Marquis in New York City, staring at the flashing billboards in Times Square, I am glued to the lights and mesmerized by the constant stream of images outside till the voice of the makeup artist directs my gaze to the ceiling. A few touchups later, my makeup and hair are done. I am heading downstairs to deliver my ten-minute presentation at the "Success in the New Economy" conference.

My heart pounds a little faster as I recall listening to publisher Steve Forbes's one-hour keynote just a few hours ago. As I march down the hallway, I roll my shoulders back, take a few deep breaths, and visualize a magical swirl of energy that connects me with my audience. Somebody's skillful hands attach a tiny microphone to my dress. I walk up onto the stage and become blinded by the lights and cameras.

I begin: "Opportunity often comes disguised, or so they say. My business breakthrough came disguised as a junk email message—talk about not missing your chance." I proceed to tell a funny story of how an email message from Craig Valentine announcing his World Class Speaking Coach certification program got swept away into my junk folder by the evil email filters. By chance I discovered my future business breakthrough among the promises of best deals, wonder pharmaceutical products, and exorbitant sums of money about to be wired to me by unknown rich relatives in foreign lands.

I continue to speak about the power of storytelling in business to "melt the ICE" for greater *impact, connection,* and *earnings.* Ten minutes fly by. Even though my presentation is over, its journey into the virtual world of multimedia is only beginning.

In this chapter you will learn how to boost your virtual presence as a speaker by:

- telling your story across multiple media channels
- generating buzz through multisensory content
- taking your virtual audience behind the scenes of your life as a speaker
- co-creating stories with your audience
- remixing and repurposing your content in multimedia

Transmedia Storytelling: Develop Compelling Content across Multiple Media Platforms

Technology offers speakers an opportunity to spread their messages across multiple media channels. Compelling storytelling forms the foundation of World Class Speaking. Speakers are used to telling their stories in various formats: live keynotes, seminars, webinars, radio and TV shows. A novel approach is to use transmedia storytelling—to break down a story into elements and map them to several virtual platforms. The use of the second screen is a common example when viewers of a television program, for instance, share comments about the program via a mobile application on their tablets or smartphones. The second screen can offer interactivity, game capabilities, and some exclusive content to enhance the regular TV programming.

> *Just as there is an art and science to pairing wine and cheese, finding a perfect combination of content and media channel requires strategy and practice.*

In transmedia, each mode of communication is carefully chosen to unfold the story further and create its unique experience for the audience. Just as there is an art and science to pairing wine and cheese, finding a perfect combination of content and media channel requires strategy and practice. The following questions can guide your choice:

1. How does this channel of communication contribute to the story and your audience's experience?
2. What message is created or reinforced by this combination of the content and platform?
3. How does this media channel engage your audience?

Bring the Buzz: Use Multimedia, Multisensory Content to Captivate Your Audience

Attention is the currency of our information-inundated world. Buzz-worthy ideas grab attention and give people something to get excited about, something to discuss and share. World Class speakers pique the curiosity of their audience before the story begins. Transmedia can help you generate buzz about your upcoming presentations across multiple media platforms that your audience already uses. Think of it as a hop-on/hop-off tour through your story where your audience chooses where to stop, what to look at, and when to get back on the bus.

I recently had the honor of meeting Brian Tracy, the legend of personal and professional development, and appearing as a guest on *The Brian Tracy Show*. I posted several updates and shared photos on social media about the taping of the show to generate more excitement about what was yet to come. I also wrote a blog post about my experiences at the event. A digital copy of the interview will be edited and repurposed for promotional materials.

You can use the following buzz-generating strategies in your transmedia story:

Care to share. Keep your foundational phrases under 140 characters. Tweetable foundational phrases will get you more exposure and build your brand as they speak to your values, core messages, and perceptions. You can also post these phrases on Facebook and ask your fans to vote on their favorite quotations by "liking" them. The favorite phrases, chosen by your audience, can be included in printed postcards or calendars. This enables your fans to have a voice in your transmedia story.

Create a dynamic speaker reel. The content you build online can provide you with some great material for your speaker reel to showcase your strengths as a speaker, including:

- video and audio clips from your speaking engagements
- video testimonials from your clients
- your own narration of your bio
- photos from various events
- slides with pertinent information about your business

Your speaker reel should give event planners and prospects a good idea of what you bring to the table as a speaker. Make it available in several formats. You can include DVDs with your speaker reel in your media kits for news and TV stations and welcome packages for your clients along with other materials. You can leave such DVDs in the offices of your referral partners to promote your business. You can also run it on TV screens during trade shows and expos or even in your own office reception area.

Give content generously. Answer questions and share your expertise on forums, listserves, LinkedIn, and Facebook groups. As you contribute more valuable content, you will become a "go-to" person for your topic. When you expand your virtual presence, you grow your credibility and visibility, get notified of media opportunities, and book more speaking business.

I once received an email from a member of a LinkedIn group after I posted a comment on one of the discussion threads. Something in my comment triggered his memory of an image I had shared in the same group many months before. He wasn't sure but thought I might be the one who had shared it, so he emailed me to see if I could give him the source of that image. This story illustrates how your brand can be associated with and reinforced by the content you share—in addition to the fact that visuals are memorable.

Behind the Scenes: Grant Your Virtual Audience Exclusive Access to Your Life as a Speaker

The day before the "Success in the New Economy" conference, I used the photo- and video-sharing platform Instagram to post photos of the restaurant where the reception took place, the ambiance, and yes even the food. Visuals are an important part of your evolving transmedia story. I love to use Instagram for visual storytelling because it allows you to capture those "snapshots of the moment"—often mundane but also funny, puzzling, memorable aspects of your reality. It is a perfect tool to set the scene, or what World Class speakers call "circumstance." Your Instagram followers will be able to see your pictures in their feeds, like them, comment on them, reshare them, and post links to your Instagram photos on social media.

"Behind-the-scenes" information is like a VIP pass for your audience into your world as a speaker. People want exclusive content because it makes them feel closer to you. They feel like they know you better and therefore they can trust you more. Think about reality TV. You can use transmedia storytelling to launch your own miniseries. If you look at my Instagram from June 2013, you will see the makeup set and gorgeous views of Times Square from the window. These pictures are my memories now, but they were the scene at the time. I brought my virtual audience with me on that journey.

> *"Behind-the-scenes" information is like a VIP pass*
> *for your audience into your world as a speaker.*

Introduce "behind-the-scenes" elements of your transmedia story through photos, illustrations, maps, and video clips. You can even aggregate them into a cohesive virtual story via the platform Storify.com.

Share photos of the venues where you speak and places you visit. If you travel a lot and post pictures on Twitter while using a location-enabled service, the free application Tweeted Trips will automatically create a map of your recent tweets with accompanying photos that you can edit and post or later include as visuals in your presentations.

Introduce the characters of your stories to your audience in advance through photos or illustrations. During the launch of Bookphoria "Transmedia Solutions for Authors" we posted the drawings of our characters for the business animation we were creating. You can engage your virtual audience members by asking them to name your characters, create captions for your illustrations, or choose a favorite sketch. You can also develop cartoons showing your main characters in action.

Have a little fun with your own speaker persona to add humor to your transmedia story. The free mobile application Bitstrips enables you to create your own virtual avatar and then generate status comics that can describe your mood or the happenings of your day. You can share these comics on Bitstrips itself or on Facebook. If your friends use Bitstrips, you can have comics with friends as your co-stars. You can also design and use your virtual avatar as an element of branding on your websites, social media, presentation slides, and other information products.

Audience-Generated Content: Think Forward and Call Back

Transmedia storytelling engages your virtual audience and encourages it to co-create content with you. The asynchronous nature of transmedia allows you to connect with your audience before live presentations and follow up after the events. World Class speakers use teasers and callbacks to drive their point home. Virtual platforms offer opportunities to prepare your audience members in advance for what they are about the experience, as well as to callback to your main messages long after your presentation is over. Here is how you can both think forward and call back:

- Ask questions and collect opinions in advance, and use your audience's comments in your upcoming presentations. For example, my business partner and I used Survey Monkey—a free platform that allows you to create and publish surveys—to ask authors about their attitudes toward multimedia. We later used the results of the survey to promote our transmedia for authors. An infographic was designed to showcase the results in presentations. Getting such feedback from your target market is invaluable when you prepare for speaking engagements. You can use your audience's language to describe their pains, gains and benefits.
- Have a conversation with your virtual audience. TweetChat.com is a free platform that allows Twitter users to have a real-time conversation about their topics of interest. You can initiate your own chats or join the existing chats to establish new connections, raise your virtual visibility, and gain insights about the challenges and hot topics across various target groups.
- At an event, you can engage your fellow attendees by asking a question and recording their short answers through smartphone video applications such as Vine or Instagram. Vine is a free platform that enables you to record six seconds of looping video clips. Instagram allows videos between three and fifteen seconds in length. You can later run those video clips during your live presentations to encourage a discussion among your audience members. And don't forget to collect video testimonials.

Plato said, "You can discover more about a person in an hour of play than in a year of conversation." Technology allows you to "gamify" the speaking business to bring more fun and interactivity to your audience. Play delights the brain as it boosts creativity, imagination, and decision making. At the core of each game experience there is a problem to be solved and an opportunity of getting a reward. For example, you can encourage your audience members to submit their own Then/Now/How stories virtually for a chance to win a prize. You can award special badges to honor your most active community members. Rewards cause the release of the feel-good neurotransmitter dopamine in the brain, which is implicated in our intrinsic motivation and desire to learn.

Multimedia Information Products: Remix and Repurpose

One of the benefits of transmedia storytelling is that it allows you to grow and leverage your content for live speeches and presentations, as well as information products. You can test and fine-tune it with your audience's direct participation.

Recycle your content across different platforms. You can use a blog post as a script for an audio or video piece. Turn your transmedia photos and videos into visuals for your presentations. You can transcribe your interviews and discussions and post the transcripts on your blog or website. Alternatively, you can use them as a foundation for a workbook or guide that you can package along with the videos to create an information product for sale.

Create multimedia learning modules for live and virtual presentations and information products. To create professional multimedia modules, I use Camtasia Studio, a screen-recording and video-editing software that enables you to turn your PowerPoint slides and any onscreen activity into videos. You can add your own narration to it. You can also import an mp3 audio or HD camera video, add transitions, animations, and other features to customize and edit your content. It is a great way for speakers and experts to share their expertise, grow business, and create additional income streams based on information products and online courses.

Transmedia storytelling reaches diverse groups through their preferred ways of interacting with information. World Class Speaking principles thrive in multimedia. As a speaker, you can boost your virtual presence by:

- telling your story across multiple media channels
- generating buzz through multisensory content

- taking your virtual audience behind the scenes of your life as a speaker
- co-creating stories with your audience
- remixing and repurposing your content in multimedia

Speak your mind virtually and be heard!

Anastasia Pryanikova, MA, JD, is the founder of E-Studio LLC, a coaching, training, and consulting company that translates neuroscience insights into tools and solutions in the areas of communication, conflict management, public speaking, presenting, and transmedia storytelling. She shares her tips on brain-friendly public speaking and presenting at http://brainalchemist.com.

47

Creating and Delivering World Class Teleseminars for Fun and Profit

Daniel R. Moirao

Most entrepreneurs would be shocked if they realized how much money they have access to but are leaving behind without the simple tool of a teleseminar to market their talent. In this chapter you will learn how to accomplish more with a one-hour teleseminar than most entrepreneurs accomplish in a month of laborious marketing efforts. You will discover how to use the simple technology of the telephone to:

- structure your content to make you a recognized thought leader in your niche
- generate more qualified leads and build a list that will keep you busy for months
- attract new clients, offer programs that help sell products, and leave your audience wanting more
- leverage the teleseminar into information products for profits—while you sleep

A teleseminar is simply a phone call that you invite your audience to take part in. It can be an interview, a lecture, or just a Q&A jam session. A teleseminar is an opportunity to put your mojo on display, show off your personality (and talent), and get real-time feedback from your participants. It is also an opportunity to learn from others about your topic or available resources.

Structure Your Content to Make You a Recognized Thought Leader

If you had asked me three years ago to write a chapter about creating and delivering World Class teleseminars, my response would have been, "Yeah, right! Who me? I have nothing to talk about to a sea of faceless participants!" But then the National Speakers Association asked me to become the teleseminar host for the Storyteller's PEG (Professional Experts Group). All I had to do was locate recognized speakers who would share their expertise on the power of storytelling in public speaking. Twelve months, one hour a month, with two pages of leads… Sure, I could ask questions and talk to leaders in the industry, no problem.

Little did I know that I would become the name behind the phone. After twelve intriguing interviews, the listeners sought me out to coach and guide them in finding their stories. Suddenly I was the expert! *I became the expert by facilitating the words of the true experts.* What I learned was that people seek out and buy from individuals they feel comfortable with, people they know and trust. Each month was a different speaker, but I was the common voice who brought the pros to them.

Becoming a thought leader in your niche doesn't necessarily mean that you are the expert on the topic. What it does mean is that you are the most receptive and understanding of your customers' needs. You have found where their pain rests, what keeps them up at night, and you have a cure. To create and deliver World Class teleseminars:

- **Find your audience's need.** What do they want to know? Develop your content to answer their questions. Bring them to a new place or provide a list of actions for them to take.
- **Comb through content in your topic area.** Provide quick synopses of articles from other leaders in your industry.

Spark the discussion and give your industry something to think about. The power of a teleseminar is the power of the platform. He who controls the mic controls the thought!

> *The power of a teleseminar is the power of the platform.*
> *He who controls the mic controls the thought!*

Generate Qualified Leads and Build a List That Will Keep You Busy

One day I had the opportunity to transport Darren LaCroix from event to event. Watching him in action proved to be a learning experience. Darren is a master at product development and list generating. He never left a group without several pages of new leads. At teleseminars you won't be able to pass around a paper and pencil to get names and email addresses, or collect business cards, but the wise marketer knows that the opening tease will spark interest in your topic. Then the sign-in will secure you the contact information you need to follow up. If people landed on your page and took the time to give you their name and email address, they have some interest in you and/or your topic. If they don't attend your teleseminar, they may attend a later event.

Here are a few tips to advertise and generate leads that will build your list:

- **Create a landing page (website) for your teleseminar.** People are busy, short on time and attention. This may be your most important marketing tool so put in the effort that sets you apart from the crowd. What will your audience gain by listening to your call? The answer to a pressing question? The secret to a particular technique? The solution to some problem they may be facing? Keep your copy to a minimum. Set the context, state what the call is about, tell visitors what they will learn, and give your call to action.

- **Establish your email list.** Create a separate list or campaign for your teleseminar. GetResponse is online system I have used. Create an event-specific signup, confirmation email, and auto-responder series to keep tabs on the activity and interest in your event. In the confirmation email, provide the number to call, the pin number to access your event, and any other ways they could listen (via webcast or Skype). I also include a prompt to "like" me on Facebook or a click to Tweet that includes the hook for the call. Get prospects to market for you with a link to the landing page.

- **Send out your invitations** (if they aren't already clamoring at your door). Promote your teleseminar in as many different ways as possible. Utilize social media, and if you already have a blog use it! Don't forget your existing email list.

Attract New Clients, Offer Programs That Help Sell Products, and Leave Your Audience Wanting More

A teleseminar is as simple as hosting a conference call. (A webinar by contrast is a teleseminar on steroids, complete with a PowerPoint presentation, maybe video segments, voting polls, etc.) The beauty of a teleseminar—aside from its simplicity—is that it provides your audience with a sample of what it is like to work with you live. It also promotes your services and educates your market. Because of their simplicity teleseminars can become a regular part of your marketing strategy. In less than one hour you can offer your audience solutions and prove your value to them.

When you use the right tools, teleseminars can be completely free. In fact, if you are paying for a service provider you are paying too much. FreeConferenceCalling. com has been my provider by choice. Having experimented with several, I have yet to be "dropped" from the call. I can see where my callers are calling from, I can see how many callers are present, and I can record, monitor questions and answers, and use many other handy tools provided (it will even store recorded calls for you).

If your teleseminar will be a revenue generator, allow your participants easy access to a payment method such as PayPal. After one call providing an overview of my services as a certified World Class Speaking Coach, I generated twelve follow-up calls, secured four prepaid clients, and garnered several months of income. My participants came from around the globe, and that was my first teleseminar on this topic. I have the recording and have yet to finish editing it (the perfectionist side of me!) to make it into a sellable product. Not bad for one hour's worth of work. While marketing I secured nearly 150 email addresses that are now a part of my mailing list.

Promote your event. Lewis Howes, an expert in the world of webinars, offers the following actions in his four-day marketing plan. They apply to teleseminars as much as they do to webinars.

- Hold your teleseminars on a Tuesday or Thursday, somewhere around the noon hour or at 9 p.m., which for most folks is near the lunch hour or after dinner. Consider your time zone. Your lunchtime may be someone else's 9 a.m. wakeup call, or 9 p.m. could be somebody's midnight bedtime! Don't change the date and/or time of the call once you go public. You will create confusion and even annoyance. Being an expert is a fragile thing.

- On Sunday or Monday before the event, send an email to your list telling why they will benefit from signing up for your teleseminar. Have your automated system send another email to unopened emails eight hours later with yet another compelling headline.

- Post it on your social media: LinkedIn groups, Twitter, Facebook page created just for this event. Use the share buttons from the registration page to get others to sign up.

- Return to your contact list again and target the entire list with a different, shorter message and a few new points describing the benefits. Provide a hint that there will be a free access offer—only if they attend your event live.

- Send to those unopened emails again with a different header. For those who have signed up, send them a reminder email with something catchy like "Are you joining us for lunch?" or "You're going to join us right? We are starting in ten minutes."

- Hold the call. Have a backup facilitator. At the scheduled time for one of my calls there was a police emergency at my place of business and I could not conduct the call myself. Thank goodness for my backup.

- During the teleseminar use a strong call to action and an irresistible offer to the next step. Make a special offer for a product, program, or service that you can fulfill. I have even heard some teleseminar hosts make it sound spontaneous: "Hey, you've been a great bunch of folks and I want to do something special for you. For you on the call and for you only I will offer my complete program, which normally sells for $1997, at a reduction of 95 percent. If you register within the next two hours from the end of this call, you pay only $98.97!" It sounds spontaneous, but no doubt it was planned all along.

- After the teleseminar, follow up, follow up, follow up! Contact those who attended your call. If you did a call to action, remind them. If you made a special deal for your products or services, remind them of the deal and the deadline you set. For those who did not attend, have the recording ready for sale; you might let them in on the deal you made for the attendees if they purchase your recording.

Everyone here is now on your mailing list and will be waiting eagerly for your next teleseminar, webinar, keynote, or presentation. Be ready with your next step! And don't forget to ask for feedback and testimonials; these help with marketing future calls and establish you as the expert in your field.

Leverage the Teleseminar into Information Products for Profits—While You Sleep

Teleseminars serve multiple purposes. They generate income, establish credibility, produce unlimited exposure, and can be reproduced and regenerated as CDs, eBooks, audio files, and other products that will continue to generate publicity and income. For a minimum fee you can have your teleseminars transcribed, and with some editing you have an article that gives you even more exposure. Run a series of teleseminars on a common theme and each seminar becomes a chapter for a new book.

My tenure as the Storyteller's PEG teleseminar host generated a potential book from that year alone (these are owned by the National Speakers Association, so not a product I can produce). Take each of your interviews, transcribe them, edit them, maybe write an introductory chapter and conclusion, and it's done.

The questions and answers generated in the teleseminar will guide you where to take your topic next. These can become your focus for a keynote or breakout session, or maybe you find the coaching niche (the pain others are feeling around your topic) that branches off into yet another segment of your business. Suddenly clients are clamoring at your door 24/7. Have this all available on your website, and wake up each morning to check your profits after a good night's sleep—much like the stockbroker who checks his or her stock profits every morning.

> *With a minimum investment of time and money, teleseminars provide an extraordinary amount of exposure and an unprecedented return on your investment.*

Teleseminars are taking the business world by storm. With a minimum investment of time and money, teleseminars provide an extraordinary amount of exposure and an unprecedented return on your investment. Teleseminars:

- **Automatically establish you as the expert.** When you teach what you know, you're qualified as a thought leader in your field.
- **Are amazingly affordable.** The Internet and the simple technology of a phone make teleseminars both easy and inexpensive to produce, deliver, and promote
- **Are convenient to your audience.** Teleseminars can be attended and conducted from home or work, eliminating the necessity for travel and travel accommodations. I even conducted several off the side of the road on more than one occasion.
- **Are technologically easy even for the techno-phobic.** There is little to no effort to jump on a call. Anyone who can use a phone can participate.
- **Are an easy way to increase your client base.** Every person who registers is one more person you add to your list of prospects, making this one of the fastest list-building tools you can use.
- **Anybody and everybody can attend.** Gone are the limits of available seats, geographical location, time and travel. You as the teleseminar host decide how many attendees you want to accommodate without any of the restrictions of space.
- **Help you generate viral buzz about you, your topic, and your event.** Teleseminars allow you to generate anticipation and a need for your topic without ever leaving your home.
- **Help you add to your testimonials and endorsements.** Customer satisfaction is one of the best marketing tools any entrepreneur can have. Testimonials provide you with free advertisements and endorsements. One good deed creates another.

One simple call can take your business to levels never before imagined. So what number do I call to hear your next teleseminar?

Daniel Moirao is the CEO of Dr. Dan Presents. Dr. Dan is a leader of leaders, guiding leaders through four frames of leadership that promote sustainability for productivity and profit and leaving a lasting legacy. He has been the CEO of organizations ranging from two hundred to over two thousand employees and is recognized as a true statesman and an outstanding educator.

48

Wowing with Webinars the World Class Speaking Way

Amelia "Mimi" Brown

Congratulations! You have just delivered a phenomenal speech at a conference in a country outside the United States, commanding a standing ovation from audience members who yearn for another day, another hour, another moment of your speech. The audience is so impressed with your speech that you sell all your videos, books, and other promotional products after the speech. Wow! Standing ovations and sold-out promotional products usually signify that speakers will be in high demand—it's a goal that all speakers want to achieve.

Now let's imagine you delivering this phenomenal speech to the same audience from any room of your choice inside your home, or perhaps inside your office selling large quantities of promotional products, and then merely one hour later delivering this speech to a different audience in another part of the country selling more of your promotional products. If you're thinking *Is it really possible to have multiple speaking engagements on the same day in various parts of the world and to sell promotional products too?* the answer is yes. The perfect opportunity for you to become a World Class speaker really does exist. The perfect opportunity to reach a mass audience is available for you right now.

Let's get started wowing your audience with webinars to take your speaking business to the next level. This chapter will explain:

- what webinars are
- what you need to get started
- how webinars can skyrocket your business
- how to integrate webinars into your marketing strategy
- the World Class webinar process
- a checklist to help you get started
- suggestions for software and service vendors

What Are Webinars?

Webinars are a great communication tool for customers because they yield three powerful elements: prospect interaction and audio and visual elements, including video. Webinars, also known as Web conferences, are lectures, meetings, seminars, or training sessions presented on the Internet and designed to be shared with remote locations—anywhere, anytime. Webinars allow speakers to present information and share documents in real time. The session can include speeches, handouts, video, interactive questions and answers, and the option to record.

What You Need to Get Started

1. A powerful and passionate message that you know the world needs to hear
2. A way to accept payment, such as PayPal or Google Wallet
3. A website or blog site (setting up a blog is not within the scope of this chapter, but I personally use WordPress as the platform for my website and blog)

How Webinars Can Skyrocket Your Business

Dr. Nido Qubein, one of the most sought-after leadership speakers, once wrote, "You are not in the speaking business, you are in the business of speaking." The use of webinars can skyrocket your business in a big way.

Like any business, it is imperative that you stay ahead of your competition. The speaking marketplace is very crowded. Every speaker is vying for his or her voice to be heard—to be booked across the world. Webinars make it possible for speakers to gain a competitive edge by allowing speeches to be delivered live or through a streaming video, as well as the use of slideshow presentations, ultimately separating most speakers from the World Class communicators.

> *The use of webinars can skyrocket your business in a big way.*

The top five ways webinars can skyrocket your speaking business include:

- **Generating qualified leads.** Webinars deliver a higher quality of leads. People who are already interested in what you are offering have opted in. They are warm and ready to be convinced. When you provide a solid pitch, your conversion rates can easily double other methods. Typical conversion rates average around 1 percent. A great webinar can achieve 4 percent conversions or a conversion rate that is 400 percent greater than the norm.

- **Creating an instant product.** Webinars are a great way to create quick products. You can use the recording again and again. If you don't already have a product, this is a wonderful way to get started. You can save the webinar and use it as a way to market yourself. You can also turn it into an e-book. During the webinar, you can reference clips from a video or pages from a book you are trying to promote. At the end of the seminar direct the audience to a purchase page or give them more information on how they can obtain the product.

- **Positioning you as an authority.** In an oversaturated market, standing out from the competition is extremely important. You receive instant credibility when you host webinars. People will start to see you as the subject matter expert in your area of expertise.

- **Allowing you to connect with your "tribe" across the world.** As a speaker you can deliver live or streaming video speeches to more than one hundred participants during a single session anywhere in the world at any hour of the day or night, as well as receive instant feedback and questions and answers from participants.

- **Keeping key expenses low.** Webinars provide businesses with a way to save thousands of dollars on conference or seminar-related expenses. Rather than renting out a convention hall or large room for the audience to gather in, you can conduct the webinar from your office and attendees can watch and interact from wherever they please. This also eliminates the need for costly travel.

Integrating Webinars into Your Marketing Strategy

Marketing strategies and social media have been united for years to promote people, places, and things—and more specifically to promote businesses' speaking engagements. If marketing plans are the blueprint to achieve a successful speaking business, then webinars are the desired sales tools for generating World Class exposure and increasing customer loyalty. Integrate webinars into your marketing plans to:

- **Generate new leads and build contacts.** Requiring participants to register upon receiving the electronic invitations may generate sales leads. Be sure to follow up.
- **Create awareness and exposure.** Use your website, social media, and email messages to promote your webinar and to maximize opportunities.
- **Build contact lists.** Host free webinars to attract people and to instantly build contact lists.
- **Promote your products.** Inform participants about books or videos available for purchase.
- **Increase profit.** Host fee-based webinars and offer recorded downloads for sale.
- **Target a specific content.** Establish your expertise by delivering informational content targeted to a specific audience.

World Class Webinar Process

So far you have learned about webinars and how these online conferences can be a valuable marketing tool for promoting your speeches. It is also a good business practice to follow a process to guide you through the steps of effective webinar delivery. Using a webinar process will enable you to collect information to better communicate your intentions and avoid mistakes before the actual session takes place. It will also help you to deliver a strong first impression and produce the desired end results, including increased attendance and profits. Before initiating your webinar, consider the following process:

- Choose a relevant topic and use a searchable headline.
- Choose your target audience and the capacity size.
- Determine how and why your speech is beneficial to the target audience, and deliver on your promises.
- Create the content to add value, but eliminate irrelevant details for timing issues. Get to the point. Keep in mind that everyone's time is valuable and attention spans are short.
- Practice running a test webinar to ensure it will run smoothly, including content flow, timing, and technology. Make adjustments as necessary.
- Use your website, blog, social media, email lists, and even YouTube video promotion to distribute information to promote the webinar.
- Run the actual webinar and present offers to the audience.
- Send email thank-you and follow-up messages, and make sales calls if appropriate.

Checklist to Help You Get Started

Your webinar will be a success with proper planning and preparation to determine in advance what will work and what will not. A checklist helps you to avoid common mistakes.

- **Webinar platform.** Webinars are often sold as a service, hosted on a Web server controlled by the vendor. Type "webinar software" in the Google search engine for a number of Web conferencing results. Webinar platforms allow speakers to give online speeches when they do not own the equipment to host a webinar. Decide if you will purchase hardware or use a hosting platform. Compare cost and reviews. Factors that affect the cost include bandwidth, number of people attending the session, and the platform you choose to host the webinar. Decide which options are suitable for your budget.
- **Live speeches, on-demand services, or recorded downloads.** Live webinars will allow your audience to ask questions and give feedback in real time. The audience for live webinars can only view the speech once, but the speaker can decide to make the live webinar available as a download and choose to give access to on-demand services.

- **Marketing plan.** Determine your target audience and how you will convince them to register and attend your webinar. Make sure your plan has a competive edge.
- **Presentation.** Your webinar must achieve your objectives as well as benefit your audience. Select a topic the audience *needs* to know about. Use a title that will capture your topic and appeal to your audience. Include an introduction and conclusion, and allot time for a Q&A period.
- **Follow-up plan.** Create an opt-in box on your lead-generation page or website. Send followup messages to all who have registered. Include thank-you messages to attendees and followup messages to those who registered but did not attend. Consider using an external responder, newsletter, or broadcast service, including aWeber, GetResponse, MailChimp, ConstantContact, iContact, Infusionsoft, Autoresponse Plus, VerticalResponse, or Office Auto Pilot.

> *Your webinar will be a success with proper planning and preparation to determine in advance what will work and what will not.*

Suggestions for Software and Service Vendors

There are thousands of webinar service vendors, with some more expensive than others but not necessarily better. Webinar services are not cheap, but compared to expenses for travel, hotel, venue, and materials, it is much more cost effective. Do research before you make your final decision to choose a webinar service vendor. Check out the vendor's history, level of service, requirements, and response time before signing up. Requirements include: high-speed Internet connection, PC computer, updated browser, computer speaker or headsets for audio, and microphone.

One of the reasons to use a service provider is because the vendor provides extra services such as notice of meetings. Basic services can cost about $50 a month. Webinar services may charge by the hour for each participant, and some webinar software can be used if your webinar vendor has a number of programs suitable for different users. Speakers can also get their own server, add the software, and run the meetings and webinars themselves. Some suggestions for webinar platforms include:

- **GoToWebinar.com.** One of the industry standard platforms used by the serious webinar host, it is a very expensive platform that offers a thirty-day free trial. GoToWebinar offers chat, screen, share polls, and allows for different presenters to be a part of your conference.
- **InstantTeleSeminar.com.** This platform is another popular choice. No downloads are required. Allows you to schedule and do pre-recorded webinars, upload your own audio files for replays, and load replays of audio onto your site. Offers a twenty-one-day free trial.
- **MeetingBurner.** Offers free account for up to ten people, but no recording. A fifty-person room includes recording and integration with aWeber at an affordable rate. On the bottom of the page it offers: pay as you go, no long-term contracts, no termination fee, cancel at any time. You can maintain a free account and upgrade when you need to have all the features. Then at the end of the month you can downgrade.
- **FuzeMeeting.** Invitations can be scheduled and sent out directly from this platform. Other features include video streams and content sharing. Offers a one-day usage fee of $10 if you are not going to record the session and do not do many webinars. There is also a thirty-day free trial.
- **WebEx.com.** Solid packages for an eight- to twenty-five-person room. Well-known Cisco solution that accommodates individuals, small to medium businesses, and large businesses.
- **Instant Presenter.** All packages include high-quality video, logo branding, and different user interfaces. No option for screen sharing on larger conferences. Monthly cost per number of attendees tend to be expensive.
- **Global Meet.** Audio and Web conferencing can be used without passcodes, dial-in numbers, or guest downloads. It also has an iPhone app, as well as a thirty-day trial.
- **Calliflower.** A pay-as-you-go platform with a couple of plans, including a basic plan for a five-person team. No long-term contracts or commitments. Fourteen-day trial.
- **AnyMeeting.** Free platform but advertisements will be seen on your screen periodically.

- **MegaMeeting.com.** Choice of VoIP or text messaging to participate in the conference. This platform can be used for a onetime fee instead of an ongoing subscription service. Thirty-day trial.
- **Microsoft Live Meeting.** Allows desktop sharing, PowerPoint presentations, recordings, and playback. Accommodates meetings up to 1,250 participants. Choose a per-use fee or flat rate. Thirty-day trial.
- **Adobe Connect.** Offers a hosted service for individuals that can only be purchased online and supports Web meetings and webinars.
- **GatherPlace.net.** Toll-free conferencing and the ability to record sessions for audiences up to two thousand. This platform offers a free trial.
- **FreeScreenSharing.** A free online meeting service as part of FreeConferenceCall designed for screensharing, Web conferencing, product demonstrations, webinars for up to ninety-six people, and no cost. Only the audio conferencing portion may be recorded.
- **InterCall.com.** Provides integrated audio and video, eliminating the need to send links and dial-in numbers. Software to help manage and promote your webinar is included. Free trial is offered.
- **TalkingCommunities.com.** PC-based platform that allows you to lease one room or purchase the rights to a server with multiple roooms.
- **ClickWebinar.** Platform for videoconferencing and webinars for up to one thousand people. Offers a standard feature set including whiteboard annotation, moderated chat, and polling.
- **Skype 5.3 for Windows.** Offers screensharing, phone-card-like calling with Skype to Go, WiFi access, and video calling.

Webinars are not only a great way to sell your products or services but also an amazing way to add value and communicate to your target market. You can easily make a lot of money fast while also educating, informing, and adding value to your prospects.

Amelia "Mimi" Brown is an award-winning speaker, trainer, and coach specializing in the art and craft of selling. She teaches entrepreneurs and women business owners how to build better relationships that build better business, so they can sell more and live big. Check out her website at www.thesalesmaven.com.

49

Finding Your Voice in Social Media

Henrik Brameus

You know that your voice is important in your speaking. The words you use and the way you deliver them decides your impact. In the same way, your voice in social media will decide your impact. Many people tend to do social media as a part of their overall strategy, but rather do it as a side project.

Do you see social media as the magic bullet to getting free publicity and gaining new customers? I have bad news. There are no magic bullets. Social media is a means to an end, not the end itself. Done right, social media is a huge asset. Don't focus on the quantity of your audience, focus on the quality. If you do that, your audience will grow because you add value.

In the next few pages you will learn:

- why social media is good for your business
- how to design a strategy for using social media
- what social media platforms you want to use
- some ideas for how not to annoy people on social media

Social Media Is Good for Your Business

To win business you need to earn the trust of your customer. For anybody to trust you, they have to be familiar with you. To become familiar with you, they have to get to know about you in the first place. In the physical world, the way you would do this is to go and meet people face-to-face, talk to them about their needs, show what you can do to help, get them to trust your abilities, and finally win their business.

The same principle applies to social media. The difference is scale. By using social media you can immediately talk to a large portion of the world. Done right it will build your reputation and help you get new customers. Even if it doesn't give you customers directly, it will increase the chance that you will be found on the big search engines.

It's true that social media is no magic bullet, but with a well-constructed effort you can build your credibility and extend your reach with a modest investment. That will help you gain new clients and increase your value on the market. That is good for your business.

> *Social media is no magic bullet, but with a well-constructed effort you can build your credibility and extend your reach with a modest investment.*

Strategies for Using Social Media

Why would you want to spend time and effort on social media? Maybe you've heard countless times from people who have tried social media with little or no success. In most cases it's because the effort is not part of a bigger strategy. People focus too much on being on social media and not enough on why they are there. To me, Patricia Fripp, NSA hall of fame speaker, hits the nail on the head when she says "you are not a professional speaker but an expert who speaks." Talk about your expertise.

Of course, speaking is not enough. You need somebody to speak to. You need an audience. How do you get an audience? Through being interesting, engaging, and helpful. That is what your strategy needs to support, in addition to being in line with your overall marketing plan.

First you need to decide how much time you are going to spend. If you look at it as a daily task, you will be more successful. The more time you set off, the more social networks you will be able to engage with. Always remember that quality is more important than quantity, though.

To start off, set aside fifteen to thirty minutes per day for social media. I would recommend spending the first few weeks exploring different social networks. Find groups or people that are talking about your area of expertise. Hang around a few days to see if it's a good fit. You need to feel comfortable engaging in conversation because that is what makes social media social.

Once you have found your network(s) it's time to start participating. Follow some of the influential people in the community. Answer when somebody asks a question you know the answer to. Comment when somebody posts something worthwhile, and occasionally share something you have read that you think would be of interest to the community. If you read a lot and post a little you are more likely to come across as easy to deal with, and listening more than speaking will make you look more competent and knowledgeable. The goal should not be to impress but to engage and help. Making this a daily habit will communicate consistency and reliability. It will also let your passion for your area of expertise shine through over time.

A question I get asked is how much of your personal life you should share, and whether you should have separate accounts for personal and professional purposes. I discussed this with Marc Menninger, author of *Outrank Your Competition*. He thinks you should keep everything together. His reasoning is that people who would like to hire you want to know the whole person, and that includes your hobbies and personal interests in addition to your area of expertise. My preference is for separation. To me mixing personal and professional sides can cause confusion, and we don't want our audience confused. You know which way is best for you.

Choose Your Social Media

I know that some people will object to websites and email as social media. I think that they are fantastic tools for creating conversations and sharing knowledge. They are cost effective ways of showing your value and increasing your credibility. Here are some areas you can explore to get deeper into social networking.

Website and Blog

A website can be a great conversation starter. It's your combination brochure and contact information. Keep it simple, and make sure it's up-to-date.

It's even better if you have a blog on your website. However, having a successful blog requires consistency. In the book *APE: Author Publisher Entrepreneur—How to Publish a Book*, Guy Kawasaki points out that you need to write a new post at least once a week to maintain consistency. It's hard work but good writing practice, and an excellent way of collecting stories and ideas for your own book.

Email

Email marketing can be a very efficient way to communicate with your audience. An auto-responder with good information is an excellent way to attract new audiences. A newsletter where you also answer questions adds a level of conversation to your email communications. Also make sure you include a link and a teaser to any blog posts you have written since your last email.

In all cases of email marketing, be sure to follow the laws of the countries where your subscribers live. Being stricter than the law is better.

Twitter

The first few times you go on Twitter it can be overwhelming and confusing. At first you have almost nothing because you are not following anybody. Then you start following a number of people, and suddenly it feels like drinking from a fire hose. It never stops. If that suits you, then you have a fantastic tool for getting a lot of information about many different topics. There are even informal chats based around hashtags, such as #writetoinspire.

Facebook

Everybody is on Facebook. Almost, anyway. To build an audience on Facebook you have to remember to share your professional posts publicly. The easiest way is to create a page for you or your company and then post updates, links, events, photos, and so forth to that page. You can also change your settings so people can follow you without having to friend you. That way you know they will not get your private messages.

Google+

Google+ has a reputation for attracting nobody but geeks. Although the network doesn't have the same penetration as Facebook or Twitter, it still has many attractive features. One of the main draws is that it's integrated with the largest search engine in the world. Google+ also allows for long posts, and Guy Kawasaki suggests you can use it instead of a blog. There are also numerous interest groups for conversations and reputation building.

Linkedin

LinkedIn is a very good tool for job hunting and business development. If you are a one-person company or otherwise very small, it's a good place to have a presence, but it's much harder to build a reputation there than on the three platforms above.

YouTube

YouTube is the second largest search engine on the Internet, which carries a lot of heft. There is also some level of interaction, although the actual discussion on a topic is usually limited. The challenge is to stay interesting enough and to post videos with the frequency you need to keep your audience engaged.

> *Don't post anything you might have to apologize for later.*

Social Media without Annoying People

The reason social media carries both promise and bad experiences is that it's free, fast, and everywhere, but at the same time it can very easily be annoying. To be successful, follow these guidelines:

- Listen and read more than you post.
- Don't do social media as a popularity contest. Start with one network until you get the hang of it.
- Don't just repost other people's materials. Even if you forward something, add comments of your own so that you become a curator rather than a forwarder.
- Keep it short and in your own voice.
- Keep it regular.
- Don't post all updates to all networks.
- Be helpful and polite. Make sure that you add value to your community.

- Disclose your interests. If you are getting paid by somebody you are endorsing, tell people.
- Stay above the fray. You don't want to be known as negative or aggressive.
- Don't post anything you might have to apologize for later.
- Talk about your passions.
- Make sure all posts are visible to the world.
- Be patient. Building trust and reputation takes time.

Henrik Brameus is a certified World Class Speaking digital marketing specialist. You can reach him at Henrik@speakprofessionally.net.

50

World Class Speaking as a Philosophy of Life

Ben Thorkelson

Would you like to have a productive and creative life that is focused on achieving your full potential? You can take World Class Speaking skills and principles off the stage and use them to create a better life. Consider this:

> Watch your thoughts; they become words.
> Watch your words; they become actions.
> Watch your actions; they become habits.
> Watch your habits; they become character.
> Watch your character; it becomes your destiny.

This passage has been attributed to thinkers from Lao Tzu to Margaret Thatcher. The message is that what and how we think shapes who we are and who we will become. Your behavior is guided by your collected beliefs, ideas, and attitudes. That collection of concepts is your personal philosophy.

The Greek philosopher Socrates said, "The unexamined life is not worth living for a human being." He meant that we should examine and choose the beliefs that shape our lives. This is important because every action we take begins with a thought. While we cannot always choose our circumstances we can choose how we respond to them. Therefore to become a happy, productive, and successful person, you need to think like a happy, productive, successful person.

> *To become a happy, productive, and successful person,*
> *you need to think like a happy, productive, successful person.*

World Class Speaking principles and techniques can help you define a personal philosophy that will improve your thinking and your life. This chapter will explore:

- foundational phrases for effective thinking
- liberating creativity by working within structure
- being inspired by being "you focused"
- next steps to where you want to go

Foundational Phrases for Effective Thinking

Does this sound familiar: "a concisely expressed principle or rule of conduct, or a statement of a general truth"? That is the definition of a maxim in Webster's New World Dictionary. Philosophers use maxims as a shortcut to describe a line of reasoning or belief. Sometimes these phrases are also referred to as aphorisms, proverbs, or just sayings. When they become commonly used they are known as clichés. In World Class Speaking a concise phrase that sums up the main idea of a message in ten words or less is a *foundational phrase.*

A foundational phrase can remind an audience of the important message in a speech; it can also remind you of lessons about life. These lessons may be drawn from your own experience or they may be lessons learned from a mentor, teacher, or author. Craig Valentine gave us the phrase *"Let your long road be their shortcut."* This sums up the idea that your story can provide a way for your audience to avoid the same struggle. Many sources credit Benjamin Franklin with the phrase "If you fail to plan, you plan to fail." That phrase is a sage reminder about the importance of planning that applies to any activity.

Sometimes a phrase from a friend will help you achieve clarity about what is happening. The startup stage of my business became a frantic period of activity. I had turned my life into a constant whirl of meetings and networking sessions. One day I stole an hour for coffee with a friend who happens to be a coach. After I described my crazy schedule Teresa looked at me and asked, "Is all this activity like eating soup with a fork?"

Since then I use this phrase whenever I consider adding something to my schedule. By challenging the value of my activity this simple question helps me choose where I apply my energy. It fits very well with Craig Valentine's foundational phrase *"What gets recorded gets rewarded."*

Foundational phrases are useful because they are concise, memorable, and easily repeatable. Every culture in every age has contributed to the store of these meaningful sayings. In some cases we know the author. In many cases the phrase has outlived the author's fame. The old adage "You don't have to reinvent the wheel" applies to the idea that you can repurpose existing foundational phrases or maxims to fit your life. This brings us to working with existing forms and structures.

Liberating Creativity by Working within a Structure

World Class Speaking provides structures for building a speech. There is the 9 Step Create Your World Class Speech model. The PARTS formula provides the structure of an individual point. The Edge of Their Seats Storytelling Model provides a classic structure for telling a story. We call them structures and models but they are really sets of rules and instructions that guide you through a process. The two important benefits to working within a structure are *accelerated skills development* and *enhanced creativity*.

Using a structured system saves time and energy by ensuring you practice effective techniques. It also enables you to assess your abilities, making it possible to focus more on skills that need improvement. Working with a structure ensures development of strong fundamental skills before advanced techniques.

If you are working with a coach, they can use their knowledge of the structure to provide you with important feedback exactly when you need it. Getting good feedback and correcting deficiencies as they happen can rapidly accelerate your learning. The greater your mastery of techniques the easier it is to use them creatively. Using a proven structure can free you to be more creative.

Have you ever hoped for greater inspiration? How many times have you been told to "think outside the box"? That is a common cliché about creativity that leads to misconceptions about the value of structure and rules. When most people hear the words rules and instructions they think of them as constraints.

Early in my design career I wanted to become more innovative and creative. Initially I thought I should "think outside the box." I should reject conventions, rules, and structure. I thought inspiration would come from some combination of intuition and talent. Then I learned two very important lessons.

The first lesson came from a conversation with my father. I was caught in the early transition from manual art to digital art. I was frustrated because the struggle to learn new techniques was interfering with my pursuit of inspiration. My father had been through multiple changes in the graphics industry. He laughed and said, "Good design is not about your favorite artistic techniques. It's not even really about you being cleverly creative. Good design is about helping a client deliver their message."

The second lesson came from observing the senior designers in the art department. I realized they were working with a consistent structured process. These artists were working with a set of rules! Instead of thinking outside the box, their creative process started by redefining the box.

This creative process began by defining the result the client needed. Any requirements and parameters about the job were clearly described. Then the designer tried to discover what would provide the desired result. To do this they would try to learn as much as possible about the client and their customers. The creative process considered every step from concept to production to delivery. Sometimes a solution presented itself quickly. Sometimes they would use brainstorming techniques like word association and mental maps. Working within those parameters, the artist created a solution that put a desired vision in the minds of the audience. That vision could be tied to a specific call to action.

The result of my colleagues' work was often unique. However, the process they used to achieve that result was consistent. The process was like a vehicle they could drive to explore routes to any destination. When you travel by car you don't start by reinventing the wheel before each trip. My colleagues did not reinvent the creative process with every job. By using a consistent structured approach they were able to quickly generate several possible answers. Then they could efficiently select the best and reject those less suitable. Watching them use the process I learned that sources of inspiration are always abundant and available. I just needed to practice better techniques for noticing them.

Remember, inspiration is the result of noticing interesting aspects of things and relationships or potential relationships. Opportunities for inspiration are all around you.

The designer's creative process is very similar to the structures used in World Class Speaking to create a keynote. You can take the structures used in World Class Speaking and adapt them to almost any kind of communication, from a keynote to a one-on-one conversation. In any creative design process and in World Class Speaking, knowing your audience is crucial.

Being Inspired by Being "You Focused"

Being "you focused" does not mean being focused on you the speaker. It means using language as if your audience were one individual and customizing your message to their interests. Creating a custom message means you must learn all you can about your audience.

When you step off the stage it can be beneficial to stay "you focused." Unless you are a hermit you have to interact with people. Do you treat them as individual humans, or do you deal with them like anonymous drones? People tend to be very touched when you pay honest attention to them. Sometimes it is amazing how much cooperation can be obtained by a little caring interest in someone. You may not have time to fully interact with everyone, but never underestimate the value of a simple smile.

Being "you focused" instead of "me focused" is also important if you do any networking. There is an old saying that goes: "If you want to be the most interesting person in the room, be the most interested person in the room." You will have better conversations if you try to get to know people instead of forcing them to know you.

> *There is an old saying that goes: "If you want to be the most interesting person in the room, be the most interested person in the room."*

Top salespeople and negotiators know the power of client research. When you can clearly identify a person's needs or desires it changes the dynamics of the relationship.

Instead of trying to satisfy your need to sell them something, you shift to helping them buy something they need.

Giving value first and freely builds trust even if all you give is information that provides a different perspective. This is the principle behind the SWAP (Selling Without Annoying People) technique. Knowing your audience means you can give something that matters to them.

Creative professionals use audience research to find the questions that need to be answered. The design process described earlier does not work well without valid information about the audience. Designers and negotiators often talk about "getting into someone's head." They are talking about seeing things from the other person's perspective and trying to understand how they think and might react.

Being more "you focused" and less "me focused" allows you to start seeing the people around you as unique individuals. When you remember that no two people can share an identical experience you can start exploring their unique perspectives. Every person you see is a potential source of inspiration. The Mona Lisa was the result of Leonardo da Vinci noticing something as subtle as an enigmatic smile.

Discovering the inspiration provided by the people around you is a big step to leading a creative life. Achieving your full potential does not come from the steps you have taken. It comes from always taking another step.

Next Steps to Where You Want to Go

A World Class speaker is like a guide that takes their audience on a journey to a specific destination. The conclusion to a World Class speech includes a next step that will help the audience act upon the main message. Everything that goes into the speech delivers the audience to the conclusion so they can take the next step and continue the journey.

Planning to live a creative, productive, and happy life is a lot like planning a speech, or maybe a series of speeches. It is essential to set specific goals that will help you achieve your full potential. Sometimes it is easy to get distracted from large goals that are a long way off. Knowing your next step and taking it will get you where you want to go.

Aspiring to an important goal makes you like a climber on Mount Everest. Climbing Mount Everest is a daunting task. It is impossible to do in one continuous effort. Instead climbers break the climb into stretches between several basecamps. At the highest altitudes climbers adopt a strange rhythmic gait called a rest step. For safety and to conserve energy they literally pause between each step. The final assault on Mount Everest is conquered one careful step at a time.

If you think deliberately about your activities you can avoid stepping off the path you have set for yourself. Doing things step-by-step allows you to see progress instead of being intimidated by a daunting goal. Celebrating the completion of each step is very motivating. Here again you can apply Craig Valentine's phrase *"What gets recorded gets rewarded."*

If you are deliberate about planning each step you can decide when to move forward and when to rest. Everyone needs downtime, but if you actively choose when and how you rest and relax it will be more beneficial. It also won't waste what should be productive time, and you will make better progress.

Taking World Class Speaking off the stage and into your life can help you develop a personal philosophy. Creating and using foundational phrases can help us be clear about life lessons. Working with proven structures can liberate our creativity. Inspiration can come from respecting and caring for the people around us. Personal achievement comes through always planning and taking the next step. These are a few of the ideas you can find in World Class Speaking that will make your life stand up to examination. You might say that World Class Speaking can lead to World Class Being.

Ben Thorkelson is a graphic arts consultant, writer, speaker, and certified World Class Speaking coach. Ben lives and works in Calgary, Alberta, next to the Canadian Rockies. When he isn't working he's riding motorcycles in the Rockies with his favorite riding partner—his wife, Margaret.

Get Your Free
World Class Speaking In Action
Audio Toolkit (valued at $97)

www.WorldClassSpeakingInAction.com

Plus a special offer for the readers of this book!

Learn from some of the top speaking coaches in the world how to...

- Craft an unforgettable message that hits home with your audience
- Deliver your speech in a way that keeps your audience on the edge of their seats
- Sell your message so your audience takes that exact next step you want them to take

For more information on Craig Valentine
Visit www.CraigValentine.com

For more information on Mitch Meyerson
Visit www.MasteringOnlineMarketing.com